CU00705237

Electric Welding

ELECTRIC WELDING

ELECTRIC WELDING

BY

ETHAN VIALL

EDITOR AMERICAN MACHINIST

*Member American Society of Mechanical Engineers, Society of Automotive Engineers,
American Institute of Electrical Engineers, Franklin Institute, American Welding
Society. Author of Manufacture of Artillery Ammunition, United States
Artillery Ammunition, United States Rifles and Machine Guns,
Broaches and Broaching, Gas-Torch and Thermit Welding.*

FIRST EDITION
THIRD IMPRESSION

McGRAW-HILL BOOK COMPANY, Inc.
NEW YORK: 370 SEVENTH AVENUE
LONDON: 6 & 8 BOUVERIE ST., E. C. 4
1921

PREFACE

Few fields afford a greater opportunity for study to the mechanic, the student, or the engineer, than that of electric welding. Arc welding, with its practical, every-day, shop applications for repair and manufacture, is in some respects crowding closely into the field in which the gas-torch has seemed supreme. With the development of mechanical devices for the control of the arc, the range of application to production work has greatly increased.

Resistance welding presents in its various branches some of the most interesting scientific and mechanical problems to be found anywhere. Spot-welding—butt-welding—line-welding—all occupy a particular place in our manufacturing plants today, and new uses are being constantly found.

In the gathering and arranging of the material used in this book, particular care has been taken to classify and place various subjects together as far as possible. This is not only convenient for reference purposes, but enables the reader to easily compare different makes and types of apparatus. In most cases, the name of the maker of each piece of apparatus is mentioned in the description in order to save the time of those seeking information.

No time or pains have been spared in the endeavor to make this the most comprehensive book on electric welding equipment and practice, ever published. Every possible source of information known to the long-experienced editor has been drawn upon and properly credited.

It is hoped that this book will prove a permanent record of electric welding as it is today, and also be an inspiration and source of information for those engaged in practice, research or development.

ETHAN VIALL.

New York City,
November, 1920.

71937

v

CONTENTS

CHAPTER VII

CHAPTER VIII

CHAPTER IX

CHAPTER X

Relation of Microstructure to the Path of Rupture—Effect of
Heat Treatment Upon Structure—Persistence of ''Plates''
After Annealing—Thermal Analysis of Arc-Fused Steel—
Summary.

CHAPTER XI

The General Electric Automatic Arc Welding Machine—The
Welding Head—Set-Up for Circular Welding—Set-Up for
Building Up a Shaft—Diagram of Control of Feed Motor—
Some Work Done by the Machine—Repaired Crane Wheels—
Welded Hub Stampings—Welded Rear Axle Housings—Welded
Tank Seam—The Morton Semi-Automatic Machine—Methods
of Mechanically Stabilizing and Controlling the Arc—Examples
of Work Done by the Morton Machine—The G.E. Electric-Arc
Seam Welding Machine.

CHAPTER XII

Resistance Welding Machines—Butt-Welding Machines—Cur-
rent Used in Butt-Welding—How the Secondary Windings of
the Transformer are Connected—Typical Butt-Welding Ma-
chine with Main Parts Named—How the Clamping Jaws are
Operated—Annealing Welds—Portable Wire Welding Ma-
chines—Examples of Butt-Welding Jobs—Welding Copper and
Brass Rod—Welding Aluminum—Typical Copper Welds—
T-Welding—Welding Band Saws—Automobile Rim Welding—
The ''Flash-Weld''—Welding Heavy Truck Rims—Welding
Pipe—The Type of Clamp Used for Pipe—The Approximate
Current Used for Pipe Welding—The Winfield Butt-Welding
Machines—Cost of Butt-Welds—The Federal Butt-Welding
Machines—Welding Motor Bars to the End Rings—Welding
Valve Elbows on Liberty Motor Cylinders—An Automatic
Chain-Making Machine—Electro-Percussive Welding—How the
Machine is Made—Uses of Percussive Welding—Power Con-
sumed and Time to Make a Percussive Weld.

CHAPTER XIII

Spot-Welding—Three Desirable Welding Conditions—Welding
Galvanized Iron and Other Metals—Mash Welding—Details of
Standard Spot-Welding Machines—Foot-, Automatic-, and

CHAPTER XIV

CHAPTER XV

CHAPTER XVI

ELECTRIC WELDING

CHAPTER I

ELECTRIC WELDING—HISTORICAL

All electric welding may be divided into two general classes —arc welding and resistance welding. In each class there are a number of ways of obtaining the desired results. Arc welding is the older process, and appears to have been first used by de Meritens in 1881 for uniting parts of storage batteries. He connected the work to the positive pole of a current supply capable of maintaining an arc. The other pole was connected to a carbon rod. An arc was struck by touching the carbon rod to the work and withdrawing it slightly. The heat generated fused the metal parts together, the arc being applied in a way similar to that of the flame of the modern gas torch.

Of the several methods of arc welding, there are the Zerner, the Bernardos, the Slavianoff and the Strohmenger-Slaughter processes, as well as some modifications of them. The different methods are named after the men generally credited with being responsible for their development. The LaGrange-Hoho process is not a welding process at all, as it is merely a method of heating metal which is then welded by hammering, as in blacksmith work. It is sometimes called the "water-pail forge."

The Zerner process employs two carbon rods fastened in a holder so that their ends converge like a V, as shown in Fig. 1. An arc is drawn between the converging ends and this arc is caused to impinge on the work by means of a powerful electromagnet. The flame acts in such a manner that this process is commonly known as the electric blowpipe method. The Zerner process is so complicated and requires so much skill that it is practically useless. A modification of the Zerner process, known as the "voltex process," uses carbon rods containing a small percentage of metallic oxide which is converted into metallic vapor. This vapor increases the size of the arc and to some extent prevents the excessive carbonizing of the work. This process, however, is about as impractical for general use as the other.

The Bernardos process employs a single carbon or graphite

Fig. 1.—The Zerner Electric "Blow-Pipe."

rod and the arc is drawn between this rod and the work. A sketch of the original apparatus is shown in Fig. 2. This is commonly called the carbon-electrode process. In using this method it is considered advisable to connect the carbon to the negative side and the work to the positive. This prevents the carbon of the rod from being carried into the metal and a softer weld is produced.

In the Slavianoff process a metal electrode is used instead

of a carbon. This process is known as the metallic-electrode process.

The Strohmenger-Slaughter, or covered electrode, process is similar to the Slavianoff except that a coated metallic elec-

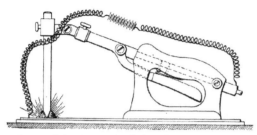

Fig. 2.—Original Bernardos Carbon Electrode Apparatus.

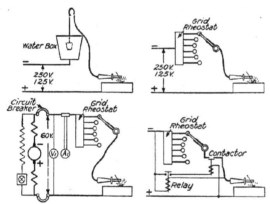

Fig. 3.—Arc Welding Circuits as First Used.

trode is used. In this process either direct or alternating current may be used.

Some of the early methods of connecting up for arc welding are shown in Fig. 3.

The LaGrange-Hoho heating process makes use of a wooden tank filled with some electrolyte, such as a solution of sodium or potassium carbonate. A plate connected to the positive wire is immersed in the liquid and the work to be heated is connected to the negative wire. The work is then immersed in the liquid. When the piece has reached a welding temperature it is removed and the weld performed by means of a hammer and anvil

Resistance Welding.—The idea of joining metals by means of an electric current, known as the resistance or incandescent process, was conceived by Elihu Thomson some time in 1877.

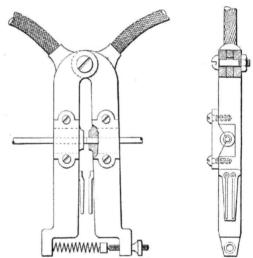

Fig. 4.—First Practical Electric Butt Welding Device, Patented by Elihu Thomson, Aug. 10, 1886.

Little was done with the idea from a practical standpoint for several years. Between 1883 and 1885 he developed and built an experimental machine. A larger machine was built in 1886. He obtained his first patent on a device for electric welding Aug. 10, 1886. The general outline of this first device is shown in Fig. 4. The first experiments were mostly confined to what is now known as butt welding, and it was soon found that the jaws used to hold the parts heated excessively. To remedy this water-cooled clamping jaws were developed.

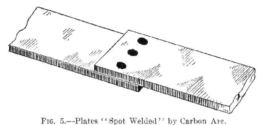

FIG. 5.—Plates "Spot Welded" by Carbon Arc.

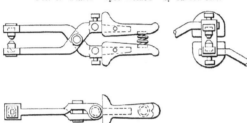

FIG. 6.—The DeBenardo Carbon Electrode Spot Welding Apparatus.

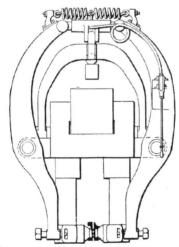

FIG. 7.—The Kleinschmidt Apparatus, Using Copper Electrodes.

Closely following the butt welding came other applications
of the resistance process, such as spot, point or projection, ridge
and seam welding. Percussive welding, which is a form of
resistance welding, was developed about 1905. Since spot welding is such an important factor in the manufacturing field today

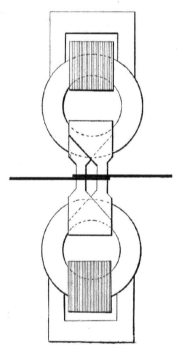

FIG. 8.—Bouchayer's Spot Welding Machine, Using Duplex Copper
Electrodes.

the evolution of this process, as indicated by the more prominent
patents, will be of considerable interest: Fig 5 shows plates spot
welded together by means of the carbon arc. This was patented
by DeBenardo, May 17, 1887, Pat. No. 363,320. The claims
cover a weld made at points only. The darkened places indicate

where the welds were made. Fig. 6 shows the apparatus made by DeBenardo for making "spot welds," as they are known today. He patented this in Germany, Jan. 21, 1888. Carbon electrodes were used. This patent was probably the first to cover the process of welding under pressure and also for passing the current through the sheets being welded. The German patent number was 46,776—49.

The apparatus shown in Fig. 7 is known as the Kleinschmidt patent, No. 616,463, issued Dec. 20, 1898. The patent claims cover the first use of pointed copper electrodes and raised sections, or projections, on the work in order to localize the flow of the current at the point where the weld was to be effected.

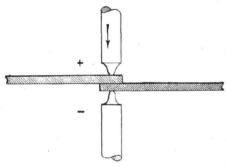

Fig. 9.—Principle of the Harmatta Process, Using Copper Electrodes.

Considerable pressure was also applied to the electrodes and work by mechanical means.

Fig. 8 shows diagrammatically Bouchayer's spot welding machine, patented in France, March 13, 1903, No. 330,200. He used two transformers, one on each side of the work. Duplex copper electrodes were used, and if the transformers were connected parallel one spot weld would be made at each operation. If the transformers were connected in series two spot welds would be made.

Fig. 9 illustrates the principle of the Harmatta patent, No. 1,046,066, issued Dec. 3, 1912. This is practically the same as the DeBenardo patent, No. 46,776—49, except that copper electrodes are used. However, it is under the Harmatta patent that a majority of the spot welding machines in use today are made.

Fig. 10 illustrates the principle on which the Taylor patent is founded. This patent was issued Oct. 16, 1917, No. 1,243,004. It covers the use of two currents which are caused to cross the path of each other in a diagonal direction, concentrating the heating effects at the place of intersection.

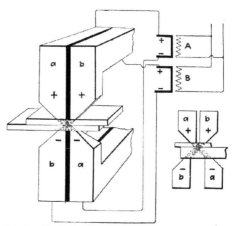

Fig. 10.—The Taylor Cross-Current Spot Welding Method.

From the foregoing it will be seen that spot welds, as this term is now understood, can be produced in a number of ways, none of which methods are identical. As a matter of fact, spot welds can be produced by means of the gas torch or by the blacksmith forge and anvil, although these methods would not be economical.

CHAPTER II

ARC WELDING EQUIPMENT

Electric Arc Welding is the transformation of electrical energy into heat through the medium of an arc for the purpose of melting and fusing together two metals, allowing them to melt, unite, and then cool. The fusion is accomplished entirely without pressure. The heat is produced by the passage of an electric current from one conductor to another through air which is a poor conductor of electricity, and offers a high resistance to its passage. The heat of the arc is the hottest flame that is obtainable, having a temperature estimated to be between 3,500 and 4,000 deg. C. (6,332 to 7,232 deg. F.).

The metal to be welded is made one terminal of the circuit, the other terminal being the electrode. By bringing the electrode into contact with the metal and instantly withdrawing it a short distance, an arc is established between the two. Through the medium of the heat thus produced, metal may be entirely melted away or cut, added to or built up, or fused to another piece of metal as desired. A particularly advantageous feature of the electric arc weld is afforded through the concentration of this intense heat in a small area, enabling it to be applied just where it is needed.

Direct-current is now more generally used for arc welding than alternating-current.

When using direct-current, the metal to be welded is made the positive terminal of the circuit, and the electrode is made the negative terminal.

Regarding alternating-current it is obvious that an equal amount of heat will be developed at the work and at the electrode, while with direct-current welding we have considerably more heat developed at the positive terminal. Also in arc welding the negative electrode determines the character of the arc, which permits of making additions to the weld in a way that is

9

not possible with alternating-current. Inasmuch as the work always has considerably greater heat-absorbing capacity than the electrode, it would seem only reasonable that the direct-current arc is inherently better suited for this work.

Two systems of electric arc welding, based on the type of electrode employed, are in general use, known as the carbon (or graphite) and the metallic electrode processes. The latter

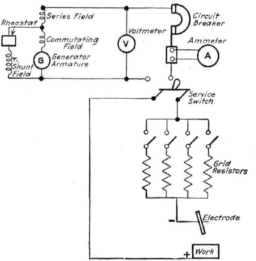

Courtesy of the Westinghouse Co.

FIG. 11.—Simple Schematic Welding Circuit.

process is also sub-divided into those using the bare and the covered metallic electrodes.

A simple schematic layout for an arc-welding outfit is shown in Fig. 11.

The Carbon Electrode Process.—In this process, the negative terminal or electrode is a carbon pencil from 6 to 12 in. in length and from $\frac{1}{4}$ to $1\frac{1}{2}$ in. in diameter. This was the original process devised by Bernardos and has been in more or less general use for more than thirty years. The metal is made the positive terminal as in the metallic electrode process in order that the greater heat developed in this terminal may be applied just where it is needed. Also, if the carbon were positive, the tendency would be for the carbon particles to flow into the weld and thereby make it hard and more difficult to machine.

The current used in this process is usually between 300 and 450 amp. For some special applications as high as from 600 to 800 may be required, especially if considerable speed is desired. The arc supplies the heat and the filler metal must be fed into the weld by hand from a metallic bar.

The class of work to which the carbon process may be applied includes cutting or melting of metals, repairing broken parts and building up materials, but it is not especially adapted to work where strength is of prime importance unless the operator is trained in the use of the carbon electrode. It is not practical to weld with it overhead or on a vertical surface but there are many classes of work which can be profitably done by this process. It can be used very advantageously for improving the finished surface of welds made by metal electrodes. The carbon electrode process is very often useful for cutting cast iron and non-ferrous metals, and for filling up blowholes.

The Metallic Electrode Process.—In the metallic electrode process, a metal rod or pencil is made the negative terminal, and the metal to be welded becomes the positive terminal.

When the arc is drawn, the metal rod melts at the end and is automatically deposited in a molten state in the hottest portion of the weld surface. Since the filler is carried directly to the weld, this process is particularly well adapted to work on vertical surfaces and to overhead work.

If the proper length of arc is uniformly maintained on clean work, the voltage across the arc will never greatly exceed 22 volts for bare electrodes and 35 volts for coated electrodes. The arc length will vary to a certain degree however, owing to the physical impossibility of an operator being able to hold the electrode at an absolutely uniform distance from the metal throughout the time required to make the weld.

It is very essential that the surfaces be absolutely clean and free from oxides and dirt, as any foreign matter present will materially affect the success of the weld.

When using a metallic electrode, the arc which is formed by withdrawing it from the work, consists of a highly luminous central core of iron vapor surrounded by a flame composed largely of oxide vapors. At the temperature prevailing in the arc stream and at the electrode terminals, chemical combinations occur instantaneously between the vaporized metals and the atmospheric gases. These reactions continue until a flame of incandescent gaseous compounds is formed which completely envelopes the arc core. However, drafts created by the high temperature of the vapors and by local air currents tend to remove this protecting screen as fast as it is formed, making it necessary for the welder to manipulate the electrode so that the maximum protective flame for both arc stream and electrode deposit is continuously secured. This can be obtained automatically by the maintenance of a short arc and the proper inclination of the electrode towards the work in order to compensate for draft currents.

Selection of Electrodes.—The use of a metallic electrode for arc welding has proved more satisfactory than the use of a carbon or graphite electrode which necessitates feeding the new metal or filler into the arc by means of a rod or wire. The chief reason for this is that, when the metallic electrode process is used, the end of the electrode is melted and the molten metal is carried through the arc to be deposited on the material being welded at the point where the material is in a molten state produced by the heat of the arc. Thus a perfect union or fusion is produced with the newly deposited metal.

Wire for metallic arc welding must be of uniform, homogeneous structure, free from segregation, oxides, pipes, seams, etc. The commercial weldability of electrodes should be determined by means of tests performed by an experienced operator, who can ascertain whether the wire flows smoothly and evenly through the arc without any detrimental phenomena.

The following table indicates the maximum range of the chemical composition of bare electrodes for welding mild steel:

Carbon trace up to	0.25%
Manganese trace up to	0.99%
Phosphorous not to exceed	0.05%
Sulphur not to exceed	0.05%
Silicon not to exceed	0.08%

The composition of the mild steel electrodes, commonly used, is around 0.18 per cent carbon, and manganese not exceeding 0.05 per cent, with only a trace of phosphorus, sulphur and silicon.

The size, in diameter, ordinarily required will be $^1/_8$ in., $^5/_{32}$ in., and $^3/_{16}$ in. and only occasionally the $^2/_{32}$ in.

These electrodes are furnished by a number of firms, among whom are John A. Roebling's Sons Co., Trenton, N. J.; American Rolling Mills Co., Middletown, Ohio; American Steel and Wire

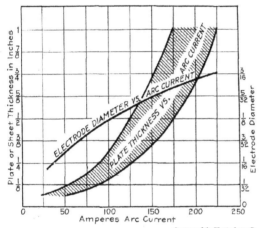

Courtesy of the Westinghouse Co.

Fig. 12.—Relation of Approximate Arc Currents and Electrode Diameters.

Co., Pittsburgh; Ferride Electric Welding Wire Co., New York City; Page Woven Wire Co., Monessen, Pa.; John Potts Co., Philadelphia.

A coated electrode is one which has had a coating of some kind applied to its surface for the purpose of totally or partially excluding the atmosphere from the metal while in a molten state when passing through the arc and after it has been deposited.

The proper size of electrode may be determined from Fig. 12 from which it will be seen that the class of work and current used are both factors determining the size of the electrode for welding steel plates of various thicknesses. To find the diameter of the metallic electrode required, select, for example, a three-eighths plate, and follow horizontally to the "Thickness of the Plate Curve." The vertical line through this intersection represents about 110 amp. as the most suitable current to be used with this size of plate. Then follow this vertical line to its intersection with the "Diameter of Electrode" curve which locates a horizontal line representing approximately an electrode $^5/_{32}$ in. in diameter. In a similar manner, a $^1/_2$-in. plate requires about 125 amp. and a $^5/_{32}$-in. electrode.

The amount of current to be used is dependent on the thickness of the plate to be welded when this value is ¾ in. or less. Average values for welding mild steel plates with direct current are indicated by the curve referred to above in connection with the selection of the electrode of proper size. These data are also shown in Table I.

TABLE 1.—APPROXIMATE CURRENT VALUES FOR PLATES OF DIFFERENT THICKNESS

Plate Thickness in Inches	Current in Amperes	Electrode Diameter in Inches
1/16	20 to 50	1/16
1/8	50 to 85	3/32
3/16	75 to 110	1/8
1/4	90 to 125	1/8
3/8	110 to 150	5/32
1/2	125 to 170	5/32
5/8	140 to 185	5/32
3/4	150 to 200	3/16
7/8	165 to 215	3/16
1	175 to 225	3/16

It should be borne in mind, however, that these values are only approximate as the amount of current to be used is dependent on the temperature of the plate and also upon the type of joint. For example, when making a lap weld between two ½-in. steel plates at ordinary air temperature of about 65 deg. F. it has been found that the extra good results were obtained by using a current of about 225 amp. and a $^3/_{16}$-in. diameter electrode. The explanation for the high current permissible is the tremendous heat storage and dissipation capacity of the lapped plates which makes the combination practically

FIG. 13.—Carbon-Arc Welding, Using King Mask.

FIG. 14.—Metallic-Arc Welding, Using a Hand Shield.

equivalent to that of a butt weld of two 1-in. plates. For that reason the above values will be very greatly increased in the case of lap welds which require practically twice the amount of current taken by the butt welds.

When the proper current value is used there will be a crater,

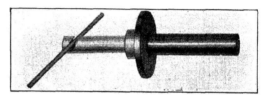

Fig. 15.—Simple Form of Electrode Holder.

or depression, formed when the arc is interrupted. This shows that the newly deposited metal is penetrating or "biting into" the work.

The difference between the carbon and the metallic electrode processes can be seen in Figs. 13 and 14. In Fig. 13 the welder

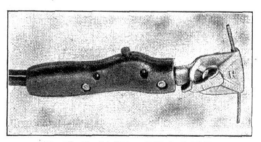

Fig. 16.—Special Make of Electrode Holder.

is using a carbon electrode and feeding metal into the weld from a metal rod held in his left hand. In Fig. 14 the metal rod is held in a special holder and not only carries the current but metal from it is deposited on the work.

Electrode holders should be simple, mechanically strong, and so designed as to hold the electrode firmly. It should be practically impossible to burn or damage the holder by accidental contact so that it will not work. Small, flimsy or light projecting parts are almost sure to be broken off or bent. Fig. 15 shows one of these holders that answers the requirements. However, any of the companies selling arc welding apparatus will be able to supply dependable holders.

A holder made by the Arc Welding Machine Co., New York, is shown in Fig. 16 and in detail in Fig. 17. The metal rod is clamped in by means of an eccentric segment operated by a thumb lever. If the rod should freeze to the work it will not pull out of the holder, but will be gripped all the tighter. The

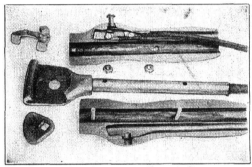

FIG. 17.—Details of Special Electrode Holder.

welding current enters at the rear end of the composition shank, passes along the shank to the head of the tool, and from there directly into the electrode. It will be noted that there are no joints in this tool except where the cable is soldered into the shank. There is a relatively large contact surface between the electrode and the holding head, which precludes any possible heating at this point. The trigger is intended for remote control employed with the closed circuit system. Whenever this holder is used on other systems, the trigger is omitted.

Cable.—For arc welding service the cables leading to the electrode holder should be very flexible in order to allow the operator full control of the arc.

The following sizes of cable have been found by the General

Electric Co. suitable for this service, due account being taken of the intermittent character of the work.

It is extra flexible stranded dynamo cable, insulated for 75-v. circuit, with varnished cambric insulation, covered with weather-proof braid.

Amperes	Size of Cable	Circular Mills
Up to 200	225/24	90,000
Over 200 Up to 500	375/24	150,000
Over 500 Up to 1,000	650/24	260,000

It will be noted in Figs. 13 and 14, that two different ways of protecting the eyes are shown. One man has a helmet and

Fig. 18.—King Face Masks With and Without Side Screens.

the other uses a shield held in the hand. Conditions under which the welders work, and their personal preferences, largely dictate which type is to be used. However, no welder should ever attempt arc welding without a protecting screen fitted with the right kind of glass. Cheap glass is dear at any price, for the light rays thrown off from the arc are very dangerous to the eyesight. The guard should be so made as to not only protect the eyes from dangerous light rays, but should also protect the face and neck from flying sparks of metal.

A very good face mask made by Julius King Optical Co., New York, is shown in Fig. 18. These masks are made of fiber and provision is made for a free circulation of air between the front and the face, not only keeping the operator cool, but preventing the tendency of the lenses to fog. The masks are supported by bands over the head and it is said that weight

FIG. 19.—King Hand Shields.

FIG. 20.—Method of Using Screens to Protect Others.

is not apparent and that they are as comfortable to wear as a cap. Two styles are made—with and without side screens. The one without screens may be had with combination lenses tinted for acetylene or electric welding or with any other tint for specific work. The one with side screens, providing side vision,

FIG. 21.—Individual Stalls for Instruction Work.

is fitted either with combination lenses or with clear Saniglass lenses. A hand shield is shown in Fig. 19.

In arc welding in the open, other workmen or onlookers are liable to injury as well as the welders, so screens should be placed around the work to conceal the light rays from the view of others besides the welder. Such an arrangement is shown in Fig. 20.

Where repetition work is to be done, it is well to provide individual stalls or booths, somewhat similar to the one shown in Fig. 21. These were designed for use in the welding schools under the supervision of the Lincoln Electric Co. For actual shop work, curtains or screens should be provided back of the welders.

It must be remembered also, that owing to the presence of ultra-violet rays, severe flesh burns may result with some people if proper gloves and clothing are not worn—especially when using the carbon arc.

Selecting a Welding Outfit.—Welding outfits may be of the stationary or the portable type. These may also be divided into motor-generator sets and the "transformer" types. Both d.c. and a.c. current may be used primarily, depending on the apparatus employed and the source of current available.

Regarding the selection of any particular outfit J. M. Ham, writing in the *General Electric Review* for December, 1918, says:

Few things electrical have in so short a period of time created such wide-spread interest as that of arc welding. Engineers having to do with steel products, in whatever form produced or in whatever way employed, have investigated its uses not only as a building agent when applied to new material but as a reclaiming agent for worn or broken parts. In both cases its possibilities as a means of greatly increasing output and in saving otherwise useless parts at a small fraction of their original or replacement value has proved astounding.

Out of these investigations have grown several systems of arc welding.

To exploit these is the duty of the sales department and the measure of its success depends upon the quality of service rendered.

The difficulties of giving service are perhaps not fully appreciated. Where so many systems have been called for and where so many individual ideas have to be met, the problems of the manufacturer become multiplied.

During a period of freight congestion when locomotives were in unprecendented demand, an engine was run into the repair shop with slid flat spots on each of the eight driving wheels, and orders were issued to return it ready for service in record time. In three hours repairs had been completed by means of the electric arc (to have put on new tires would have required three to four days) and the locomotive was out on the road. Many other achievements as remarkable as these have been obtained.

It would seem that having demonstrated the success of arc welding for a given line of work, others similarly engaged would be keen to take advantage of it; but that is true only in part, possibly because this is a "show me" age.

When it becomes apparent to the investigator of arc welding possibilities that the process fulfills his requirements, the question of what system to employ confronts him; salesmen are on the job to tell him about their particular specialties. He is informed that the real secret of welding is having the proper electrode (the salesman's special kind); it must be covered or bare, as the case may be, and contain certain unnamed ingredients. The merits of the direct-current system are extolled. Alternating-current outfits are advocated by others, it being claimed that they bite deeper and weld if the arc is held. The prospective buyer retires with a headache to think it over.

There is no mystery about arc welding. It is being done with all sorts of outfits and many varieties of electrodes. It can even be done from power lines with resistance in series with the arc. But these systems differ widely in essentials, just as in the case of automobiles. We can buy a cheap car or an expensive car, and in either event we get just about what we pay for.

The arc-welding set must pay its way. It must earn dividends and conserve materials, and when properly selected and applied does both of these things to a degree quite gratifying. To the discriminating purchaser it is not sufficient merely to know that an outfit will make a weld, he wants to know if it is the best weld that can be made, if it can be made in the shortest possible time, and whether the ratio between cost of the entire system to the savings affected is the lowest obtainable. He doubtless will, if the work is of sufficient magnitude to warrant, establish a welding department with a trained arc welding man in charge, and see that this department stands on its own feet. By so doing he places responsibility on a man who knows what to do and how to do it—a friend rather than a foe of the system. He will, other things being anything like equal, respect the opinion of the operator in the selection of the system to be employed, because it is better to provide a man with tools he is familiar with and prefers to use, rather than to force him to use something with which he is unfamiliar or which he regards with disfavor.

Obviously, the purchaser wishes to know that the companies he is dealing with are reliable and responsible, that the experience back of the salesmen is sufficient to warrant faith in his product. It is important to know the amount of power required per operator and whether drawing the needed amount from his own lines or from those of the power company will interfere with the system, and if so to what extent, and what, if any, additional apparatus will be needed to correct the trouble. Having determined these things to his satisfaction, he can install his arc-welding system with a considerable degree of assurance that there will be a decided saving in time, men, and money, and a genuine conservation of materials.

EYE PROTECTION IN IRON WELDING OPERATIONS

In the *General Electric Review* for Dec., 1918, W. S. Andrews says in part:

Radiation from an intensely heated solid or vapor may be divided under the three headings:

(1) Invisible infra-red rays
(2) Visible light rays
(3) Invisible ultra-violet rays.

There is no clear line of demarcation between these divisions, as they melt gradually one into the other like the colors of the visible spectrum. When the heated matter is solid, such as the filament of an incandescent lamp, the visible spectrum is usually continuous, that is, without lines or bands; but when it is in the form of a gas or vapor, as in the iron arc used for welding operations, the spectrum is divided up into bands or is crossed by lines which are characteristic of the element heated.

The radiations under the foregoing three headings, although of common origin, produce very diverse effects upon our senses. Thus, the infra-red rays produce the sensation of heat when they fall on our unprotected skin, but they are invisible to our eyes. The visible light rays enable us to see; but we have no sense that perceives the ultra-violet rays, so that we know of them only by their effects.

The intense glare emitted in the process of arc welding consists of a combination of all these rays, and special safety devices are required to protect the operator from their harmful effects.

For welding with acetylene and for light electric welding, it may be necessary only to protect the eyes with goggles fitted with suitable colored glasses.

A hand shield made of light wood, and which has a safety colored glass window in the center is also sometimes used. This device is used for medium weight electric welding done with one hand. The shield serves the double purpose of protecting the eyes of the operator and also shielding his face from the heat rays and the ultra-violet radiation, which might otherwise cause a severe sunburn effect.

For heavy electric welding, which requires the use of both hands, it is common practice for the operator to protect his eyes and neck with a helmet fitted with a round or rectangular window of safety glass. These helmets are usually made of some strong light material such as vulcanized fiber and are designed so that they can be slipped on and off easily, the weight resting on the shoulders of the operator.

There are a great many different kinds of special safety glasses on the market, and many combinations of ordinary colored glass are also in common use, so a brief discussion of this very important subject is in order.

It is well known that the normal human eye shows considerable chromatic aberration towards the red and blue-violet ends of the spectrum and that this defect is completely corrected in regard to the middle colors. It, therefore, naturally follows that a much clearer definition of an object is obtained by combinations of yellow-green light than by red alone, or especially by blue or violet light alone. The eye is also more sensitive to the yellow and green rays than it is to the red and blue rays; or in other words, yellow-green light has the highest luminous efficiency. This may easily be verified by looking at a sunlit landscape or fleecy clouds in a blue sky through plates of different colored glass. A glass of a light amber color or amber slightly tinted with green will clearly bring out details that are hardly observable without the glass, and which will be obscured entirely by a blue or violet glass. It is therefore obvious that in order to obtain *the clearest definition or visibility with the least amount of glare*, the selection of the *color tint* in safety glasses should properly be decided by an expert; but the *depth of tint or*, in other words, the *amount of obscuration* may be determined best by the operator himself, owing to the individual difference in visual acuity which will permit one man to see clearly through a glass that would be too dark for another man.

When the invisible infra-red rays encounter any material which they cannot penetrate, or which is opaque to them, they are absorbed and are changed into heat. Hence, they are frequently termed heat rays. It is, therefore, very necessary to guard the eyes from these rays; and although they are absorbed to a certain extent by ordinary colored glass, this is not sufficient protection against any intense source. There are, however, several kinds of glass, which, although fairly transparent to visible light, are wonderfully efficient in absorbing heat. The effects of even low-power heat rays, when generated in close proximity to the eyes for considerable time, are often serious, as is evidenced by the fact that glass blowers, who use their unprotected eyes near to hot gas flames of weak luminous intensity, are frequently afflicted with cataract which might be positively avoided by wearing properly fitted spectacles.

In selecting colored glasses, great care should be taken to discard all samples that show streaks or spots, as these defects are liable to produce eye-strain. The glass should be uniform in color and thickness throughout, and the colored plate should be protected from outside injury by a thin piece of clear glass that can easily be renewed.

Table II indicates roughly the percentage of heat rays transmitted by various colored glasses of given thickness. The source of heat used was a 200-watt, gas-filled Mazda lamp operating at a temperature of about 2400 deg. C. Although the figures are substantially correct for the samples tested, they would necessarily vary somewhat for other samples of different thickness and degrees of coloration, so that they can be taken only as a general guide for comparative purposes. Examination of the table will show that the last three, or commercial samples, all show better than 90 per cent exclusion of the heat rays.

TABLE II.—QUALITIES OF VARIOUS KINDS OF GLASS

Kind of Glass	Thickness in Inches	Per Cent Heat Rays Transmitted
Clear white mica	0.004	81
Clear window glass	0.102	74
Flashed ruby	0.097	69
Belgium pot yellow	0.126	50
Cobalt blue	0.093	43
Emerald green	0.100	36
Dark mica	0.007	15
Special light green glass	0.095	10
Special dark glass	0.096	4
Special gold-plated glass	0.114	0.8

As to the invisible ultra-violet rays, they are principally to be feared not only because they are invisible, but because we have no organ or sense for detecting them, and we can only trace their existence by their effects. In all cases, however, when we are forewarned of their presence, they are very easily shielded, for there are only a few substances which are transparent both to visible light and to ultra-violet radiation. Foremost among these latter substances, because it is most common, is clear natural quartz or rock crystal, from which the so-called "pebble" spectacle lenses are made. Fluorite and selenite are also transparent to ultra-violet rays, but these crystalline materials are rare and not in common use. However, a moderate thickness of ordinary clear glass, sheets of clear or amber mica, and of clear or colored celluloid or gelatine are opaque to these dangerous rays. As a case in point, it is well known that the mercury vapor lamp, when made with a quartz tube, is an exceedingly dangerous light to the eye, being a prolific source of ultra-violet radiation, so that when it is used for illumination, it is always carefully enclosed in an outer globe of glass. When the mercury vapor lamp, however, is made with a clear glass tube it is a harmless, if not very agreeable, source of light, because the outer tube of clear glass is opaque to the ultra-violet rays that are generated abundantly within it by the highly luminescent mercury vapor.

When operating with a source of light that is known to be rich in ultra-violet rays, such as the iron arc in welding operations, it is not sufficient to guard the eyes with ordinary spectacles because these invisible rays are capable of reflection, just the same as visible light, and injury may easily ensue from slanting reflections reaching the eye behind the spectacle lenses. Goggles that fit closely around the eyes are the only sure protection in such cases. Also, when using a hand shield it should be held close against the face and not several inches away from it.

It may here be mentioned that the invisible ultra-violet rays, when they are not masked or overpowered by intense visible light, produce the curious visible effect termed "fluorescence" in many natural and artificial compounds. That is, these rays cause certain compounds to shine with various bright characteristic colors, when by visible light alone they may appear pure white or of some weak neutral tint. Thus, natural willemite, or zinc silicate, from certain localities (which may also be made artificially) shows a bright green color under the light from a disruptive spark between iron terminals; whereas this compound is white or nearly so by visible light. Also, all compounds of salicylic acid, such as the sodium salicylate tablets which may be bought at any drug store, are pure white when seen by visible light, but show a beautiful blue fluorescence under ultra-violet rays. Many other chemical compounds could be mentioned which possess this curious property, but the above substances will suffice to illustrate the effect of fluorescence produced by ultra-violet rays, and by which these rays may be thereby detected. It must, however, be noted that these substances will only show their fluorescent colors very faintly when viewed by the light of the low-tension iron arc used in welding, because the intense visible light of this arc will overpower the weaker effect of the invisible ultra-violet rays. The true beauty of fluorescent colors can only be seen under a high-tension disruptive discharge between iron terminals, the visible light in this case being weak while the ultra-violet rays are comparatively intense.

Summarizing the effective means for eye protection against the various harmful radiations that are particularly associated with welding operations:

(1) The intense glare and flickering of the visible rays should be softened and toned down by suitably colored glasses, selected by an expert and having a depth of coloration which shows *the clearest definition combined with sufficient obscuration of glare,* which last feature can be best determined by the individual operator.

(2) When infra-red rays are present to a dangerous degree, a tested heat-absorbing or heat-reflecting glass should be employed, either in combination with a suitable dark colored glass, when glaring visible light is present, or by itself in cases where the visible rays are not injuriously intense.

(3) In guarding the eye from the dangerous ultra-violet rays, it must be carefully noted that "pebble" lenses are made from clear quartz or natural rock crystal, and this material being transparent to these rays offers *no protection* against their harmful features. On the other hand, ordinary clear glass is a protection against these rays when they are not very intense, but dark-amber or dark-amber-green glasses are absolutely protective. Glasses showing blue or violet tints should be avoided, excepting in certain combinations wherein they may be used to obscure other colors.

CHAPTER III

DIFFERENT MAKES OF ARC WELDING SETS

In showing examples of different makes and types of arc welding sets, only enough will be selected to cover the field in a general way, and no attempt whatever will be made to make the list complete.

The General Electric Co., Schenectady, N. Y., puts out the

Fig. 22.—General Electric 3-KW., 1700-R.P.M., 125-60-20-V. Compound-wound Balancer-Type Arc Welding Set.

constant energy metallic electrode set shown in Fig. 22. This, however, is but one type of its machines as this company makes a varied line covering all needs for welding work. Two of their commonly used, up-to-date sets are illustrated in Figs. 131 and 132, Chapter VIII.

This particular machine combines high arc efficiency and light weight. The balancer set is of the well-known G-E standard "MCC" construction. It is built for operation on 125-v., d.c. supply circuits, which may be grounded on the positive side only, and is rated "MCC" 3 kw., 1,700 revolution, 125/60/20 v., compound-wound, 150 amperes, RC-27-A frames, the two armatures being mounted on one shaft and connected in series across the 125-v. supply circuit, one welding circuit terminal being taken from the connection between the two armatures and the other from the positive line. By this means each machine supplies part of the welding current and, consequently, its size and weight is minimized. The design of the fields and their connections is such that the set delivers the voltage required directly to the arc without the use of resistors or other energy-consuming devices. The bearings are waste packed: this type of bearing

FIG. 23.—Welding Control Panel for Balancer Set.

being desirable in a set which is to be made portable either for handling by a crane or for mounting on a truck.

The welding control panel for the balancer set is shown in Fig. 23. This panel consists of a slate base, 24-in. square, which is mounted on 24-in. pipe supports for portable work and on 64-in. pipe supports for stationary work.

The entire set consists of one ammeter, one voltmeter, one dial switch, two field rheostats (motor and generator) one starting equipment with fuse, one reactor mounted on the pipe frame work of panel. The ammeter and voltmeter are enclosed in a common case. The ammeter indicates current in the welding circuit and the voltmeter is so connected that by means of a double-throw switch, either the supply line voltage or the welding line voltage can be read.

The dial switch is connected to taps in the series field of

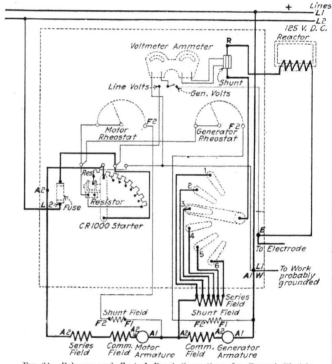

Fig. 24.—Balancer and Control Panel Connections for General Electric Constant-Energy Constant-Arc Set.

the generator, the field being connected to oppose the main field. This feature provides the current control by which six steps are obtained of the approximate values of 50, 70, 90, 110, 130 and 150 amp., which enables the operator to cover a very wide range.

In addition, if intermediate current values are required, they can be obtained by means of the generator field rheostat.

A small reactor is used to steady the arc and current both on starting and during the period of welding.

Arc welding is usually done on metal which is grounded and this is especially unavoidable in ship work, where the ship structure is always well grounded. Since successful operation requires that the positive terminal be connected to the work the supply circuit should be safely grounded on the positive side.

Where a 125-v., d.c. supply system is not available, standard

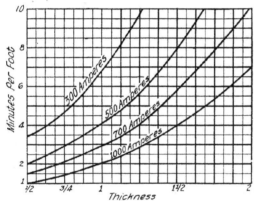

Fig. 25.—Carbon Electrode Cutting Speeds for Different Thicknesses of Plate.

"MIC" or "MCC" sets are furnished to supply power at 125 v., the motor being either 3-phase, 60-cycle, 220, 440 or 550 v., or d.c., 230 or 550 v., and in three capacities, 5½ kw., 7 kw., and 15 kw. With each motor generator set there is supplied a panel containing generator field rheostat and motor starter, which may be mounted beside the balancer panel. A diagram showing the balancer and control panel is shown in Fig. 24.

The constant energy arc-welding equipment supplies, to the arc, practically constant energy throughout the welding range for metallic electrode welding only. If the arc is lengthened slightly the voltage increases and the current decreases, the total

TABLE III.—DATA FOR METALLIC ELECTRODE BUTT AND LAP WELDS

BUTT WELDS BY METALLIC ELECTRODE—LAP WELDS WILL BE APPROXIMATELY THE SAME AS TWO BUTT WELDS—POWER 3C. PER KW. HR.;—LABOR 30C. PER HR.—ELECTRODE 5C. PER LB.

Thickness of Metal	Diameter Electrode	Speed Ft. per Hr.	Amperes	Mean Kw. at 60 Volts	Mean Kw. at 70 Per Cent Eff.	Approx. Electrode per Hr. Lb.	Power per Hour c.	Labor c.	Electrode c.	Total per Hr. c.	Total per Ft. c.
1/16	1/16	20	High 50 / Mean 40 / Low 30	1.8	2.0	0.9	6.0	30	4.5	40.5	2.0
1/8	1/8	16	90 / 70 / 50	1.4	3.6	1.4	10.8	30	7.0	47.8	3.0
1/4	1/8 or 3/16	10	125 / 100 / 70	2.0	5.1	3.1	15.3	30	15.5	60.8	6.1
3/8	3/16 or 1/4	6.5	150 / 125 / 100	2.5	6.4	3.6	19.2	30	18	67.2	10.3
1/2	1/4	4.3	150 / 140 / 120	2.8	7.2	3.8	21.6	30	19	70.5	16.4
5/8	1/4	2.8	150 / 125	3.0	7.7	3.4	23.1	30	17	70.1	25.4

NOTE.—The figures given for power, labor and material are arbitrary and may be changed to suit local conditions.

energy being practically constant. As the voltage required by the arc varies, the generator readjusts itself to this condition and automatically supplies the required voltage; the remainder being utilized by the motor end of the set. The interchange of voltage between the motor and generator is practically instantaneous, no perceptible lag occurs. This feature is valuable when metal drops from the electrode and causes an instantaneous increase in current. The commutation is sparkless and the weld-

Fig. 26.—Wilson Two-Arc, 300 Amp., "Plastic Arc" Welding Set.

ing circuit may be short-circuited without injury to the machine.

In connection with welding with an outfit of this kind, the practical man and student will find Table III of considerable interest. For sheet steel cutting using the carbon arc, the chart Fig. 25 is given.

The Wilson Outfit.—The Wilson "plastic arc" process and apparatus was first developed in railroad work by the Wilson Welder and Metals Co., New York, in order to enable the welder to control the heat used. By this system it is claimed

that any number of operators can work from one large machine
without one welder interfering in any way with the work of
another. Each operator can have properly controlled heat and
a steady arc at the point of application. This system was

FIG. 27.—Welding and Cutting Panel for Wilson Set.

largely used in the repair of the damaged engines on the German ships which were seized by us. By regulating the heat
it is claimed that any metal can be welded without preheating.

  A two-arc set is shown in Fig. 26 and a close-up of a control
panel in Fig. 27.

This outfit consists essentially of a constant voltage generator driven by any constant-speed motor, all mounted on a common bedplate. The regulation of the welding current is maintained by means of a series carbon pile acting as a series resistance of varying quantity under the action of increasing or decreasing mechanical pressure. This pressure is produced by means of a series solenoid operating mechanically on a lever and spring system which varies the pressure on the carbon pile inversely as the current in the main circuit. This establishes a constant current balance at any predetermined adjustment between a maximum and minimum range designed for. The change in adjustment is controlled by the operator at the point of work by means of a small pilot motor which shifts the lever center of the pressure mechanism, thereby raising or lowering the operating current. This system maintains a constant predetermined current at the arc regardless of the arc length. The operation of the mechanism is positive and quick acting. A special series choke-coil is mounted on the control panel for use as a cutting resistance.

"Plastic Arc" Dynamotor Unit.—The "plastic arc" welding unit illustrated in Fig. 28, while embodying the same fundamental principles as the foregoing, is a later model. This set is composed of a dynamotor and current control panel. The generator is flat-compound wound, and maintains the normal voltage of 35 on either no load or full load.

The control panel has been designed to provide a constant-current controlling panel, small in size, of light weight, simple in operation and high in efficiency. The panel is of slate, 20 in.$\times$27 in., and on it are mounted a small carbon pile, a compression spring, and a solenoid working in opposition to the spring. The solenoid is in series with the arc so that any variation in current will cause the solenoid to vary the pressure on the carbon pile, thereby keeping the current constant at the value it is adjusted for.

Three switches on the panel provide an easy means of current adjustment between 25 and 175 amperes. The arrangement of the welding circuit is such that 25 amperes always flow through the solenoid when the main switch is closed, whether the welding current is at the minimum of 25 amperes or the maximum of 175 amperes. The balance of the welding current is taken care of in by-pass resistances shunted around the solenoid.

This outfit can be furnished as a dynamotor unit, with standard motor characteristics as follows: 110 volts or 220 volts direct current, or 220 or 440 volts, 60 cycle, 2 or 3 phase, alternating current; also as a gasoline-driven unit, or it can

Fig. 28.—''Plastic-Arc'' Dynamotor Welding Unit.

be furnished without a motor, to be belt driven. The normal generator speed is 1800 r.p.m. The net weight is 800 lb. with direct-current motor, 807 lb. with alternating-current motor, 1200 lb. with gasoline engine, and 550 lb. as a belted outfit without motor. The sets can be mounted on a truck for easy portability if desired.

The Lincoln Outfit.—The portable arc-welding outfit illustrated in Fig. 29 is the product of the Lincoln Electric Co., Cleveland, Ohio. The outfit is intended for operation where electric current is not available and consists of a 150-amp. arc-welding generator direct connected to a Winton gasoline engine. An interesting feature of the machine is the method used to insure a steady arc and a constant and controllable heat. A compound-wound generator is used, the series wind-

Fig. 29.—Lincoln Self-Contained Portable Set.

ings of which are connected to oppose the shunt field, the two windings being so proportioned that the voltage increases in the same ratio that the current increases, thus limiting the short-circuit current. Another important effect of this is that the horsepower, and therefore the heat developed for a given setting of the regulator switch shown on the control board above the generator remains practically constant. It is claimed that this method of control gives considerably more work

on a given amount of electricity than where the machines use
the ballast resistance. Additional arc stability is insured by
the stabilizer at the right of the illustration, this being a highly
inductive low-resistance coil connected in the welding circuit
and serving to correct momentary fluctuations of current.

Westinghouse Single-Operator Electric Welding Outfit.—
The single-operator electric arc-welding equipment shown in
Fig. 30 is manufactured by the Westinghouse Electric and
Manufacturing Co., East Pittsburgh, Pa. The generator

FIG. 30.—Westinghouse Single-Operator Portable Outfit.

operates at arc voltage and no resistance is used in circuit
with the arc. The generator is designed to inherently stabilize
the arc, thereby avoiding the use of relays, solenoid control-
resistors, etc.

The generator has a rated capacity of 175 amp. and is
provided with commutating poles and a long commutator,
which enable it to carry the momentary overload at the instant
of striking an arc without special overload device. Close adjustment of current may be easily and quickly made, and, once

made, the amount of current at the weld will remain fixed within close limits until changed by the operator. There are twenty-one steps provided which give a current regulation of less than 9 amp. per step and make it much easier for a welder to do vertical or overhead work.

The generator is mounted on a common shaft and bedplate with the motor. A pedestal bearing is supplied on the commutator end and carries a bracket for supporting the exciter which is coupled to the common shaft. Either d.c. or a.c. motors can be supplied. Where an a.c. motor is used leads

Fig. 31.—U. S. L. Portable, A-C. Motor-Generator Set.

are brought outside the motor frame for connecting either 220- or 440-v. circuits. An electrician can change these connections in a few minutes' time. This feature is desirable on portable outfits which may be moved from one shop to another having a supply circuit of different voltages. For portable service, the motor-generator set with the control panel is mounted on a fabricated steel truck, equipped with roller-bearing wheels. The generator is compound-wound, flat compounded, that is, it delivers 60 v. at no-load and also at full-load.

The U. S. Light and Heat Co.'s Outfit.—The portable outfit, Fig. 31, is made by the U. S. Light and Heat Corp., Niagara Falls, N. Y. It is 28 in. wide, 55 in. high, 54 in. long, and will pass through the narrow aisle of a crowded machine shop. It weighs 1,530 lb. complete. In case a d.c. converter is used, the weight is about 125 lb. less. Curtains are provided to keep out dirt. A substantial cable reel is provided carrying two 50-ft. lengths of flexible cable for carrying the current to the arc. The reel is controlled by a spring which prevents the paying out of more cable than the welder needs. The outfit is made in several models to use 4 kw., 110-220-440-550 v., 2 and 3 phase, 25 and 60 cycle.

The Arc Welding Machine Co.'s Constant-Current Closed-Circuit System.—The constant-current closed-circuit arc welding

Fig. 31A.—The Arc Welding Machine Co.'s Outfit.

system developed by the Arc Welding Machine Co., New York, permits the use of an inherently regulating generator with more than one arc on a single circuit. This system is claimed to be especially adapted to production welding applications.

The method has all the advantages of series distribution, namely, the size of wire is uniform throughout the system and carries a uniform current, independent of the length of the circuit as well as of the number of operators. The circuit is simply a single wire of sufficient cross-section to carry the current for one arc, run from the generator to the nearest arc, from there to the next, and so on back to the generator. Wherever it is desired to do welding, a switch is inserted in the line, and a special arc controller provided with suitable connections is plugged in across the switch whenever work is to be done. These controllers may be made portable or permanently mounted at the welding station.

The set shown in Fig. 31A consists of two units: The generator proper which furnishes the energy for welding, and the regulator which automatically maintains the current at a constant value. The regulator is excited from a separate source, and, by varying its excitation with an ordinary field rheostat, the main welding current may be set at any value within the range of the machine that is desired, and once set it will automatically maintain that value.

Each arc that is operated on the system is equipped with an automatic controller which serves two essential purposes:

1—It maintains at all times the continuity of the circuit, so that one arc cannot interfere with any of the others when it comes on, or goes out of, the circuit.

2—It controls automatically the heat which can be put into the metal of the weld.

The current through the arc, together with the size of the electrode, determines the flow of metal from the electrode, and this current is adjusted by shunting a portion of the main current around the arc. The regulation characteristic of the arc may be adjusted by a series parallel resistance, which is one of the special features. When doing work on very thin, light metals, especially where the weld must be tight, it is necessary that fusion take place from the first instant the arc is struck. If the heat of the arc is exactly right for continuous operation, it will not be enough at the first instant, and if it is sufficient to produce fusion at once, then it will be too much a few seconds later. On this account a special type of controller is used for such work which provides for automatic reduction at a definite time after the arc is actually started, and continuing for a definite time and at a definite rate. Both periods of time and the rate and magnitude of the current change are adjustable.

For a given flow of metal through the arc the temperature of the metal is determined by the length of the arc, that is, by the voltage. With this controller, the length of the arc limited by the voltage is adjusted to suit the work and the operator, and if exceeded, the arc is short-circuited automat-

ically and remains short-circuited until the welder is ready
to begin again.

Provision is also made for stopping the arc at will without
lengthening it. Therefore it is claimed that with this system
it is impossible to draw a long arc and burn the metal. The
arc is not broken when the welding operation is stopped, but
is killed by a short-circuit which is placed across it.

FIG. 32.—Zeus Arc-Welding Outfit.

Stopping an arc by short-circuiting and limiting the heat
production in the same way is a patented feature.

"Zeus" Arc-Welding Outfit.—The "Zeus" arc-welding outfit shown in Fig. 32 is a product of the Gibb Instrument Co.,
1644 Woodward Ave., Detroit, Mich. In this device the motor-
generator customarily used has been supplanted by a trans-

former with no moving parts. The outfit is built on a unit system, which allows the installation of a small outfit, and if the work becomes heavier a duplicate set may be connected in parallel. One of the features of the machine is the arrangement for regulation. It is not necessary to change any connection for this purpose, as a wheel connected with a secondary and placed on the top of the case raises and lowers this secondary, and provides the regulation of current necessary for

Fig. 33.—Arcwell Outfit for Alternating Current.

different sizes of electrodes. The inherent reactance of the outfit automatically stabilizes the arc for different arc lengths.

The Arcwell Outfit.—The Arcwell Corporation, New York, has on the market an electric welding apparatus built for operation on alternating current of any specified voltage or frequency. It is shown in Fig. 33. It differs from the company's standard outfit in that it is being put out expressly for the use of smaller machine shops and garages, its capacity not being sufficient to take care of heavy work on a basis of

speed. It will do any work that can be done by the larger
machines, but the work cannot be performed as rapidly, the
machine being intended especially for use by concerns who
have only occasional welding jobs to perform. The machine
weighs approximately 200 lb. and, being mounted on casters,
it can be moved from one job to another.

Alternating-Current Arc-Welding Apparatus.—The Electric
Arc Cutting and Welding Co., Newark, N. J., is now marketing
the alternating-current arc-welding outfit shown in Fig. 34.

This illustration shows the entire apparatus for use on a

Fɪɢ. 34.—Apparatus Made by the Electric Arc Cutting and Welding Co.

single-phase circuit, the current being brought in through the
wires seen protruding at the lower left corner.

The device consists principally of a transformer with no
moving parts and is claimed to last indefinitely. In this apparatus, instead of holding either current or voltage constant
as with direct-current sets, the wattage, or the product of
voltage and current, is held constant. The alternating-current
set holds the arc wattage without moving parts; hence the heat
is substantially constant for any given setting, and it is claimed
that as soon as any person becomes accustomed to the sound
and sight of the arc and can deposit the molten metal where
he desires it is impossible to burn the metal from too much
heat or make cold-shut welds from too little heat. The amount

of heat generated is controlled by means of an adjusting handle on the transformer together with taps arranged on a plugging board. It is stated that the kilowatt-hours required to deposit a pound of mild steel with this machine varies from $1\frac{1}{2}$ to $2\frac{1}{4}$.

Their largest set is a 60-cycle type weighing about 200 lb., which places it in the portable class. The set can be furnished for any a.c. power supply, but it is not advisable to use a greater voltage than 650 on the primary. The set can also be made single phase, two phase three wire, two phase four wire,

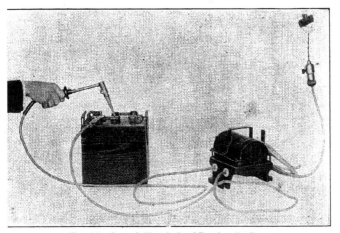

Fig. 35.—General Electric Lead-Burning Outfit.

to operate across the outside wires of the two-phase system or from a three-phase power supply. Polyphase sets are about 30 per cent heavier than the single-phase sets. In the two-phase machine balanced current can be drawn from each of the two phases by placing the sets across the outside wires. This is advocated, as it provides for leading current on one phase which brings up the total power factor of the system and a better power rate can be obtained. In polyphase circuits where more than one set is used single-phase sets can be distributed among the several phases.

The outfit can be made especially for welding and for cutting or for combination welding and cutting and can make use of bare wire, slag-covered, gaseous fluxed or carbon electrodes. An operator's mask and the electrode holder used may be seen on top of the apparatus.

General Electric Lead-Burning Transformer.—This lead-burning transformer, Fig. 35, a product of the General Electric Co., Schenectady, N. Y., can be used for lead burning, soldering electric terminals, splicing wires and tinsmith jobs, and even brazing can be done by placing the work between a blunt carbon point and a piece of cast iron. The transformer is designed to be connected to the ordinary 110-v., a.c. lighting circuit. Heavy rubber-covered terminal leads are used to convey the low-voltage, heat-producing current to the work, one terminal ending in a clip for fastening to some convenient portion of the work while the other terminal has a carbon holder arranged with an insulated handle. When the welding carbon is brought into contact with the work the pointed end becomes intensely hot and melts the metal over a restricted area. It should be noted that no arc is drawn, the end of the carbon point being heated to such a temperature that the metal in the vicinity is melted. The device uses about 800 watts while in actual use, the consumption dropping to $4\frac{1}{2}$ watts when the point is removed from the work. It is stated that the device is very convenient in plumbing, roofing and tank-building jobs, as well as other such work.

CHAPTER IV

TRAINING ARC WELDERS

Writing on the training of arc welders, in the *American Machinist*, April 15, 1920, O. H. Eschholz, research engineer of the Westinghouse Electric and Mfg. Co., Pittsburgh, says:

Many industrial engineers are now facing the problem of developing competent welders. This situation is attributed to the rapid growth of the metallic electrode arc-welding field as the result of the successful application of the process to war emergencies. The operator's ability, it is now generally conceded, is the most important factor in the production of satisfactory welds. To facilitate the acquirement of the necessary skill and knowledge, the following training course considers in their proper sequence the fundamental characteristics and operations of the bare metallic electrode arc-welding process.

It is well known that the iron arc emits a large quantity of ultra-violet radiation. Protection from the direct rays is usually afforded by the use of hand shields. Many uncomfortable burns, however, have been traced to reflected radiation. To secure adequate protection from both direct and reflected light it is necessary for the welder to use a fiber hood equipped with suitable glasses. Paper No. 325 of the Bureau of Standards on "Spectroradiometric Investigation of the Transmission of Various Substances" concludes that the use of amber and blue glasses will absorb most of the ultra-violet as well as infra-red radiation. To protect the operator from incandescent particles expelled by the arc, closely woven clothing, a leather apron, gauntlets and bellows-tongued shoes should be worn.

If the welding booth is occupied by more than one welder, it will be found desirable to equip each operator with amber or green-colored goggles to reduce the intensity of accidental "flashes" from adjacent arcs after the welder has removed his hood.

The Welding Booth.—The difficulty of maintaining an arc is greatly increased by the presence of strong air currents. To avoid the resulting arc instability, it is desirable to inclose the welder on at least three sides, with, however, sufficient ventilation provided so that the booth will remain clear from fumes. By painting the walls a dull or matte black the amount of arc radiant energy reflected is reduced.

The electrode supply and means of current control should be accessible to the operator. When using bare electrodes the positive lead should be firmly connected to a heavy steel or cast-iron plate, mounted about 20 in. above the floor. This plate serves as the welding table.

Welding Systems.—Many commercial sets compel the operator to hold a short arc. This characteristic favors the production of good welds but increases the difficulty of maintaining the arc. By increasing the stability of the arc through the use either of covered electrodes, series inductances or increased circuit voltage and series resistance, the acquisition of the purely manipulative skill may be accelerated.

The Electrode Holder.—The electrode holder should remain cool in service, shield the welding hand from the arc, facilitate the attachment and release of electrodes, while its weight, balance and the drag of the attached cable should not produce undue fatigue. A supply of different types of covered and bare electrodes should be carried by the welding school so that the operator may become familiar with their operating and fusing characteristics.

The degree of supervision the welder is to receive determines the source of operator material. If the welding operations are to be supervised thoroughly and the function of the welder is simply that of uniting suitably prepared surfaces, the candidate may be selected from the type of men who usually become proficient in skilled occupations. If, however, the responsibility of the entire welding procedure rests upon the operator, he should be drawn from members of such metal trades as machinist, boilermaker, blacksmith, oxy-acetylene welder, etc. Some employers find it expedient to use simple eye and muscular co-ordination tests to determine the candidate's ability to detect the colors encountered in welding and to develop an automatic control of the arc.

With adequate equipment provided, the operator may be instructed in the following subjects:

1. Manipulation of the arc.
2. Characteristics of the arc.
3. Characteristics of fusion.
4. Thermal characteristics.
5. Welding procedure.
6. Inspection.

Arc Manipulation.—A sitting posture which aids in the control of the arc is shown in Fig. 36. It should be noted that

FIG. 36.—Correct Welding Posture and Equipment.

by resting the left elbow on the left knee the communication of body movements to the welding hand is minimized, while by supporting the electrode holder with both hands the arc may be readily directed. During the first attempts to secure arc control covered electrodes may be used, as these greatly increase arc stability, permitting the welder to observe arc characteristies readily. It is suggested that throughout the training period the instructor give frequent demonstrations of the welding operations as well as occasionally guide the apprentice's welding arm.

Arc Formation.—With the welding current adjusted to 100 amp. and a $5/_{32}$-in. covered electrode in the holder, the operator assumes the posture shown and lowers the electrode until contact is made with a mild-steel plate on the welding table, whereupon the electrode is withdrawn, forming an arc. If an insulating film covers either electrode surface or the current adjustment is too low, no arc will be drawn. With the arc obtained the operator should note the following characteristics of arc manipulation.

Fusion of Electrodes.—The fusion of electrodes is frequently called "sticking" or "freezing." It is the first difficulty encountered and is caused either by the use of an excessive welding current or by holding the electrodes in contact too long before drawing the arc. This fusing tendency is always present because the welding operation requires a current density high enough to melt the wire electrode at the arc terminal. When such fusion occurs the operator commits the natural error of attempting to pull the movable electrode from the plate. If he succeeds in separating the electrodes, the momentum acquired, unless he is very skillful, is sufficient to carry the electrode beyond a stable arc length. If, however, the wrist of the welding hand is turned sharply to the right or left, describing the arc of a circle having its center at the electrode end, the fused section is sheared and a large movement of the electrode holder produces an easily controllable separation of the arc terminals.

Maintenance of Arc.—After forming the arc the chief concern of the welder should be to maintain it until most of the electrode metal has been deposited. If the movable electrode were held rigidly, the arc would gradually lengthen as the electrode end melted off until the arc length had increased sufficiently to become unstable and interrupt the flow of current. To maintain a constant stable arc length it is necessary for the operator to advance the wire electrode toward the plate at a rate equal to that at which the metal is being deposited. For the novice this will prove quite difficult. However, if the initial attempts are made with covered electrodes, which permit greater arc-length variations than bare electrodes, the proper degree of skill is soon acquired.

When the operator succeeds in maintaining a short arc length for some time, the covered electrode should be replaced by a $5/32$-in. diameter bare electrode, the welding current increased to 150 amp. or 175 amp. and either reactance included in the circuit or the voltage of the welding set increased. With increase in manipulative skill the reactance coil may be short-circuited or the supply voltage reduced to normal and practice continued under commercial circuit and electrode conditions.

Further instruction should not be given until the candidate is able to maintain a short arc during the entire period required to deposit the metal from a bare electrode 14 in. long, $5/32$ in. in diameter, on a clean plate $\frac{1}{2}$ in. in thickness when using a welding current of 150 amp. The arc voltage may be used as a measure of the arc length. The average arc voltage during the test should be less than twenty-five, as this corresponds to a length of approximately $\frac{1}{8}$ in. Some operators meet this test in the first hour of their training, others require two or three days' practice. If arc-length control is not obtained within the latter period, the instructor may safely conclude that the apprentice is physically unfitted for the occupation of arc welding. If the test is satisfactory, training should be continued, using bare electrodes but with such stabilizing means as inductance or resistance again inserted in the circuit.

Control of Arc Travel; Direction and Speed.—The plate arc terminal and the deposited metal follow the direction taken by the pencil electrode. The difficulty of forming deposits varies with the direction. The first exercise should consist in forming a series of deposits in different directions, as shown in A, Fig. 37, until the operator develops the ability to form a series of straight, smooth-surfaced layers. Additional skill may be acquired by the practice of forming squares, circles and initials.

The speed of arc travel determines the height of the deposit above the parent metal. A second exercise should require the formation of deposit strips having heights of $1/16$, $1/8$ and $3/16$ in. The normal height of a deposit when using a welding current of 150 amp. and a bare electrode of $^5/_{32}$ in. diameter is approximately ⅛ in.

Weaving.—If the electrode end is made to describe the arc of a circle across the direction of deposit formation, the width of the deposit may be increased without changing the height of the deposit. This weaving movement also facilitates slag flotation and insures a more complete fusion of the deposited metal to the parent metal. *B* and *C*, Fig. 37, illustrate the appearance of deposits formed with and without weaving of the electrode.

A third exercise should consist in forming layers of equal

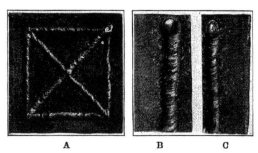

| A | B | C |

FIG. 37.—Control of Arc Direction Exercise.

(*A*) Exercise to develop control of arc direction. (*B*) Effect of weaving electrode across direction of deposit. (*C*) Effect of not weaving. These deposits were formed with the operator and plate in the same relative position, necessitating a change in the direction of arc travel for the deposition of each layer. Note that this direction is indicated by the position of the crater terminating each strip as well as by the inclination of the scalloped surface.

heights, but having widths of ¼, ⅜, ½ and ¾ in. when using an arc current of 150 amp. and a $^5/_{32}$-in. diameter bare electrode.

As the welder should now be able to control direction, height and width of deposits while maintaining a short arc, he should be given the fourth exercise of forming tiers of parallel, overlapping layers until inspection of the surface and cross-sections of the built-up material indicates good fusion of the metal as well as absence of slag and blowholes.

Arc and Fusion Characteristics.—The arc is the welder's tool. Its function is to transform electrical energy into highly concentrated thermal energy. This concentrated energy serves to melt both the parent and the deposited metals at the electrode terminals, the arc conveying the liquefied pencil into the crater formed on the material to be welded.

The plate arc terminal will always appear as a crater if a welding current is used. This crater is formed partly by the rapid volatilization of the liquefied material and partly by the expulsion of fluid metal due to the explosive expansion of occluded gases suddenly released or of gases formed by chemical reaction between electrode materials and atmospheric gases. To secure good fusion the deposited metal should be dropped into the crater. This is facilitated by the use of a short arc. On welding, the operator should frequently note the depth of arc crater and manipulate the arc so that the advancing edge of the crater is formed on the parent metal and not on the hot deposited metal.

Polarity.—When using bare electrodes the concentration of thermal energy is greater at the positive than at the negative terminal. Since in most welding applications the joint has a greater thermal capacity than the pencil electrode, more complete fusion is assured by making the former the positive electrode. The difference in concentration of thermal energy may be readily illustrated to the welder by having him draw an arc from a $^1/_{16}$-in. thick plate with the plate first connected to a negative and then to the positive terminal. If a current of approximately 60 amp. is used with a $^1/_{16}$-in. diameter electrode, he will be able to form a deposit on the plate, if the plate is the negative terminal. On reversing the polarity, however, the energy concentration will be sufficient to melt through the plate, thus producing a "cutting arc."

An arc stream consists of a central core of electrically charged particles and an envelope of hot gases. The electrode material is conveyed in both liquid and vapor form across the arc, a spray of small globules being discernible with some types of electrodes. Since atmospheric gases tend to diffuse through this incandescent metal stream, it is obvious that some of the conveyed material becomes oxidized.

Through the maintenance of a short arc, not exceeding $\frac{1}{8}$ in., the resulting oxidation is a minimum because enveloping oxide of manganese vapor and carbon dioxide gas, formed by the combination of atmospheric oxygen with the manganese and carbon liberated from the electrodes, serves as a barrier to restrict the further diffusion of atmospheric gases into the arc stream. Fig. 38 illustrates the degree of protection afforded the conveyed metal when using short and long arcs. With the latter convection currents deflect the protecting envelope from the arc stream. The effect of arc length on rate of oxidation may be clearly indicated to the welder by forming deposits with a ¼-in. arc and a ⅜-in. arc on a clean plate.

The surface of the first deposit will be clean and smooth, as shown at *a*, Fig. 39. The surface of the second deposit will be irregular and covered with a heavy coating of iron oxide, as shown at *b*. All oxide formed during welding should be

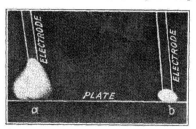

Fig. 38.—Long and Short Welding Arc.
Large arc stream causes excessive oxidation.

floated to the surface, since its presence in the weld will reduce the strength, ductility and resistance to fatigue of the joint.

Stability.—The ease of maintaining an arc is determined by the stabilizing characteristics of the electrical circuit and the arc gases. As noted above, increased stability may be obtained by the use of series inductance or higher circuit voltage with increased series resistance, higher arc currents and covered electrodes. A high-carbon-content electrode, such as a drill rod, gives a less stable arc than low-carbon content rods, owing apparently to the irregular formation of large volumes of arc-disturbing carbon-dioxide gas. Bare electrodes after long exposure to the atmosphere or immersion in weak acids will be found to "splutter" violently, increasing thereby the difficulty of arc manipulation. This "spluttering" is apparently caused by irregular evolution of hydrogen. If the electrode is coated with lime, its stability improves.

The evident purpose of a welding process is to secure fusion between the members welded. The factors that determine fusion in arc welding are arc current, electrode current density, thermal capacity of joint sections and melting temperatures of electrode and plate materials. By observing the contour of the surface of the deposited metal as well as the depth of the arc crater the welder may determine at once whether such conditions under his control as arc current, electrode current

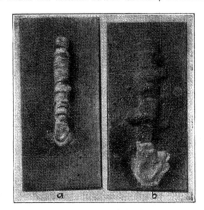

FIG. 39.—Deposit Obtained with Short Arc and Long Arc.

Note that surfaces of deposit and plate in (*a*) are comparatively clean, while those in (*b*) are heavily coated with iron oxide.

density and electrode material are properly adjusted to produce fusion.

The fifth exercise should consist of forming a series of deposits with arc currents of 100, 150 and 200 amp., using electrodes with and without coatings having different carbon and manganese content. Cross-sections of the deposits should then be polished and etched with a 10 per cent nitric-acid solution and the surface critically examined for such evident fusion characteristics as penetration and overlap, comparing these with the surface characteristics.

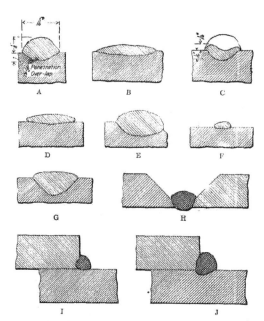

FIG. 40.— Overlap and Penetration Studies.

(*A*) Typical section through a normal layer formed by depositing metal from a mild-steel electrode on a mild-steel plate. Note the contour of the deposit as well as that of the fused zone and the slight overlap and correct depth of deposit penetration. Parent-metal crystal structure is altered by thermal changes.

(*B*) Typical section through a deposit formed when holding a long arc. Excessive overlap and no penetration exist. Most weld failures may be attributed to the operator maintaining occasionally or continuously too long an arc.

(*C*) Section through crater formed on completing deposit strip. The depth of the crater is a measure of the depth of penetration.

(*D*) Excessive overlap secured with a pencil electrode (drill rod) having a lower melting temperature than the parent metal (mild steel).

(*E*) Elimination of overlap obtained by using a pencil electrode (mild steel) having a higher melting temperature than the parent metal (cast iron).

(*F*) Incomplete fusion obtained with a low arc current.

(*G*) "Cutting" secured through use of high arc current.

(*H*) Section indicates proper selection of welding current and electrode diameter to secure fusion.

(*I*) Poor fusion caused by too rapid flow thermal energy from deposit through plates.

(*J*) Adequate fusion obtained by increasing arc terminal energy to compensate for increased rate of heat flow.

Overlap and Penetration.—Examination of the boundary line between the deposited and plate metals in A and B, Fig. 40, reveals that the penetration decreases in both directions from the center of the layer, no fusion being evident at the edges of the deposit, the contour betraying the extent of this overlap. As shown in C the penetration may be estimated from the crater depression.

An exaggerated overlap obtained in welding a mild-steel plate with a high-carbon-content steel rod, having a lower melting point than the plate, is shown in D. The re-entrant angle of the deposit edge is plainly evident. E illustrates a condition of no overlap in depositing metal from a mild-steel electrode upon a cast-iron plate having a lower melting point. F and G show respectively the effect of using too-low and too-high arc currents.

The effect of heat conductivity, heat-storage capacity, expansion and contraction of the parent metal and contraction of the hot-deposit metal must be studied.

Heat Conductivity and Capacity.—The effect of any of these factors is to increase the flow of thermal energy from the plate arc terminal and therefore to reduce the amount of metal liquefied. To maintain a given rate of welding speed it therefor becomes necessary to increase the arc current with increase in thickness or area of joint.

A welding current of 150 amp. will produce satisfactory penetration on welding the apex of scarfed plates $\frac{1}{2}$ in. thick shown in H. If the joint is backed by a heavy steel plate, increasing thereby both its thermal capacity and conductivity, a higher current, in the neighborhood of 175 amp. to 200 amp., will be required for the same penetration. If a lap joint is made as in I and the same current used as in H, the flow of heat will be so rapid that poor fusion will result. By increasing the current to 225 amp., J, the desired penetration, as indicated by crater depth, will be obtained with the maintenance of a high welding speed.

Expansion and Contraction of Parent Metal.—The welding operation necessarily raises the temperature of the metal adjacent to the joint, producing strains in the structure if it does not expand and contract freely. This condition is particularly marked when welding a crack in a large sheet or plate. The plate in the region of the welded section expands, the strains produced react on the cold metal at the end of the crack to open it further, with the result that as the welding proceeds the plate continues to open at a rate about equal to the welding speed. One inexperienced welder followed such an opening for 7 ft. before adopting preventive measures. The simplest of these is to drill a hole at the end of the crack and follow an intermittent welding procedure which will maintain the plate at a low temperature. Under exceptional conditions, such as welding cracks in heavy cast-iron plates or cylinders, it is advisable to preheat and anneal the regions stressed. A second example is offered by the warping obtained on building up the diameter of a flanged shaft. The face of the flange adjacent to the shaft becomes hotter than that opposite, producing internal stresses which warp the flange to a mushroom shape. Preheating of the flange will prevent this.

Contraction of Deposited Metal.—The contraction of deposited metal is the most frequent cause of residual stress in welds and distortion of the members welded. The magnitude of "locked-in" stresses depends upon the welding procedure and the chemical constituents of parent and deposited metals. If the deposit is thoroughly annealed, practically no stress will remain. On adopting a welding sequence in which the joint is formed by running tiers of abutting layers, each newly applied layer will serve partly to anneal the metal in adjacent layers. If mild-steel plate, with less than 0.20 per cent carbon, is welded in this way, the locked-in stresses should be less than 5,000 lb. per square inch. With increase in carbon content the locked-in stresses will increase. If welded joints of high-carbon steels are not permitted to cool slowly, they will often fall apart when the joint is given a sharp blow.

To illustrate this characteristic, the following exercises are suggested:

Exercise 1—Deposit a layer 1 ft. long on a strip of steel about $^2/_{16}$ in. thick, $^1/_2$ in. wide, using 150 amp. direct current and a $^5/_{32}$-in. bare electrode. The longitudinal contraction of the deposit will bend the strip of metal as shown in Fig. 41.

Exercise 2—Deposit a layer of metal around the periphery of a wrought-iron tube. The contraction of the deposit will cause the tube to decrease in diameter.

Exercise 3—Place two plates, ¼ in. thick, 2 in. wide, 6 in. long, ⅛ in. apart, and deposit a layer of metal joining them together. The transverse contraction on cooling will pull the plates out of line.

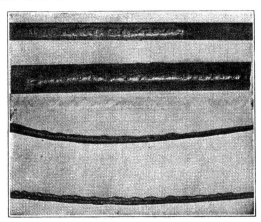

Fig. 41.—Warping of the Parent Metal Caused by the Transverse Contraction of the Deposited Layers.

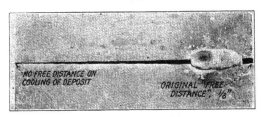

Fig. 42.—Reduction of "Free Distance" Caused by Transverse Contraction.

Illustrates the necessity of rigidly clamping the joint members, or of assembling them by an increasing distance from the end to be first welded, to equalize the movement caused by the contraction of the deposited metal, if the desired "free distance" is to be maintained throughout the welding operation.

Exercise 4—If two plates, ¼ in. thick, 6 in. wide and 6 in. long, spaced ⅛ in., are welded by depositing a short layer extending ¼ in. from the one end, it will be found that when

the deposit has cooled the resulting transverse contraction will
not only warp the plates as in Exercise 3, but will also draw
them together as shown in Fig. 42, thereby decreasing the free
distance between plates.

Welding Procedure.—Satisfactory welds will be obtained
only when the sections to be welded are properly scarfed or
cut out and the surfaces on which the deposits are formed
cleaned before and during the welding operation. The scarfs
may be machined or cut with a cold chisel or the carbon arc.
The surfaces of the deposited layers may be cleaned with a

Fig. 43.—Welds Showing Poor and Good Fusion.

Section through one-half of a welded joint showing poor fusion obtained at apex
of V as the result of assembling the joint sections without a "free distance." Section
through one-half of a welded joint showing excellent fusion obtained as a result
of the use of a "free distance" of ⅛ in., thus permitting the operator to maintain a
short arc when welding the bottom of the V. Failures of deep welds may be usually
attributed to the use of too small a "free distance," low welding current, improper
cleaning of scarf faces or incomplete slag flotation.

chisel or wirebrush, although the use of a sandblast is preferable. The joint sections should be separated by a free distance
of about ⅛ in. in order that the bottom of the V may be accessible to the welder.

The scarf angle and free distance vary inversely. Both
are determined by the depth of the V. If the character of the
work is such that it is not practicable to separate the joint
sections, the V should be cut at the bottom to form a 90-deg.
angle, this angle being reduced to 60 deg. as the surface is
approached; otherwise the scarf angle may be reduced along
the entire length to 60 deg., excepting in the case of very deep

welds. It is usual practice now to scarf plate welds to 60 deg. and separate the sections $\frac{1}{8}$ in. for V's up to $\frac{1}{2}$ in. in depth.

At the left in Fig. 43 is shown the poor fusion obtained at the bottom of the V on welding a 1-in. square bar, scarfed 60 deg., without the use of a free distance. At the right is shown the satisfactory union obtained with the use of free distance of $\frac{1}{8}$ in. Whenever a butt joint is accessible to horizontal welding from both sides, it is preferable to scarf the sections to a double-bevel, double-V joint.

The choice of arc current is determined by the thermal conductivity and capacity of the joint as previously discussed, a convenient criterion being the depth of arc crater. The arc current selected should be of such a value that on welding the given sections the depth of the arc crater or "bite" is never less than $^1/_{16}$ in.

Electrode Current Density.—To maintain a uniform flow of the metal, neither too slow, which causes excessive penetration, nor too fast, which produces excessive overlap, an electrode diameter should be chosen such that the current density is approximately 8,000 amp. per square inch. For the usual sizes of bare wire available this corresponds to the following welding currents:

———Arc Current (Amp.)———			Electrode
Normal	Maximum	Minimum	Diameter (in.)
225	275	190	3/16
155	190	125	5/32
100	125	70	1/8
60	70	45	3/32

If covered electrodes are used, the direct-current rating for the wires should be decreased roughly to 60 per cent of these values. If bare wires are used on alternating current, the rating should be increased from 20 to 40 per cent.

The first layer should thoroughly fuse the apex of the V. Wherever possible inspect the reverse side, as the deposited metal should appear projecting through. Subsequent layers should be fused then to the preceding layers or to the scarfed face. The final surface should be from $^1/_{16}$ to $^1/_8$ in. above that of the adjacent sections. This welt increases the strength of the joint or permits the joint surface to be machined to a smooth finish. If the weld is to be oil-tight, the metal projecting through the abutting sections on the reverse side as a result of the first step in filling the section should be chipped out and the resulting groove filled with at least one layer of deposited metal. This extension of the procedure is frequently used in the welding of double-bevel joints where the joint is to have a "100 per cent" strength.

If a vertical seam is to be welded, sufficient material should first be deposited to produce a shoulder so that the added metal may be applied on an almost horizontal surface to facilitate the welding operation.

If an overhead seam is to be welded, the operation is simplified by placing on the upper side of the joint a heavy steel plate covering the apex of the V. A shoulder is then formed by an initial deposit of metal, the operator continuing to add metal to the corner so produced and the vertical face of the shoulder.

The considerations pointed out under the section on thermal characteristics determine whether it is necessary to preheat and anneal the joint. The method used in filling the scarfed section is determined by the preference for either the rigid or non-rigid system.

When using the rigid system both sections of the joint are clamped firmly to prevent either member from moving under the stresses produced by the expansion and contraction obtained during the welding operation. If a proper welding sequence is not followed, the accumulation of "locked-in" stresses on cooling may be sufficient to rupture the welded area. To minimize these stresses it is the usual practice to tack the plates together at the apex of the scarf with short deposits at about 1-ft. intervals, and then to deposit single layers in alternate gaps, each tier being completed before adding a second tier at any section. This procedure tends to maintain a low average temperature of the joint and plate, thereby decreasing the amount of expansion, while the deposition of the metal in layers serves partly to anneal the metal beneath and materially reduce "locked-in" stresses.

In the non-rigid system both members of the joint are free to move. To prevent the edges of the plate from overlapping or touching as shown in Fig. 42, the initial free distance is made great enough to equalize the movement of the plates caused by the contraction of the hot deposited metal. On welding long seams of $\frac{1}{2}$-in. plate the contraction is limited by maintaining a spacing block $^5/_{16}$ in. wide, approximately 1 ft. ahead of the welded section. With a "free distance" of $\frac{1}{8}$ in. the contraction stresses draw the plates together a distance of $^3/_{16}$ in. This modification converts the non-rigid into a semi-rigid system.

Inspection.—No direct, non-destructive means are available for readily determining the strength and ductility of welds. A number of indirect methods, however, are in commercial use which give a fair measure of weld characteristics if intelligently applied. They consist in estimating the degree of fusion and porosity present by critically inspecting the surface of each layer and in noting the depth of liquid penetration through the completed section.

In examining each layer the amount of oxide present, smoothness and regularity of the surface, its contour, freedom from porosity and depth of crater should be noted. After a little experience these observations will give the inspector a good indication of the manipulative ability of the welder and of the degree of fusion obtained, as discussed above.

A succession of unfused zones will produce a leaky joint. These sections may be detected by flooding one surface of the joint with kerosene, using a retaining wall of putty, if necessary, as the liquid penetrates through the linked areas and emerges to stain the opposite side.

Brief Terminology.—The following terms are used most frequently in arc welding:

Free distance.—The amount that the joint sections are separated before welding.

Overlap.—The area of deposited metal that is not fused to the parent metal.

Parent metal.—The original metal of the joint sections.

Penetration.—The depth to which the parent metal is melted by the arc—gaged by the depth of the arc crater.

Recession.—The distance between the original scarf line and the average depth of penetration parallel to this line obtained in the completed weld.

Re-entrant angle.—The angle between the original surface of the parent metal and the overlapping, unfused deposit edge.

Scarf.—The chamfered surface of a joint.

Tack.—A short deposit, from $\frac{1}{2}$ to 2 in. long, which serves to hold the sections of a joint in place.

Weaving.—A semi-circular motion of the arc terminal to the right and left of the direction of deposition, which serves to increase the width of the deposit, decrease overlap and assist in slag flotation.

Welt.—The material extending beyond the surface of the weld shanks to reinforce the weld.

QUESTIONS AND ANSWERS

What does the welder's equipment consist of?

Welding generator, electrode holder with cables, welding booth, helmet or shield, gauntlets, high shoes with bellows tongue, heavy clothing or leather apron, proper electrodes.

What is the most important precaution the operator should observe?

To protect his eyes and body from the radiant energy emitted by the arc.

How is the operator prevented from drawing too long an arc after the electrode "freezes" to the work?

By twisting the wrist sharply to the right or left, thereby shearing the fused area.

What is the essential factor in securing the maintenance of the arc?

The electrode should be advanced to the work at the rate at which it is being melted.

What is the test of an operator's manipulative ability?

He should be able to hold an arc no longer than $\frac{1}{8}$ in., having a voltage across it less than twenty-five during the period required to deposit the metal from a $\frac{5}{32}$-in. diameter bare electrode, 12 in. long on 150 amp. direct current.

What is meant by "free distance," "overlap," "parent metal," "penetration," "recession," "re-entrant angle," "scarf," "tack," "weaving" and "welt"?

Given under "Terminology."

What function does the arc perform?

It transforms electrical energy into thermal energy.

What polarity should the welder use on welding all but thin sections with bare electrodes?

The pencil electrode should be negative.

How may the amount of oxide formed be reduced to a minimum?

By holding a short arc and the use of electrodes containing a small quantity of carbon (0.18 per cent) and manganese (0.50 per cent).

How may an operator determine the degree of fusion obtained (a) by inspecting the surface, (b) by inspecting the cross-section of deposit?

(a) By examining the contour of the surface, noting the re-entrant angle and estimating the overlap; observing the depth of crater and estimating the penetration.

(b) By directly observing the depth of penetration of recession, the overlap and porosity or blow holes.

What are the factors in arc welding that determine the degree of fusion?

Arc current, arc length, electrode current density, electrode material, freedom of weld from oxides.

How may a welder determine when he is using the proper welding current?

By the depth the arc melts the material welded. The crater should be not less than $^3/_{16}$ in. in depth.

What is the most important thermal characteristic encountered in welding?

Contraction of the hot deposit.

How may strains produced by this characteristic be minimized?

By adopting a correct welding procedure, either non-rigid or rigid, which serves partly to anneal the metal and reduce "locked-in" stresses.

What is the effect of holding too long an arc with the metallic electrode?

The use of a long arc produces a poor deposit, due to insufficient penetration, and also produces a large amount of oxide which reduces both the strength and ductility of the joint.

What size of bare electrodes corresponds to welding currents of approximately 225, 155, 100 and 60 amp. on welding with direct current?

Sizes $^1/_{16}$, $^3/_{32}$, $^1/_8$ and $^3/_{32}$ in. respectively.

How should joint sections be prepared for welding?

The surfaces should be cleaned thoroughly and the faces of the joint scarfed to an angle of 60 to 90 degrees with the edges separated a free distance of approximately $\frac{1}{8}$ in. in the rigid welding process, and an additional $^3/_{16}$ in. per foot from the point welded for each foot length when using the non-rigid system.

What surface characteristics denote fusion?

Surface porosity, amount of oxide coating, depth of arc crater, surface contour, compactness, regularity and re-entrant angles.

CHAPTER V

CARBON-ELECTRODE ARC WELDING AND CUTTING

In the *American Machinist* of Sept. 9, 1920, O. H. Escholz, research engineer of the Westinghouse Electric & Manufacturing Co., dealt with the various phases of carbon arc welding and cutting as follows:

Carbon or graphite electrode arc welding is the oldest of the electric fusion arc processes now in use. The original process consisted in drawing an arc between the parent metal and a carbon electrode in such a manner that the thermal energy developed at the metal crater fused together the edges of the joint members. This process was early modified by adding fused filling metal to the molten surface of the parent metal.

The equipment now used consists of a direct-current arc-circuit possessing inherent means for stabilizing the carbon arc, a welding hood for the operator, an electrode holder that does not become uncomfortably hot in service and suitable clothing such as bellows-tongued shoes, gauntlets and apron of heavy material.

When arc currents of less than 200 amp. are used, or when a graphite arc process is employed intermittently with the metallic electrode process, the carbon-holding adapter shown in Fig. 44 may be used with the metallic electrode holder, the shank of the adapter being substituted for the metal electrode. With very high arc currents, 750 amp. or more, special holders should be constructed to protect the operator from the intense heat generated at the arc. Typical holders are shown in Figs. 45 and 46.

Electrodes.—Although hard carbon was originally employed for the electrode material, experience has shown that a lower rate of electrode consumption as well as a softer weld may be obtained by substituting graphite electrodes. While both elec-

66

trodes have the same base and binder, the graphite electrode is baked at a sufficiently high temperature (2000 deg. C.) to graphitize the binder, thereby improving the bond and the homogeneity of the electrode. The graphite electrode is readily

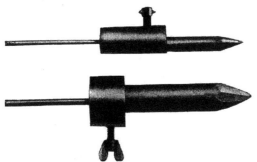

Fig. 44.—Adapters for Using Carbons in Metallic-Electrode Holder

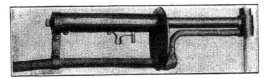

Fig. 45.—Metallic-Electrode Holder.

Fig. 46.—Carbon- or Graphite-Electrode Holder.

distinguishable by its greasy "feel" and the characteristic streak it makes on paper.

The diameter of the electrode is determined partly by the arc current. To fix the position of the carbon arc terminal, thereby increasing arc stability and arc control, all electrodes should be tapered. This precaution is particularly important when using low value of arc current or when maintaining an arc under conditions which cause distortion and instability. The following table gives electrode diameters in most common use with various arc currents:

Amperes		Diameter
50 to 150	....	$\frac{1}{4}$ in. tapered to $\frac{1}{8}$ in.
150 to 300	....	$\frac{3}{8}$ in. tapered to $\frac{1}{4}$ in.
300 to 500	....	1 in. tapered to $\frac{1}{4}$ in.
500 to 750	....	$1\frac{1}{4}$ in. tapered to $\frac{3}{8}$ in.
750 to 1000	....	$1\frac{1}{2}$ in. tapered to $\frac{1}{2}$ in.

Filler Material.—A strong, sound weld can be obtained only by using for filler metal low-carbon, commercially pure iron rods having a diameter of $\frac{3}{8}$ in. or $\frac{1}{2}$ in., depending on the welding current used. Cast iron or manganese steel filler rods produce hard welds in which the fusion between the parent and added metals may be incomplete. Short rods of scrap metal, steel turnings, etc., are frequently made use of for filler metal when the purpose of the welder is merely to fill a hole as rapidly as possible. It should be understood that welds made with such metal are weak, contain many blowholes and are frequently too hard to machine.

It is as difficult for the user of graphite arc processes as it is for the oxy-acetylene welder to estimate the degree of fusion obtained between deposited and parent metals. Therefore the operator must follow conscientiously the correct procedure, recognizing that the responsibility of executing a faulty weld rests solely with himself. He should, of course, have a working knowledge of metals, must be able to distinguish colors and possess a fair degree of muscular co-ordination, although the manipulative skill required is less than that necessitated by the metallic electrode process.

For graphite arc welding employing a filler the correct posture is illustrated in Fig. 47. The filler rod is shown grasped by the left hand with the thumb uppermost. When held in this position the welder may use the rod to brush off slag from the surface of molten metal or to advance the rod into the arc stream.

The surfaces to be welded should be chipped clean. Where

they are scarfed the angle should be wide enough to enable the operator to draw an arc from any point without danger of short-circuiting the arc. It is the practice of some welders to remove sand and slag from the metal surfaces by fusing them with the aid of the arc and then striking the fluid mass with a ball-peen hammer. This method should be discouraged since both operator and nearby workmen may be seriously injured by the flying hot particles.

Arc Manipulation.—The arc is formed by withdrawing the graphite electrode from a clean surface of solid metal or from the end of the filler rod when it is held in contact with the

Fig. 47.—Correct Welding Position when Using Carbon Arc and a Filler Rod.

parent metal. If the arc is formed from the surface of the deposited metal or from that of a molten area, slag particles may adhere to the end of the electrode, deflecting the arc and increasing the difficulty of manipulating it.

By inclining the electrode approximately 15 deg. to the vertical the control of the position, direction and speed of the arc terminal is facilitated. When the electrode is held vertically irregularities in the direction and force of convection currents deflect the arc first to one side and then to another, causing a corresponding movement of the metal arc terminal. By inclining the graphite electrode the deflecting force is constant in direction, with the result that the electrode arc stream and arc terminal remain approximately in line, as shown in Fig. 48, and may then be moved in any direction or at any speed by a corresponding movement of the graphite electrode.

Polarity.—It is common knowledge that the positive terminal of a carbon arc is hotter and consumes more energy than the negative terminal. If the graphite electrode of the welding arc is made the positive terminal, energy will be use-

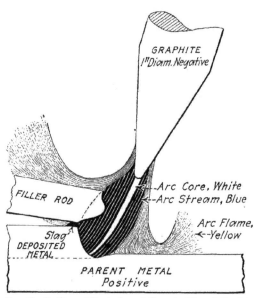

FIG. 48.—Position of Electrode and Characteristics of the Arc.

lessly consumed and the resulting higher temperature will increase the loss of **carbon** through excessive oxidation and vaporization. Moreover, for reasons well known to those familiar with the phenomena of arc formation, a very unstable arc is obtained with the iron parent metal functioning as the negative electrode. The graphite electrode should therefore always be connected to the negative terminal, reversal of polarity being detected when the arc is difficult to hold and when the carbon becomes excessively hot.

Arc Length.—Even when the graphite electrode serves as the negative arc terminal, its temperature is great enough to cause vaporization of a considerable quantity of carbon. If this carbon is permitted to be transferred to and absorbed by the fluid metal, a hard weld will result. To insure a soft metal practically all of the volatilized carbon should be oxidized. This may be accomplished by regulating the arc length so that atmospheric oxygen will have ample time to diffuse through the arc stream and combine with all of the carbon present. The correct arc length is dependent upon the welding current and the degree of confinement of the arc. Since the arc diameter varies as the square root of the current the arc length should be increased in proportion to the square root of the current. It is also obvious that when an arc is drawn from a flat, open surface the vaporized carbon is more accessible to the atmospheric gases than when it is inclosed by the walls of a blowhole. This means that to secure the same amount of oxidized carbon under both conditions the confined arc should be the longer. Many welders are not familiar with this phenomenon, with the result that metal deposited in holes or corners appears to be inexplicably hard.

The length of a 250-amp. arc should not be less than $\frac{1}{2}$ in. and that for a 500-amp. arc should not be less than $\frac{3}{4}$ in. when drawing the arc from a flat surface. The maintenance of excessive arc lengths causes the diffusion, through convection currents, of the protecting envelope of carbon dioxide, with the result that the exposed hot metal is rapidly oxidized or "burned." For most purposes a 250-amp. arc should not exceed a length of 1 in. and the length of a 500-amp. arc should not exceed $1\frac{1}{2}$ in. In view of the large variation permissible, the welder should be able to maintain an arc length which assures a soft weld metal with but little slag content.

The arc serves to transform electrical energy into thermal energy. The energy developed at the metal terminal or arc crater is utilized to melt the parent metal, while that generated in the arc stream serves to melt the filling material. If the molten filler is not properly guided and, as a consequence, overruns the fused parent metal, a poor weld will result. This

process necessitates, therefore, a constant observation of the
distribution of the fused metals as well as a proper control
of the direction of flow and speed of deposition of the filling
metal.

There are two methods in use for adding the filler with a

Fig. 49.—Starting to Build Up a Surface.

minimum overlap. One is called the "puddling" process. It
consists in melting a small area of the parent metal, thrusting
the end of the filler rod into the arc stream, where a small
section is melted or cut off, withdrawing the rod and fusing
the added material with the molten parent metal by imparting

Fig. 50.—Building-Up Process Nearly Completed.

a rotary motion to the arc. This puddling of the metals serves
also to float slag and oxidized material to the edge of the
fused area, where they may be brushed or chipped off.

The rapid building up of a surface by this method is shown
in Fig. 49. The short sections of filler rod were welded to

the sides of the casting in order to prevent the molten material from overflowing and to indicate the required height of the addition. The appearance of the nearly completed "fill" is shown in Fig. 50. One side of the added metal is lower than the others to facilitate the floating off of the slag, some of

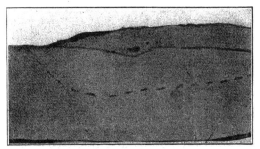

FIG. 51.—Section Through a Built-Up Weld.

FIG. 52.—Method of Depositing Filling Material in Layers.

which may be observed adhering to the edge of the plate. Fig. 51 shows a section through a weld produced in this manner, the continuous line indicating the zone of fusion and the broken line the boundary of crystal structural change produced by the temperature cycle through which the parent metal has passed as a result of the absorption of the arc energy.

Some users of this method advocate puddling short sections of the filler rod, 1 to 3 in. in length, with the parent metal. Where this is done, the filler may be incompletely fused and therefore not welded to the surface of the parent metal.

In the second method the filler material is deposited in

FIG. 53.—Layers of Deposits Smoothed Over.

FIG. 54.—Fused Ends of Filler Rods.

layers, as shown in Figs. 52 and 53, the deposits being similar to those obtained with the metallic electrode process but wider and higher. In these examples a welding current of 250 amp. with a filling rod $\frac{3}{8}$ in. in dia. were used. This method simply requires the operator to feed the filling rod continuously into the arc stream so that the molten filler deposits on the area of parent metal fused by the arc terminal while the arc travels across the surface. If the end of the rod is moved forward while resting on the surface of the newly deposited metal,

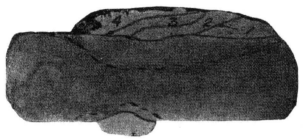

Fig. 55.—Showing the Fusion of Parent Metal and Four Layers.

most of the slag produced by the oxidation of the hot metal is floated to the sides of the deposit, where it may be brushed or chipped off.

The appearance of fused filler rod ends when correctly manipulated is shown in Fig. 54. Slag may be observed still

Fig. 56.—Flanged Edges Welded with Graphite Arc.

adhering to the bottom of one of the rods. The fusion between parent and added metal is shown in Fig. 55. Four layers of added metal are shown at the upper surface.

To remove slag or improve the appearance of the deposits

the surface of the added metal may be remelted by running the arc terminal over it, provided "burning" and hardening of the metal is avoided. Figs. 52 and 53 illustrate plainly the appearance of deposits before and after the surfacing operation.

The expedient of hammering or swaging the hot deposited metal is frequently resorted to where a refinement in the structure of the crystal grains is desirable.

Flanged Seam Welding.—Fig. 56 illustrates a useful application of the original carbon-arc process wherein no filler metal is used, the metal arc terminal serving to melt together the flanged edges.

This process is easily performed. To obtain adequate fusion the arc current selected should have such a value that the metal-arc crater nearly spans the edges of the seam. To assure the maintenance of a stable arc a small, tapered electrode should be employed, the diameter of the electrode end remaining less than $\frac{1}{8}$-in. during use.

This graphite arc process is used occasionally to form butt and lap welds by melting together the sides of the joint without the use of filler metal. Examination of sections through joints made in this manner reveals that the weld is very shallow and therefore weak.

Welding of Non-Ferrous Metals.—Copper and bronzes have been successfully welded with the graphite arc when employing a bronze filler rod low in tin and zinc and high in phosphorous, at least 0.25 per cent. The best filler material for the various analyses of parent metals has not been determined, but it is recognized that the presence of some deoxidizing agent such as phosphorus is necessary in order to insure sound welds free from oxide and blowholes. Since copper and its alloys have a high thermal capacity and conductivity, preheating of the structure facilitates the fusion of the joint surfaces. The grain of the completed weld may be refined by subjecting the metal to a suitable mechanical working and temperature cycle.

Low-melting-point metals such as lead may be welded by holding the graphite electrode in contact with the surfaces to be fused without drawing an arc, the current value used being sufficient to heat the end of the carbon to incandescence. The hot electrode tip may also be used to melt the filler rod into the molten parent metal.

Application.—The graphite arc processes may be used for the following purposes:

(1) Welding of cast steel and non-ferrous metals.

(2) Cutting of cast-iron and cast-steel risers and fins and non-ferrous metals.

(3) Rapid deposition of metal to build up a surface or fill in shrinkage cavities, cracks, blowholes and sand pockets where strength is of minor importance.

(4) Fusion of standing seams.

(5) Melting and cutting of scrap metal.

(6) Remelting of a surface to improve its appearance or fit.

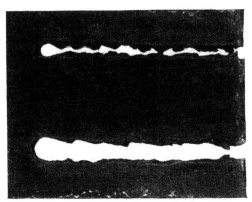

Fig. 57.—Typical Carbon-Electrode Cuts in ½-In. Ship Plate.

(7) Preheating of a metal structure to facilitate the welding operation, to reduce locked-in stresses or to alter some dimension.

(8) Deposition of hard metal or the hardening of a surface by the inclusion of vaporized carbon, such as rails, frogs and wheel treads.

(9) Automatic cutting and welding of sheet metal.

Cutting.—The manipulation of the cutting arc is exceedingly simple, the operator merely advancing the arc terminal over the section to be cut at a rate equal to that at which the molten metal flows from the cut. The cutting speed in-

creases with the value of arc current used. The **width** of the
cut increases with the arc diameter and therefore as the square
root of the arc current. Fig. 57 shows the appearance of cuts
made in ship steel plate ½ in. thick. The following data apply
in this case:

Position of Cut	Amp.	Width, in.	Length, in.	Time, min.
Upper	250	0.5	8	2½
Lower	650	0.8	8	1

Before cutting this plate the welder outlined the desired
course of the cut by a series of prick-punch marks.

When cutting deeper than 4 in. the electrode should not
come in contact with the walls of the cut and thereby short-
circuit the arc.

This process may be used for cutting both ferrous and non-
ferrous metals. It has found a particularly useful field in the
cutting of cast iron. It is often used for the "burning" out
of blast-furnace tap holes and the melting or cutting of iron
frozen in such furnaces.

CUTTING METALS

The accompanying charts illustrate the application of the
carbon electrode cutting process with a current value of 350
to 800 amperes, depending on the thickness of the metal and
the speed of cutting desired. A moderate cutting speed is
obtained at a small operating expense, adapting it particularly
for use in foundries for cutting off risers, sink heads, for cutting up scrap, and general work of this nature where a smooth
finish cut is not essential.

The cross section of these risers, etc., is frequently of considerable area, but by the use of the proper current value,
they may be readily removed.

Table IV shows the results obtained from tests in cutting
steel plate with the electric arc. The curves show the rate
of cutting cast iron sections of various shapes. Fig. 58 shows
the rate of cutting cast iron plates. Fig. 59 circular cross
sections, and Fig. 60 square blocks. The curves are based on
data secured through an extensive series of observations.

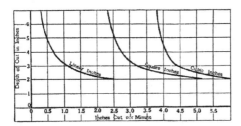

FIG. 58.—Rate of Cutting Cast Iron Plates.

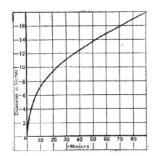

FIG. 59.—Rate of Cutting Cast Iron of Circular Cross Section.

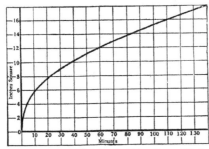

FIG. 60.—Rate of Cutting Cast Iron Square Blocks.

TABLE IV.—CUTTING STEEL PLATES WITH THE CARBON ARC

Thickness in Inches	Current in Amps.	Speed Minutes Per Ft.	Kw.-Hrs. Per Ft.
3/8	400	.50	.312
1/2	400	1.20	.75
5/8	400	2.14	1.34
3/4	400	3.00	1.88
1	600	3.75	3.50
1 3/4	600	4.32	4.10
2	600	6.75	6.30
4	600	16.90	15.50
6	800	29.00	36.20
8	800	40.50	50.00
10	800	59.00	74.00
12	800	65.00	82.00

CHAPTER VI

ARC WELDING PROCEDURE

It is presumed that the welder has a fair knowledge of the different processes of both carbon and metallic arc welding, gained from reading the previous chapters or from actual experience. However, we will recapitulate to some extent in order to make everything as clear as possible. Then we shall give some examples of the proper procedure in making welds of various kinds. For the descriptions and drawings we are principally indebted to the Westinghouse Electric and Manufacturing Co., the Lincoln Electric Co., and the Wilson Welder and Metals Co.

In order to prepare the metal for a satisfactory weld, the entire surfaces to be welded must be made readily accessible to the deposit of the new metal which is to be added. In addition, it is very essential that the surfaces are free from dirt, grease, sand, rust or other foreign matter. For this service, a sandblast, metal wire brush, or cold chisel are recommended.

During the past few years great progress has been made in the improvement of steels by the proper correlation of heat treatment and chemical composition. The characteristics of high-carbon and alloy steels, particularly, have been radically improved. However, no amount of heat treatment will appreciably improve or change the characteristics of medium and low-carbon steels which comprise the greatest field of application for arc welding. Furthermore, the metal usually deposited by the arc is a low-carbon steel often approaching commercially pure iron. It must be evident therefore that the changes of steel structure due to the arc-welding process will not be appreciable and also that any subsequent heat treatment of the medium- or mild-steel material will not result in improvements commensurate with the cost.

81

Pre-heating of medium and mild steel before applying the arc is not necessary and will only enable the operator to make a weld with a lesser value of current.

Cast-iron welds must be annealed before machining other than grinding is done in the welded sections. This is necessary because at the boundary between the original cast iron and the deposited metal there will be formed a zone of hard, high-carbon steel produced by the union of carbon (from the cast iron) with the iron filler. This material is chilled quite suddenly after the weld is made by the dissipation of the heat into the surrounding cast iron which is usually at a comparatively low temperature.

Although it is not absolutely necessary to pre-heat cast iron previous to arc welding, this is done in some instances to produce a partial annealing of the finished weld. The pre-heating operation will raise the temperature of a large portion of the casting. When the weld is completed, the heat in the casting will flow into the welded section, thereby reducing the rate of cooling.

Arc Length.—The maintenance of the proper arc length for the metallic electrode process is very important. With a long arc an extended surface of the work is covered probably caused by air drafts with the result that there is only a thin deposit of the new metal with poor fusion. If, however, the arc is maintained short, much better fusion is obtained, the new metal will be confined to a smaller area, and the burning and porosity of the fused metal will be reduced by the greater protection from atmospheric oxygen afforded by the enveloping inert gases. With increase in arc length, the flame becomes harder to control, so that it is impossible to adequately protect the deposited metal from oxidation.

The arc length should be uniform and just as short as it is possible for a good welder to maintain it. Under good normal conditions the arc length is such that the arc voltage never exceeds 25 volts and the best results are obtained between 18 and 22 volts. For an arc of 175 amp. the actual gap will be about $\frac{1}{8}$ inch.

Manipulation of the Arc.—The arc is established by touching the electrode to the work, and drawing it away to approximately $\frac{1}{8}$ in., in the case of the metallic electrode. This is best done by a dragging touch with the electrode slightly out of vertical. The electrode is then held approximately at right angles to the surface of the work, as the tendency is for the heat to go straight from the end of the electrode. This assures the fusing of the work, provided the proper current and arc length have been uniformly maintained.

A slight semicircular motion of the electrode, which at the same time is moved along the groove, will tend to float the slag to the top better than if the electrode is moved along a straight line in one continuous direction and the best results are obtained when the welding progresses in an upward direction. It is necessary in making a good weld to "bite" into the work to create a perfect fusion along the edges of the weld, while the movement of the electrode is necessary for the removal of any mechanical impurities that may be deposited. It is the practice to collect the slag about a nucleus by this

Fig. 61.—Diagram Illustrating Filling Sequence.

rotary movement and then float it to the edge of the weld. If this cannot be done, the slag is removed by chipping or brushing with a wire brush.

Filling Sequence.—When making a long seam between plates, the operator is always confronted with the problem of expansion and contraction which cause the plates to warp and produce internal strains in both plates and deposited material.

The method of welding two plates together is shown in Fig. 61. The plates are prepared for welding as previously described, and the arc is started at the point *A*. The welding then progresses to the point *B*, joining the edges together, to point *D* and back to *A*. This procedure is carried on with the first layer filling in a space of 6 or 8 in. in length, afterward returning for the additional layers necessary to fill the groove. This method allows the entire electrode to be deposited without breaking the arc, and the thin edges of the work are not fused away as might be the case if the operator should endeavor to join these edges by moving the electrode in one continuous direction. This method also prevents too rapid chilling with consequent local strains adjacent to the weld.

When making a long seam weld, for example, a butt weld between two plates, the two pieces of metal will warp and have their relative positions distorted during the welding process, unless the proper method is used.

A method was devised and has been successfully put into operation by E. Wanamaker and H. R. Pennington, of the Chicago, Rock Island and Pacific R.R. By their method the

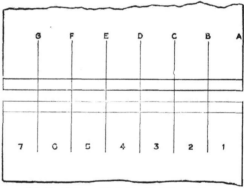

Fig. 62.—Diagram Illustrating Back-Step Method.

plates are fastened together by light tack welds about 8 in. apart along the whole seam. The operator then makes a complete weld between the first two tacks as described in the preceding paragraph, and, skipping three spaces, welds between the fifth and sixth tacks and so on until the end of the seam is reached. This skipping process is repeated by starting between the second and third tacks and so on until the complete seam is welded. The adoption of this method permits the heat, in a restricted area, to be dissipated and radiated before additional welding is performed near that area. Thus the weld is made on comparatively cool sections of the plates which keeps the expansion at a minimum.

Another method very similar to the preceding one, is known as the back-step method, Fig. 62, in which the weld is performed in sections as in the skipping process. After the pieces are tacked at intervals of 6 in. or less for short seams, the arc is applied at the second tack and the groove welded back complete to the first tack. Work is then begun at the third tack and the weld carried back to the second tack, practically completing that section. Each section is finished before starting the next.

Fig. 63 shows the procedure of welding in a square sheet or patch. Work is started at A and carried to B completely welding the seam. In order that work may next be started at the coolest point, the bottom seam is completed starting at D, finishing at C. The next seam is A to D, starting at A.

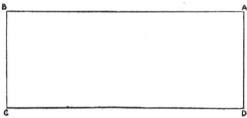

Fig. 63.—Diagram Illustrating Square Patch Method.

The last seam is finished, starting at B, and completing the weld at C.

Alternating-Current Arc Welding.—Direct current has been used for arc welding because of the fact that it possesses certain inherent advantages that make it especially adaptable for this class of work. However, the use of alternating current for arc welding has found a number of advocates.

When employing this form of energy, use is made of a transformer to reduce the distribution voltage to that suitable for application to the weld.

Inasmuch as the arc voltage is obtained directly from the distribution mains through a transformer, the theoretical efficiency is high compared with the direct-current process which requires the introduction of a motor-generator or resistor or both. The efficiency of the a.c. equipments now on the market ranges from 60 to 80 per cent. The transformer, however, is designed to have a large leakage reactance so as to furnish stability to the arc, which very materially reduces its efficiency when compared with that of the standard distribution transformer used by lighting companies.

It is difficult to maintain the alternating arc when using a bare electrode though this difficulty is somewhat relieved when use is made of a coated electrode.

Quasi Arc Welding.—The electrodes used in quasi arc welding are made by the Quasi Arc Weldtrode Co., Brooklyn, N. Y., and are known as "weldtrodes." A mild-steel wire is used with a very small aluminum wire running lengthwise of it. Around the two is wrapped asbestos thread. This asbestos thread is held on by dipping the combination into something similar to waterglass. Either a.c. or d.c. may be used, at a pressure of about 105 volts, with a suitable resistance for regulating the current. The company's directions and claims for this process are: "The bared end of the weldtrode, held in a suitable holder, is connected to one pole of the current supply by means of a flexible cable, the return wire being connected to the work. In the case of welding small articles, the work is laid on an iron plate or bench to which the return wire is connected. Electrical contact is made by touching the work with the end of the weldtrode held vertically, thus allowing current to pass and an arc to form. The weldtrode, still kept in contact with the work, is then dropped to an angle, and a quasi-arc will be formed owing to the fact that the special covering passes into the igneous state, and as a secondary conductor maintains electrical connection between the work and the metallic core of the weldtrode. The action once started, the weldtrode melts at a uniform rate so long as it remains in contact, and leaves a seam of metal fused into the work. The covering material of the weldtrode, acting as a slag, floats and spreads over the surface of the weld as it is formed. The fused metal, being entirely covered by the slag, is protected from oxidation. The slag covering is readily chipped or brushed off when the weld cools, leaving a bright clean metallic surface. In welding do not draw the weldtrode along the seam, as it is burning away all the time, and therefore it is only necessary to feed it down, but do this with a slightly lateral movement, so as to spread the heat and deposited metal equally to both sides of the joint. Care must be taken to keep feeding down at the same rate as the weldtrode is melting. On no account draw the weldtrode away from the work to make a continuous arc as this will result in putting down bad metal. The aim should be to keep the point of the weld-

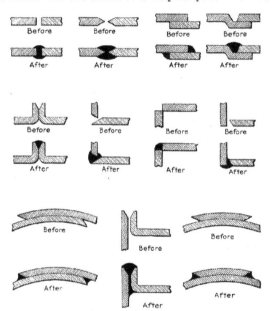

Fig. 64.—Typical Examples of Prepared and Finished Work.

trode just in the molten slag by the feel of the covering just rubbing on the work. By closely observing the operation, the molten metal can easily be distinguished from the molten slag, the metal being dull red and the slag very bright red.''

The weldtrodes are supplied ready for use in standard lengths of 18 in., and of various diameters, according to the size and nature of the work for which they are required.

Typical Examples of Arc Welding.—The examples of welding shown in Figs. 64, 65 and 66 are taken from the manual issued by the Wilson Welder and Metals Co. They will be found very useful as a guide for all sorts of work. Fig. 64

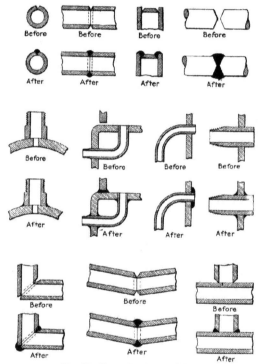

FIG. 65.—Examples of Tube Work.

shows miscellaneous plate or sheet jobs, Fig. 65 shows tube jobs, while Fig. 66 gives examples of locomotive-frame and boiler-tube welding.

As a basis for various welding calculations the following data will be found of use: On straight-away welding the ordinary operator with helper will actually weld about 75 per cent of the time.

The *average* results of a vast amount of data show that an

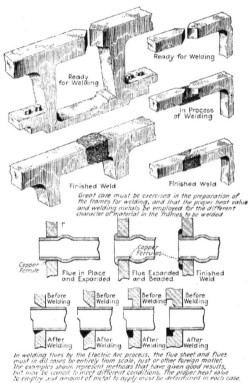

Great care must be exercised in the preparation of the frames for welding, and that the proper heat value and welding metals be employed for the different character of material in the frames to be welded

Copper Ferrule — Flue in Place and Expanded — Copper Ferrules — Flue Expanded and Beaded — Finished Weld

Before Welding — Before Welding — Before Welding — Before Welding — After Welding — After Welding — After Welding — After Welding

In welding flues by the Electric Arc process, the flue sheet and flues must in all cases be entirely from scale, rust or other foreign matter. The examples shown represent methods that have given good results, but may be varied to meet different conditions. The proper heat value to employ and amount of metal to apply must be determined in each case.

FIG. 66.—Examples of Electric Welding of Locomotive Frames and Boiler Tubes.

operator can deposit about 1.8 lb. of metal per hour. This rate depends largely upon whether the work is done out in the open or in a special place provided in the shop. For outside work such as on boats, an operator will not average in general more than 1.2 lb. per hour, while in the shop the same operator could easily deposit the 1.8 lb. stated above. This loss in speed for outside work is brought about largely by the cooling action of the air and also somewhat by the added inconvenience to the operator. The value of pounds per hour given above is based on the assumption that the work has been lined up and is ready for welding. On the average 70 per cent of the weight of electrodes is deposited in the weld, 12 per cent is burned or vaporized and the remainder 18 per cent is wasted as short ends.

Other figures prepared by the Electric Welding Committee show the possible cost of a fillet weld on a ½-in. plate, using a motor generator set and bare electrodes to be as follows:

Average speed of welding on continuous straight away work   5 ft. per hour
Amount of metal deposited per running foot.............   .6 lb.
Current 150 amps, at 20 volts = 3 kilowatts.
Motor generator eff. 50 per cent = 6 kw. ÷ 5 equals   1.2 k.w.h. per 1 ft. run
1.2 k.w.h. at 3 cents per k.w.h. equals.............   3.6 cents per ft.
Cost of electrode 10 cents per pound and allowing
  for waste ends, etc., equals....................   7.2 cents per ft.
Labor at 65 cents per hour equals...............   13.00 cents per ft.
                                                     _____
                                                     23.8 cents per ft.

Suggestions for the Design of Welded Joints.—From an engineering point of view, every metallic joint whether it be riveted, bolted or welded, is designed to withstand a perfectly definite kind and amount of stress. An example of this is the longitudinal seam in the shell of a horizontal fire-tube riveted boiler. This joint is designed for tension and steam tightness only and will not stand even a small amount of transverse bending stress without failure by leaking. If a joint performs the function for which it was designed and no more, its designer has fulfilled his responsibilities and it is a good joint economically. Regardless of how the joint is made the design of joint which costs the least to make and which at the same time performs the functions required of it, with a reasonable factor of safety, is the best joint.

The limitations of the several kinds of mechanical and welded joints should be thoroughly understood.

A bolted joint is expensive, is difficult to make steam- or water-pressure tight, but has the distinguishing advantage that

it can be disassembled without destruction. Bolted joints which
are as strong as the pieces bolted together are usually imprac-
ticable, owing to their bulk.

Riveted joints are less expensive to make than bolted joints
but cannot be disassembled without destruction to the rivets.
A riveted joint, subject to bending stress sufficient to produce
appreciable deformation, will not remain steam- or water-
pressure tight. Riveted joints can never be made as strong
as the original sections because of the metal punched out to
form the rivet holes.

There is no elasticity in either riveted, bolted or fusion-
welded joints which must remain steam- or water-pressure
tight. Excess material is required in the jointed sections of
bolted or riveted joints, owing to the weakness of the joints.

Fusion-welded joints have as a limit of tensile strength
the tensile strength of cast metal of a composition identical
to that of the joined pieces. The limit of the allowable
bending stress is also set by the properties of cast metal of
the same composition as that of the joined pieces. The reason
for this limitation is that on the margin of a fusion weld
adjacent to the pieces joined, the metal of the pieces was heated
and cooled without change of composition. Whatever properties the original metal had, due to heat or mechanical treatment,
are removed by this action, which invariably occurs in a fusion
weld. Regardless of what physical properties of the metal used
to form the joint may be, the strength or ability to resist
bending of the joint, as a whole, cannot exceed the corresponding properties of this metal in the margin of the weld. Thus,
assuming that a fusion weld be made in boiler plate, having
a tensile strength of 62,000 pounds. Assume that nickel-steel,
having a tensile strength of 85,000 lb. be used to build up the
joint. No advantage is gained by the excess 23,000 lb. tensile
strength of the nickel-steel of the joint since the joint will
fail at a point close to 62,000 lb. If appreciable bending stress
be applied to the joint it will fail in the margin referred to.

The elastic limit of the built-in metal is the same as its
ultimate strength for all practical purposes, but the ultimate
strength is above the elastic limit of the joined sections in
commercial structures.

In spite of the limitations of the fusion-welded joint it is possible and practicable to build up a joint in commercial steel which will successfully resist any stress which will be encountered in commercial work.

The fundamental factor in the strength of a welded joint is the strength of the material added by the welding process. This factor depends upon the nature of the stress applied. The metal added by the welding process, when subject to tension, can be relied on in commercial practice to give a tensile strength of 45,000 lb. per square inch. This is an average condition; assuming that the metal added is mild steel and that the operation is properly done, the metal will have approximately the same strength in compression as in tension. When a torsional stress is applied to a welded joint the resultant stress is produced by a combination of bending, tension and compression, as well as shear. The resistance of the metal to shear may be figured at $^8/_{10}$ its resistance to tensile stress. The metal added by the welding process, with the present development in the art of welding, will stand very little bending stress. A fusion-welded joint made by the electric-arc process must be made stiffer than the adjacent sections in order that the bending stress shall not come in the joint. An electric weld, when properly made, will be steam- and water-pressure tight so long as bending of members of the structure does not produce failure of the welded joint.

Little is known at the present time in regard to the resistance of an electrically welded joint to dynamic stress, but there is reason to believe that the resistance to this kind of stress is low. However, owing to the fact that in most structures there is an opportunity for the members of the structure to flex and reduce the strain upon the weld, this inherent weakness of the welded joint does not interfere seriously with its usefulness.

A few tests have been made of high-frequency alternating stresses and it has been found that using the ordinary wire electrode the welded joint fails at a comparatively small number of alternations. This is of little importance in most structures since high-frequency alternating stress is not often encountered.

Stresses in Joints.—The accompanying cuts show a number of typical joints and the arrows indicate the stresses brought

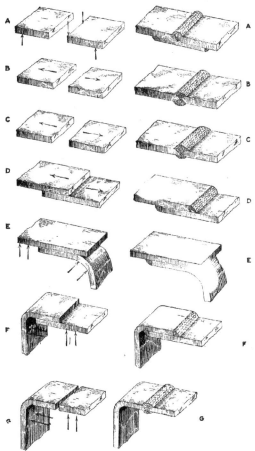

FIG. 67.—Joints Designed to Overcome Certain Stresses.

to bear on them. The proper way to weld each example is plainly shown.

In *A*, Fig. 67, it will be noted that a reinforcing plate is welded to the joint to make the joint sufficiently stiff to throw the bending outside the weld.

B shows a joint in straight tension. Since no transverse stress occurs the heavy reinforcing of *A* is not required. Just enough reinforcing is given the joint to make up for the deficiency in tensile strength of the metal of the weld.

C shows another method of building up a joint that is in

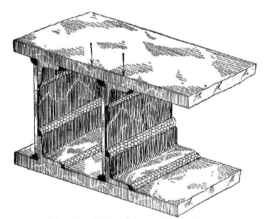

Fig. 68.—Plate and Angle Construction.

straight tension. It should be noted that in both *B* and *C* as much reinforcing is placed on one side of a center line through the plates as is placed on the other.

The original form of lap joint such as is used in riveting is shown at *D*. The method shown for welding this joint is the only method which can be used. It cannot be recommended because such a joint, when in straight tension, tends to bring the center line of the plate into coincidence with the center line of the stress. In so doing an excessive stress is placed on the welded material.

E shows the construction used in certain large tanks where a flanged head is backed into a cylindrical shell. The principal stress to be resisted by the welded joint is that tending to push the head out of the shell. The welding process indicated in the figure will successfully do this. Owing to the friction between the weld and the shell, the outer weld would be sufficient to hold the weld in place for ordinary pressure. For higher pressures the inside weld should be made in addition.

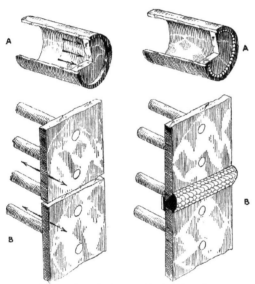

FIG. 69.—Pipe Heading and Firebox Sheet Work.

F and G show another method of welding a flanged head to the cylindrical shell. These methods are preferable to the method indicated in E. G represents the recommended practice.

Fig. 68 shows a plate and angle structure which might be used in ship construction. The particular feature to notice in the welding practice indicated, is that the vertical plates do not reach the entire distance between the horizontal plates.

This is merely a method of eliminating difficulties in welding the plates to the angle.

A in Fig. 69 shows a method of welding a head into a cylindrical pipe. The thickness of the head should be approximately twice the thickness of the wall of the pipe. The extra thickness plate is to gain sufficient stiffness in the head to make the stress on the welded material purely shear. The pressure from the inside tends to make the head assume a hemispherical shape. This would place a bending stress on the welded material if the head were thin enough to give at the proper pressure.

B shows a method of welding a crack in a fire-box sheet. The thin plate backing introduced at the weld makes the operation very much easier for the operator and produces the reinforcing of the water side of the fire-box sheet which is most desirable.

INSPECTION OF METALLIC ELECTRODE ARC WELDS

Determining the character of welded joints is of prime importance, says O. S. Escholz, and the lack of a satisfactory method, more than any other factor, has been responsible for the hesitancy among engineers of the extensive adoption of arc welding. To overcome this prejudice it is desirable to shape our rapidly accumulating knowledge of operation into an acceptable method of inspection.

Manufactured apparatus is practically all accepted on the basis of complying with a process specification rigidly enforced in conjunction with the successful reaction to certain tests applied to the finished product. Riveting impairs the strength of the joined plates, yet with a proper layout and intelligent inspection the completed structure possesses certain definite characteristics which do not require further verification. The inspector of a finished concrete structure is practically helpless, and the weakest sort of construction may be concealed by a sound surface. With careful supervision, however, the physical properties of the completed structure can be reliably gaged to the extent that the use of concrete is justified even in ship construction. With this in view, electric arc welding is susceptible to even better control than obtain in either of these structural operations.

The four factors which determine the physical characteristics of the metallic electrode arc welds are: Fusion, slag content, porosity and crystal structure.

Some of the other important methods that have been suggested and used for indicating these characteristics are:

1. Examination of the weld by visual means to determine (a) finish of the surface as an index to workmanship; (b) length of deposits, which indicates the frequency of breaking arc, and therefore the ability to control the arc; (c) uniformity of the deposits, as an indication of the faithfulness with which the filler metal is placed in position; (d) fusion of deposited metal to bottom of weld scarf as shown by appearance of under side of welded joint; (e) predominance of surface porosity and slag.

2. The edges of the deposited layers chipped with a cold chisel or calking tool to determine the relative adhesion of deposit.

3. Penetration tests to indicate the linked unfused zones, slag pockets and porosity by (a) X-ray penetration; (b) rate of gas penetration; (c) rate of liquid penetration.

4. Electrical tests (as a result of incomplete fusion, slag inclusions and porosity) showing variations in (a) electrical conductivity; (b) magnetic induction.

These tests if used to the best advantage would involve their application to each layer of deposited metal as well as to the finished weld. This, except in unusual instances, would not be required by commercial practice in which a prescribed welding process is carried out.

Of the above methods the visual examination is of more importance than generally admitted. Together with it the chipping and calking tests are particularly useful, the latter test serving to indicate gross neglect by the operator of the cardinal welding principles, due to the fact that only a very poor joint will respond to the tests.

The most reliable indication of the soundness of the weld is offered by the penetration tests. Obviously the presence of unfused oxide surfaces, slag deposits and blowholes will offer a varying degree of penetration. Excellent results in the testing of small samples are made possible by the use of the X-ray. However, due to the nature of the apparatus, the

amount of time required and the difficulty of manipulating
and interpreting results, it can hardly be considered at the
present time as a successful means to be used on large-scale
production.

The rate that hydrogen or air leaks through a joint from
pressure above atmospheric to atmospheric, or from atmospheric
to partial vacuum, can readily be determined by equipment
that would be quite cumbersome, and the slight advantage
over liquid penetration in time reduction is not of sufficient
importance to warrant consideration for most welds.

Of the various liquids that may be applied kerosene has
marked advantages because of its availability, low volatility
and high surface tension. Due to the latter characteristics
kerosene sprayed on a weld surface is rapidly drawn into any
capillaries produced by incomplete fusion between deposited
metal and weld scarf, or between succeeding deposits, slag
inclusions, gas pockets, etc., penetrating through the weld and
showing the existence of an unsatisfactory structure by a stain
on the emerging side. A bright-red stain can be produced by
dissolving suitable oil-soluble dyes in the kerosene. By this
means the presence of faults have been found that could not
be detected with hydraulic pressure or other methods.

By the kerosene penetration a sequence of imperfect structure linked through the weld, which presents the greatest
hazard in welded joints, could be immediately located, but it
should be borne in mind that this method is not applicable
to the detection of isolated slag or gas pockets nor small,
disconnected unfused areas. It has been shown by various tests,
however, that a weld may contain a considerable amount of
distributed small imperfections, without affecting to a great
extent its characteristics.

If a bad fault is betrayed by the kerosene test it is advisable to burn out the metal with a carbon arc before rewelding
under proper supervision. By the means of sandblast, steam
or gasoline large quantities of kerosene are preferably removed.
No difficulty has been encountered on welding over a thin
film of the liquid.

Electrical tests, by which the homogeneity of welds is
determined, are still in the evolutionary stages, and many difficulties are yet to be overcome before this test becomes feasible.

Some of these difficulties are the elimination of the effect of contact differences, the influence of neighboring paths and fields, and the lack of practicable, portable instruments of sufficient sensibility for the detection of slight variations in conductivity or magnetic field intensity. No simple tests are plausible, excepting those which involve subjecting the metal to excessive stresses for determining the crystal structure. Control of this phase must be determined by the experience obtained from following a prescribed process.

The inspector of metallic arc electrode welds may consider that through the proper use of visual, chipping and penetrating tests a more definite appraisal of the finished joint may be obtained than by either riveting or concrete construction. The

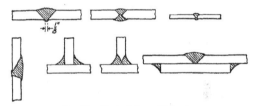

Fig. 70.—Typical Arc-weld Scarfs.

operation may be still further safeguarded by requiring rigid adherence to a specified process.

Good results are assured if correct procedure is followed.

Haphazard welding can no sooner produce an acceptable product than hit-or-miss weaving will make a marketable cloth. It is only logical that all the steps in a manufacturing operation should be regulated to obtain the best results. As it is most welders consider themselves pioneers in an unknown art that requires the exercise of a peculiar temperament for its successful evolution, and as a result welding operators enshroud themselves in the halo of an expert and do their work with a mystery bewildering to the untutored. Once in a while, due we might say to coincidences, these "experts" obtain a good weld, but more often the good weld may be attributed to the friction between slightly fused, plastered deposits.

In common with all other operations metallic electrode arc

welding is really susceptible to analysis. Regardless of the metal welded with the arc the cardinal steps are: (1) Preparation of weld; (2) electrode selection; (3) arc-current adjustment; (4) arc-length maintenance, and (5) heat treatment.

Sufficient scarfing is involved in the preparation of the weld, as well as the separation of the weld slants, so that the entire surface is accessible to the operator with a minimum amount of filling required. When necessary to avoid distortion and internal stresses, owing to unequal expansion and contraction strains, the metal is preheated or placed so as to permit the necessary movement to occur. Various types of scarfs in common use are shown in Fig. 70.

The electrode selection is determined by the mass, thickness

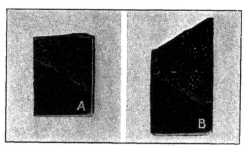

Fig. 71.—Good and Bad Welds.

and constitution of the material to be welded. An electrode free from impurities and containing about 17 per cent. carbon and 5 per cent. manganese has been found generally satisfactory for welding low and high carbon as well as alloy steels. This electrode can also be used for cast-iron and malleable-iron welding, although more dependable results, having a higher degree of consistency and permitting machining of welded sections, can be obtained by brazing, using a copper-aluminum-iron-alloy electrode and some simple flux. Successful results are obtained by brazing copper and brass with this electrode. The diameter of the electrode should be chosen with reference to the arc current used.

A great many concerns have attempted welding with too

low an arc current and the result has been a poorly fused deposit. This is due largely to the overheating characteristics of most electrode holders, or using current value, and thus leading the operator to conclude that the current used is in excess of the amount that is needed.

A, Fig. 71, shows a section through one-half of an exposed joint welded with the proper current, and *B* the effects of too low a current. The homogeneity and the good fusion of the one may be contrasted with the porosity and poor fusion of

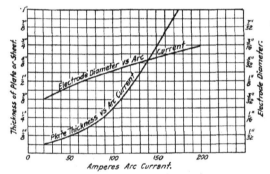

Fig. 72.—Diameters for Welding Steel Plate.

the latter. These surfaces have been etched to show the character of the metal and the welded zone.

The approximate values of arc current to be used for a given thickness of mild-steel plate, as well as the electrode diameter for a given arc current, may be taken from the curve in Fig. 72. The variation in the strength of 1-in. square welded joints as the welding current is increased is shown in Fig. 73.

Notwithstanding that the electrode development is still in its infancy the electrodes available are giving satisfactory results, but considerable strides can yet be made in the ductility of welds, consistency in results and ease of utilizing the process.

The maintenance of a short arc length is imperative. A nonporous, compact, homogeneous, fused deposit on a 1-in.

square bar from a short arc is shown in Fig. 74, *A*, and in *B* is shown a porous, diffused deposit from a long arc. Top views of these welds are shown in Fig. 75. A short arc is

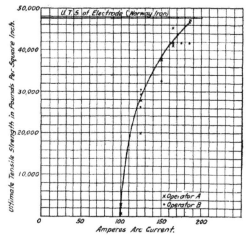

FIG. 73.—Variation in Weld Strength with Change in Arc Current.

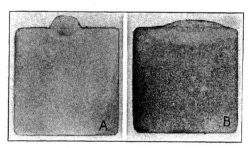

FIG. 74.—Sectional Views of Short and Long Arc Deposits.

usually maintained by a skillful operator, as the work is thereby expedited, less electrode material wasted and a better weld obtained because of improved fusion, decreased slag content and porosity. On observing the arc current and arc voltage by meter deflection or from the trace of recording instruments, the inspector has a continuous record of the most important factors which affect weld strength, ductility, fusion, porosity, etc. The use of a fixed series resistance and an automatic time-lag reset switch across the arc to definitely fix both the arc current and the arc voltage places these important factors entirely beyond the control of the welder and under the direction of the more competent supervisor.

Heat Treatment and Inspection.—The method of placing the deposited layers plays an important part on the internal strains and distortion obtained on contraction. It is possible that part of these strains could be relieved by preheating and

FIG. 75.—Top Views of Welds Shown in Fig. 74.

annealing as well as by the allowance made in preparation for the movement of the metal.

The heat treatment of a completed weld is not a necessity, particularly if it has been preheated for preparation and then subjected to partial annealing. A uniform annealing of the structure is desirable, even in the welding of the small sections of alloy and high-carbon steels, if it is to be machined or subjected to heavy vibratory stresses.

The inspector, in addition to applying the above tests to the completed joint and effectively supervising the process, can readily assure himself of the competency of any operator by the submission of sample welds to ductility and tensile tests or by simply observing the surface exposed on cutting through the fused zone, grinding its face and etching with a solution of 1 part concentrated nitric acid in 10 parts water.

It is confidently assumed, in view of the many resources at the disposal of the welding inspector, that this method of obtaining joints will rapidly attain successful recognition as a dependable operation to be used in structural engineering.

EFFECTS OF THE CHEMICAL COMPOSITION OF METALLIC ARC WELDING ELECTRODES

In order to ascertain to what extent the chemical analysis of an electrode affected the welded material in metallic arc welding, says J. S. Orton, two electrodes R and W were chosen of widely different chemical analyses, each 0.148 in. in diameter. The R electrode was within the specifications of the Welding Research Committee except that the silicon content was a little high. The analyses were as follows:

	C	Mn	P	S	Si
R wire	0.17	0.57	0.007	0.028	0.14
W wire	0.39	1.01	0.005	0.024	0.12

The silicon content was rather high, but inasmuch as it was fairly constant in both electrodes the results are comparative.

A deposit was made on a ½-in. plate by means of a metallic arc, the welded section being approximately 1 ft. long, 6 in. wide and 1 in. thick. The welding machine used was of a well-known make, with a constant voltage of 37 volts at 130 amperes. The plates used for depositing the first layer were machined away and two test bars were made from each electrode, composed entirely of welded material. The ends were rough-machined and about 4½ in. in the middle of the specimens were finished carefully.

The physical characteristics of the plates are as shown in Table V.

TABLE V.—PHYSICAL CHARACTERISTICS OF PLATES

	Tensile Strength	Elastic Limit	Elongation	RA Brinnel
R-1	57,300	43,400	8.0	15.3
2	56,050	50,500	6.0	5.9
W-1	76,200	64,000	7.5	13.0
2	72,650	60,260	5.5	7.1

After these bars were pulled, chemical analyses were taken at various points to get the values given in Table VI.

TABLE VI.—CHEMICAL ANALYSES OF SPECIMENS

	C	Mn	P	S	Si
R-1	0.12	0.23	0.012	0.019	0.10
2	0.09	0.24	0.016	0.014	0.08
3	0.11	0.26	0.014	0.020	0.08
W-1	0.23	0.84	0.014	0.012	0.02
2	0.20	0.80	0.014	0.014	0.05
3	0.20	0.88	0.013	0.013	0.02

Photographs of the different fractures are shown in Fig. 77. *W-1,* which gave the highest tensile strength, shows 100 per cent. metallic structure with a silky appearance. *R-1* shows a coarse intergranular fracture. *R-2* shows a brittle, shiny crystalline fracture with a slag inclusion at the lower left-hand and upper right-hand corners of the bars. *W-2*

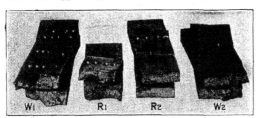

FIG. 76.—Fractures of Test Specimens.

shows partial crystalline and partial silky fracture. At the extreme right there is a portion which is not welded. This is probably the reason why *W-2* did not pull as much as the other. Undoubtedly, next to the chemical analysis, the quantity of slag in the weld has the biggest bearing on the tensile strength.

The structure of the test specimens is shown in the microphotographs of Fig. 77. In making these photographs, no attempt was made to make a complete microanalysis of the two different specimens, but rather it was intended to show the general difference in structure between the two different types of electrode. All of these photographs were taken at 150 diameters except the last two, which were taken at 100.

Photograph *R-1A* shows the general structure of the plate welded with the *R* electrode. This photograph shows a large-

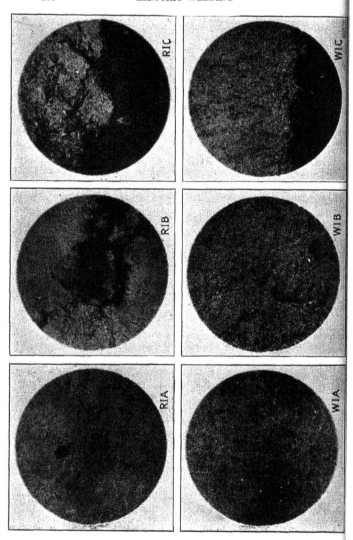

grain growth and columnar structure which are characteristic of electric welds. Photograph *W1-A* shows the general structure of the plate welded with the *W* electrode. This shows comparatively small-grain structure. The structure seems to be much better than that of *R1-A.* Photograph *R1-B* shows a portion of a test specimen which was cut out of plate *R1* and bent to an angle of 10 deg. It is interesting to note here the opening up of the welded material adjacent to slag inclusions. Photograph *W1-B* shows a portion of a small specimen cut out from sample *W1* and bent to an angle of 10 deg., the same as in the case of *R1-B.* The welded material is opening up but not in the same degree nor around the slag inclusions as in the corresponding photograph *R1-B.* Photograph *R1-C* is a profile of the fracture of the *R1* sample after bending through an angle of 15 deg. Photograph *W1-C* shows the *W1* sample after being bent through an angle of 17 degrees.

It seems just as important to specify the chemical composition of the electrode used in metallic arc welding as it is to specify the chemical composition in ordering any other type of steel.

Chemical composition seems to affect the physical properties in electrodes as well as other steel.

An excess of manganese seems to be needed in electrodes.

The relation between the carbon and manganese of an electrode should be approximately one to three.

High-carbon manganese wire tends not only to improve the weld on account of the amount of carbon and manganese in the welded material, but also on account of the type of structure which this wire lends to the deposited metal.

There is a smaller amount of oxide and slag inclusions with a high-carbon manganese wire than with a comparatively low-carbon manganese wire.

WELDING COMMITTEE ELECTRODES

After an exhaustive series of tests the Welding Committee drew up the following tentative specification for electrodes intended to be used in welding mild steel of shipbuilding quality:

Chemical Composition.—Carbon, not over 0.18 per cent; manganese, not over 0.55 per cent; phosphorus, not over 0.05

per cent; sulphur, not over 0.05 per cent; silicon, not over
0.08 per cent.

Sizes:	Fraction of Inch	Lbs. Per Foot	Foot Per Lb.	Lbs. Per 100 Ft.
	1/8	0.0416	24	4.16
	5/32	0.0651	15.35	6.51
	3/16	0.0937	10.66	9.37

Allowable tolerance 0.006 plus or minus.

Material.—The material from which the wire is manufactured shall be made by any approved process. Material made
by puddling process not allowed.

Physical Properties.—Wire to be of uniform homogeneous
structure, free from segregation, oxides, pipes, seams, etc., as
proven by micro-photographs. This wire may or may not be
covered.

Workmanship and Finish.—(a) Electric welding wire shall
be of the quality and finish known as "Bright Hard" or "Soft
Finish." "Black Annealed" or "Bright Annealed" wire shall
not be supplied. (b) The surface shall be free from oil or
grease.

Tests.—The commercial weldability of these electrodes shall
be determined by means of tests by an experienced operator,
who shall demonstrate that the wire flows smoothly and evenly
through the arc without any detrimental phenomena.

CHAPTER VII

ARC WELDING TERMS AND SYMBOLS

In order to aid the standardization of the various types of joints and welding operations the practice recommended by the Welding Committee of the Emergency Fleet Corp., for

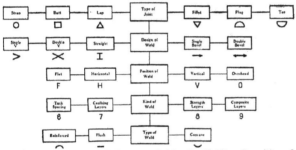

Fig. 78.—Standard Symbols Recommended by the Welding Committee of the Emergency Fleet Corporation.

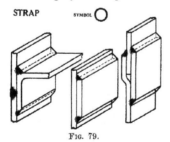

Fig. 79.

ship work, is given. The symbol chart is shown in Fig. 78 and the application of special terms and symbols is individually shown in Figs. 79 to 112 inclusive.

Fig. 79.—**A Strap weld** is one in which the seam of two adjoining plates or surfaces is reinforced by any form or shape to add strength and stability to the joint or plate. In this form of weld the seam can only be welded from the side of the work opposite the reinforcement, and the reinforcement, of whatever

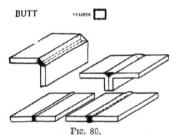

FIG. 80.

shape, must be welded from the side of the work to which the reinforcement is applied.

Fig. 80.—**A Butt weld** is one in which two plates or surfaces are brought together edge to edge and welded along the seam thus formed. The two plates when so welded form a perfectly

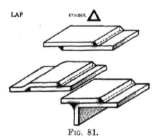

FIG. 81.

flat plane in themselves, excluding the possible projection caused by other individual objects as frames, straps, stiffeners, etc., or the building up of the weld proper.

Fig. 81.—**A Lap weld** is one in which the edges of two planes are set one above the other and the welding material so applied as to bind the edge of one plate to the face of the other plate. In this form of weld the seam or lap forms a raised surface along its entire extent.

Fig. 82.—**A Fillet weld** is one in which some fixture or member is welded to the face of the plate, by welding along

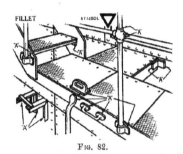

FIG. 82.

the vertical edge of the fixture or member (see welds shown and marked A). The welding material is applied in the corner thus formed and finished at an angle of forty-five degrees to the plate.

Fig. 83.—**A Plug weld** is one used to connect the metals by

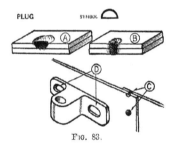

FIG. 83.

welding through a hole in either one plate A or both plates B. Also used for filling through a bolt hole as at C, or for added strength when fastening fixtures to the face of a plate by drilling a countersunk hole through the fixtures and applying the welding material through this hole, as at D, thereby fastening the fixture to the plate at this point.

FIG. 84.—**A Tee weld** is one where one plate is welded vertically to another as in the case of the edge of a transverse bulkhead A, being welded against the shellplating or deck. This is a weld which in all cases requires *exceptional* care and can only be used where it is possible to work from both sides

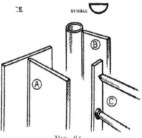

FIG. 84.

of the vertical plate. Also used for welding a rod in a vertical position to a flat surface, as the rung of a ladder C, or a plate welded vertically to a pipe stanchion B, as in the case of water closet stalls.

FIG. 85.—**A Single "V"** is applied to the "edge finish" of a plate when this edge is beveled from *both* sides to an

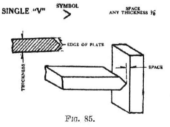

FIG. 85.

angle, the degrees of which are left to the designer. To be used when the "V" side of the plate is to be a maximum "strength" weld, with the plate setting vertically to the face of adjoining member, and only when the electrode can be applied from both sides of the work.

Fig. 86.—**Double "V"** is applied to the "edge finish" of two adjoining plates when the adjoining edges of both plates

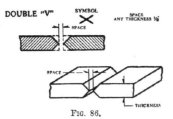

Fig. 86.

beveled from *both* sides to an angle, the degrees of which are left to the designer. To be used when the two plates are to be "butted" together along these two sides for a maximum

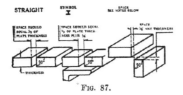

Fig. 87.

"strength" weld. Only to be used when welding can be performed from both sides of the plate.

Fig. 87.—**Straight** is applied to the "edge finish" of a plate, when this edge is left in its crude or sheared state. To be

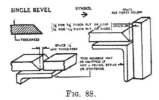

Fig. 88.

used only where maximum strength is *not* essential, or unless used in connection with strap, stiffener or frame, or where it is impossible to otherwise finish the edge. Also to be used for a "strength" weld, when edges of two plates set vertically to each other—as the edge of a box.

FIG. 88.—**Single Bevel** is applied to the edge finish of a

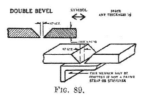

FIG. 89.

plate, when this edge is beveled from *one* side only to an angle, the degrees of which are left to the designer. To be used for "strength" welding, when the electrode can be applied

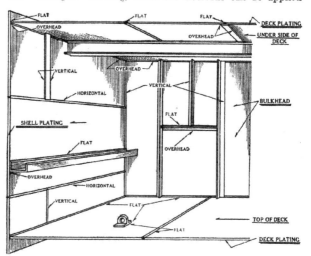

FIG. 90.

from *one* side of the plate only, or where it is impossible to finish the adjoining surface.

FIG. 89.—**Double Bevel** is applied to the edge finish of two adjoining plates, when the adjoining edges of both plates are beveled from *one* side only to an angle, the degrees of which are left to the designer. To be used where maximum strength is required, and where electrode can be applied from *one* side of the work only.

FIG. 90.—**Flat position** is determined when the welding material is applied to a surface on the same plane as the deck, allowing the electrode to be held in an upright or vertical position. The welding surface may be entirely on a plane with the deck, or one side may be vertical to the deck and welded to an adjoining member that is on a plane with the deck.

Horizontal position is determined when the welding material is applied to a seam or opening, the plane of which is vertical to the deck and the line of weld is parallel with the deck,

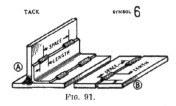

TACK   SYMBOL 6

FIG. 91.

allowing the electrode to be held in an inboard or outboard position.

Vertical position is determined when the welding material is applied to a surface or seam, whose line extends in a direction from one deck to the deck above, regardless of whether the adjoining members are on a single plane or at an angle to each other. In this position of weld, the electrode would also be held in a partially horizontal position to the work.

Overhead position is determined when the welding material is applied from the under side of any member whose plane is parallel to the deck and necessitates the electrode being held in a downright or inverted position.

FIG. 91.—**A Tack weld** is applying the welding in small sections to hold two edges together, and should always be specified by giving the *space* from center to center to weld and the *length* of the weld itself. No particular "design of weld" is necessary of consideration.

A Tack is also used for temporarily holding material in place that is to be solidly welded, until the proper alinement and position is obtained, and in this case neither the *length, space, nor design of weld* are to be, specified.

FIG. 92.—**A Caulking weld** is one in which the density of

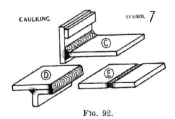

FIG. 92.

the crystalline metal, used to close up the seam or opening, is such that no possible leakage is visible under a water, oil or air pressure of 25 lbs. per square inch. The ultimate strength of a caulking weld is not of material importance—neither is the "design of weld" of this kind necessary of consideration.

FIG. 93.—**A Strength weld** is one in which the sectional

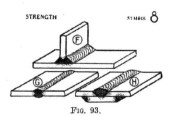

FIG. 93.

area of the welding material must be so considered that its tensile strength and elongation per square inch must equal at least 80 per cent of the ultimate strength per square inch of the surrounding material. (To be determined and specified by the designer.) The welding material can be applied in any number of layers beyond a minimum specified by the designer.

The density of the crystalline metals is *not* of vital importance. In this form of weld, the "design of weld" must be specified by the designer and followed by the operator.

Fig. 94.—**A Composite weld** is one in which both the strength and density are of the most vital importance. The *strength* must be at least as specified for a "strength weld," and the density must meet the requirements of a "caulking weld"

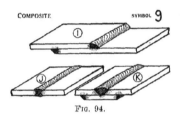

Fig. 94.

both as above defined. The minimum number of layers of welding material must always be specified by the designer, but the welder must be in a position to know if this number must be increased according to the welder's working conditions.

Fig. 95.—**Reinforced** is a term applied to a weld when the top layer of the welding material is built up above the plane

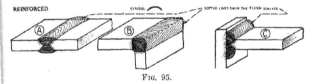

Fig. 95.

of the surrounding material as at A or B, or when used for a corner as at C. The top of final layer should project above a plane of 45 degrees to the adjoining material. This 45 degree line is shown "dotted" in C. This type is chiefly used in a "strength" or "composite" kind of weld for the purpose of obtaining the maximum strength efficiency, and should be specified by the designer, together with a minimum of layers of welding material.

FIG. 96.—**Flush** is a term applied to a weld when the top layer is finished perfectly flat or on the same plane as on the adjoining material as shown at D and E or at an angle of 45 degrees when used to connect two surfaces at an angle to each other as at F. This type of weld is to be used where a maximum tensile strength is not all important and must be

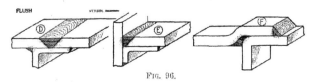

FIG. 96.

specified by the designer, together with a minimum number of layers of welding material.

FIG. 97.—**Concave** is a term applied to a weld when the top layer finishes below the plane of the surrounding material as at G, or beneath a plane of 45 degrees at an angular connection as at H and J.

To be used as a weld of no further importance than filling

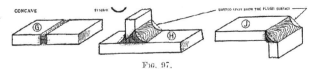

FIG. 97.

in a seam or opening, or for strictly caulking purposes, when it is found that a minimum amount of welding material will suffice to sustain a specified pound square inch pressure without leakage. In this "type of weld" it will not be necessary for the designer ordinarily to specify the number of layers of material owing to the lack of structural importance.

COMBINATION SYMBOLS

FIG. 98 shows a strap holding two plates together, setting vertically, with the welding material applied in not less than three layers at each edge of the strap, as well as between the plates with a reinforced, composite finish, so as to make the welded seams absolutely water, air or oil tight, and to

attain the maximum tensile strength. The edges of the strap
and the plates are left in a natural or sheared finish. This type
of welding is used for particular work where maximum strains
are to be sustained.

FIG. 99 shows a strap holding two plates together hori-

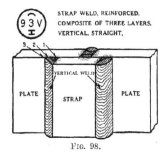

FIG. 98.

zontally, welded as a strength member with a minimum of
three layers and a flush finish. Inasmuch as the strap necessitates welding of the plates from one side only, both edges
of the plates are bevelled to an angle, the degrees of which
are left to the discretion of the designer. The edges of the

FIG. 99.

strap are left in a natural or sheared state, and the maximum
strength is attained by the mode of applying the welding
material, and through the sectional area per square inch exceeding the sectional area of the surrounding material.

FIG. 100 represents two plates butted together and welded

flat, with a composite weld of not less than three layers, and a reinforced finish. A strap is attached by means of overhead tacking, the tacks being four inches long and spaced eight inches from center to center. In this case, the welding of the plates of maximum strength and water, air or oil tight,

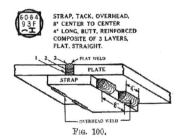

STRAP, TACK, OVERHEAD,
8" CENTER TO CENTER
4" LONG, BUTT, REINFORCED
COMPOSITE OF 3 LAYERS,
FLAT, STRAIGHT.

FIG. 100.

but the tacking is either for the purpose of holding the strap in place until it may be continuously welded, or because strength is not essential. All the edges are left in their natural or sheared state.

FIG. 101 represents a butt weld between two plates with the welding material finished concaved and applied in a mini-

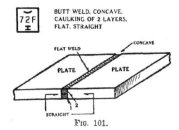

BUTT WELD, CONCAVE,
CAULKING OF 2 LAYERS,
FLAT, STRAIGHT

FIG. 101.

mum of two layers to take the place of caulking. The edges of the plates are left in a natural shear cut finish. This symbol will be quite frequently used for deck plating or any other place where strength is not essential, but where the material must be water, air or oil tight.

FIG. 102 is used where the edges of two plates are vertically butted together and welded as a strength member. The edges of adjoining plates are finished with a "double vee" and the minimum of three layers of welding material applied from each side, finished with a convex surface, thereby making the sectional area per square inch of the weld greater than that

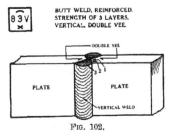

FIG. 102.

of the plates. This is a conventional symbol for shell plating or any other members requiring a maximum tensile strength, where the welding can be done from both sides of the work.

FIG. 103 shows two plates butted together in a flat position where the welding can only be applied from the top surface. It shows a weld required for plating where both strength and

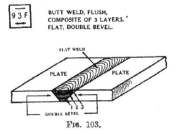

FIG. 103.

watertightness are to be considered. The welding material is applied in a minimum of three layers and finished flush with the level of the plates. Both edges of the adjoining plates are beveled to an angle, the degrees of which are left to the discretion and judgment of the designer, and should only be used when it is impossible to weld from both sides of the work.

FIG. 104 shows the edges of two plates lapping each other with the welding material applied in not less than two layers at each edge, with a concaved caulking finish, so applied, as to make the welded seams absolutely water, air or oil tight.

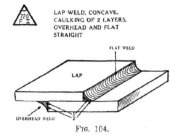

LAP WELD, CONCAVE.
CAULKING OF 2 LAYERS,
OVERHEAD AND FLAT
STRAIGHT

FLAT WELD

LAP

OVERHEAD WELD   2

FIG. 104.

The edges of the plates themselves are left in a natural or shared finish. Conditions of this kind will often occur around bulkhead door frames where maximum strength is not absolutely essential.

FIG. 105 is somewhat exaggerated as regards the bending

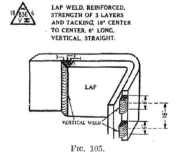

LAP WELD, REINFORCED.
STRENGTH OF 3 LAYERS
AND TACKING, 18" CENTER
TO CENTER, 6' LONG.
VERTICAL, STRAIGHT.

LAP

VERTICAL WELD

FIG. 105.

of the plates, but it is only shown this way to fully illustrate the tack and continuous weld. It shows the edges of the plates lapped with one edge welded with a continuous weld of a minimum of three layers with a reinforced finish thereby giving a maximum tensile strength to the weld, and the other edge of the plate, tack welded. The tacks are six inches long with a space of 12 inches between the welds or 18 inches from center to center of welds. In both cases, the edges of the plates are left in a natural or sheared state.

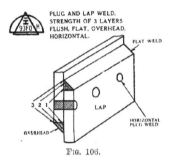

Fig. 106.

FIG. 106 shows a condition exaggerated, which is apt to occur in side plating where the plates were held in position with bolts for the purpose of alinement before being welded. The edges are to be welded with a minimum of three layers of welding material for a strength weld and finished flush,

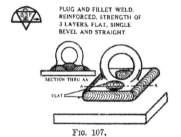

Fig. 107.

and after the bolts are removed, the holes thus left are to be filled in with welding material in a manner prescribed for strength welding. The edges of the plates are to be left in a natural or sheared state, which is customary in most cases of lapped welding.

Fig. 107 shows a pad eye attached to a plate by means of a fillet weld along the edge of the fixture, and further strengthened by plug welds in two countersunk holes drilled in the fixture. The welding material is applied in a flat position for a strength weld with a minimum of three layers

FIG. 108.

and a reinforced finish. The edges of the holes are beveled to an angle, which is left to the judgment of the designer, but the edges of the fixture are left in their natural state. This method is used in fastening fixtures, clips or accessories that would be subjected to an excessive strain or vibration

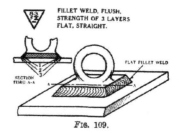

FIG. 109.

Fig. 108 shows a fixture attached to a plate by means of a composite weld of not less than three layers with a reinforced finish. The fixture being placed vertically, necessitates a combination of flat, vertical and overhead welding in the course of its erection. Although a fixture of this kind would never be required to be watertight, the composite symbol is given simply as a possibility of a combination.

FIG. 109 represents a fixture attached to a plate by a strength fillet weld of not less than three layers, finished flush.

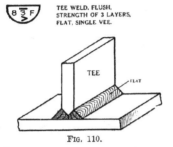

TEE WELD, FLUSH,
STRENGTH OF 3 LAYERS,
FLAT, SINGLE VEE.

FIG. 110.

The edges of the fixture are left in their natural state, and the welding material applied in the corner formed by the vertical edge of the fixture in contact with the face of the plate.

FIG. 110 illustrates the edge of a plate welded to the face of another plate, as in the case of the bottom of a transverse

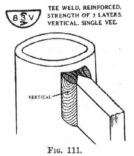

TEE WELD, REINFORCED,
STRENGTH OF 3 LAYERS.
VERTICAL, SINGLE VEE.

FIG. 111.

bulkhead being welded against the deck plating. To obtain a maximum tensile strength at the joint, the edge of the plate is cut to "single vee" and welded on both sides with a strength weld of not less than three layers, and finished flush. This would be a convenient way of fastening the intercostals to the keelsons. In this particular case, the welding is done in a flat position.

FIG. 111 shows another case of tee weld with the seam setting in a vertical position, and the welding material applied from both sides of the work. The edge of the plate is finished with a "single vee" and a minimum of three layers of welding material applied from each side, finished with a convex surface, thereby making the sectional area, per square inch of the weld, greater than that of the plate, allowing for a maximum tensile strength in the weld.

FIG. 112 represents an example of the possible combination

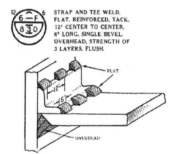

STRAP AND TEE WELD,
FLAT, REINFORCED, TACK.
12' CENTER TO CENTER,
6' LONG, SINGLE BEVEL,
OVERHEAD, STRENGTH OF
3 LAYERS, FLUSH.

FIG. 112.

of symbols. An angle iron is tack welded to the plate in the form of a strap or stiffener, though in actual practice, this might never occur. The tacks are spaced twelve inches from center to center, and are six inches long, and applied in a flat position, with a reinforced finish. As the strap prevents welding the plate from both sides, the edge of the plate is beveled, and the welding material applied for strength in not less than three layers in an overhead position and finished flush. Note that in specifying tack welds, it is essential to give the space from center to center of weld, and length of weld by use of figures representing inches placed either side of the circumscribing symbol of the combination.

CHAPTER VIII

EXAMPLES OF ARC-WELDING JOBS

Probably no mechanical job ever attracted more general attention than the repair of the German ships seized by us when we entered the World War. Even the mechanically minded Germans repeatedly declared that repairing was an impossibility, but the American engineers and mechanics showed the Hun that he had, as usual, vastly over-rated his own knowledge. One big factor in making the Hun so positive in this case, was his utter ignorance regarding the possibilities of arc welding—but he learned and in the teaching many others were also enlightened.

The work necessary on these German ships, of course, included much besides welding of the broken castings, but the welding work was of primary importance.

The principal ships on which this welding work was done were the:

U. S. Name	German name	I.H.P.	Gross Tonnage	Class of Vessel
Aeolus	Grosser Kurfurst	8,400	13,102	Transport
Agamemnon	Kaiser Wilhelm II	45,000	19,361	Transport
America	America	15,800	22,621	Transport
Antigne	Neckar	5,500	9,835	Transport
Covington	Cincinnati	10,900	16,339	Transport
George Washington	George Washington	21,000	25,570	Transport
Huron	Friedrich der Grosse	6,800	10,771	Transport
Leviathan	Vaterland	90,000	54,282	Transport
Madawaska	Koenig Wilhelm II	7,400	9,410	Transport
Martha Washington	Martha Washington	6,940	8,312	Transport
Mercury	Barbarossa	7,200	10,984	Transport
Mt. Vernon	Kronprinzessin Cecelie	45,000	19,503	Transport
Pocahontas	Prinzess Irene	9,000	10,983	Transport
Powhatan	Hamburg	9,000	10,893	Transport
President Grant	President Grant	8,500	18,072	Transport
President Lincoln	President Lincoln	8,500	18,168	Transport
Savannah	Saxonia	2,500	4.424	Repair Shop
Susquehanna	Rhein	9,520	10.058	Transport
Philippines	Bulgaria	4,200	10,924	Shipping Bd.

The total gross tonnage of the ships named was 288,780 tons, and the welding work was done by the Wilson Welder and Metals Co. of New York, using their "plastic-arc" process.

Seventy Cylinders Saved Without Replacement.—In all, there were thirty-one ships interned in the port of New York. Of these thirty-one ships, twenty-seven were German and four Austrian. Of the German ships, two were sailing vessels and four were small steamers which the Germans had not taken pains to damage materially. This left twenty-one German ships whose engines and auxiliaries were damaged seriously, ranging in size from the "Vaterland," the pride of the Hamburg-American Line, of 54,000 tons, to the "Nassovia," of 3,900 tons.

On the cylinders of the twenty vessels of German origin, not counting for the moment the turbine-driven "Vaterland," there were no less than 118 major breaks which would have entailed the renewal of some seventy cylinders if ordinary practice had been followed. In fact, such was the recommendation of the surveying engineers in their original report.

To any engineer familiar with the conditions at that time in the machine shops and foundries in the vicinity of New York, also in the drafting rooms, the problem of producing seventy cylinders of the sizes required by these vessels would seem almost impossible, and it is pretty well established that some vessels would have had to wait nearly two years for this equipment.

It must be remembered that few drawings of these engines were available, and those in many cases were not discovered until months after the repairs had started. Therefore, it would have been necessary to make drawings from the actual cylinders, and competent marine engine draftsman not already flooded with work did not exist.

The cylinders of fifteen vessels were successfully welded, while those of six were repaired by fitting mechanical patches, or, in other words, eighty-two of the major breaks were repaired by welding and thirty-six by mechanical patches.

It was not until July 12 that the final decision was made placing the transport service in the hands of the Navy and designating what ships were to be transferred from the control of the Shipping Board to that of the Navy Department. However, the first two large ships, the "Friedrich der Grosse," now the "Huron," and the "Prinzess Irene," now the "Pocahontas," were ready for sea on Aug. 20, in spite of the fact that the engines on these vessels were among the worst damaged of them all, the "Irene" having the whole side of the first intermediate valve chest broken out on each engine, the side of the high-pressure cylinder on each engine destroyed, and other smaller breaks, which, under ordinary methods, would have necessitated the renewal of four cylinders. The "Friedrich der Grosse" had the following breaks: Broken valve chest of high-pressure cylinder of each engine (valve chest cast in one with the cylinder), flanges knocked off both valve chest and cylinder covers, steam inlet nozzles knocked off both first intermediate valve chests and walls between the two valves in each check broken out, also steam inlet nozzles on both second intermediate valve chests broken off.

These two vessels were the first in which straight electric welding was used, that is, where patches were not bolted to the cylinder walls.

Method of Repair.—The nature of some of the breaks in castings is shown by the accompanying photographs, which were taken at various stages of the work.

A, Fig. 113, shows the break in the starboard high-pressure cylinder of the North German Lloyd steamer "George Washington." This break was effected by drilling a row of holes about an inch apart and knocking the piece out with a ram.

To prepare this for welding it was necessary to chisel off the surface only roughly, build a pattern of the break, cast a steel piece from the pattern, stud up the surface of the cast iron of the cylinder with a staggered row of steel studs $\frac{5}{8}$ in. in diameter, projecting $\frac{1}{2}$ in. from the cylinder, bevel the edge of the cast piece, place the piece in position as shown in *B*, and make the weld. When completed, the appearance of the work is as it appears in *C*. The broad belt of welded metal is due to the laying of a pad of metal over the rows of studs previously noted.

It cannot be too strongly insisted that tests have shown conclusively that the weld can be properly made without this pad; that is, if the approximate strength of the original metal is all that is desired—in which case the studding of the metal is

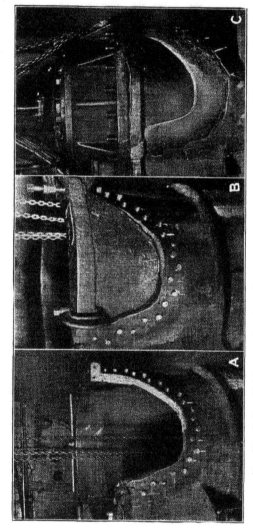

Fig. 113.—Broken High-Pressure Cylinder of U. S. S. "George Washington" and Method of Repairing.

unnecessary. But the work in these particular cases was of vital importance, due to the uses to which the vessels were to be put when in service, and also it was appreciated that this exhibition of a new application of the art in the marine engineering world required that the demonstration be satisfying, not only to the mind of the engineer, but to the eye, and ear, and when any engineer looked at that band of metal and sounded it with a hammer, he could not be but satisfied that the strength was definitely there and that the method of padding could be used in most of the situations which would arise. This at least was the effect upon all the engineers who saw the actual work.

The metal was laid on in layers in such a manner as to take care of the contraction in cooling. Each successive layer was cleaned with a wire brush before the next layer was put on. It is in the keeping of the successive layers clean and in the laying on of the metal so as to take care of the contraction that the operator's ability comes in fully as much as it does in the handling of the apparatus. The cylinders were not removed, but were repaired in place. Thus the work of fitting was reduced to a negligible quantity, and the refitting of lagging was not interfered with by projections, other than the $\frac{3}{8}$-in. pad, which is laid over the studs for extra strength. It will also be noted that these repairs can be undertaken at any place where the vessel may be lying, either at her loading dock or in the stream, since such apparatus may be carried on barges, which can be placed alongside and wires run to the work.

In this work a part consisted of the caulking of the surface of the welds which prevents porosity and also locates any brittle spots or places where poor fusion of metal has been obtained. This permits the cutting out of the bad places and replacing with good metal. The tool used was an air caulking hammer operated at 110 lb. air pressure.

Strength of Cast-Iron Welds.—Capt. E. P. Jessop, U. S. N., personally tested many welds for tensile strength in which cast iron was welded to cast steel, and in but one case was there a failure to obtain practically the original strength. This case was due to an inexperienced operator burning the metal, and was easily detected as an inferior weld without the strength test being applied.

Much has been said about the effect of the heat of welding, upon the structure or strength of cast iron, and in this particular instance the Navy engineer who had direct charge of this work, made experiments to note if there were any deleterious effects on the iron resulting from the action of the weld and reported as follows:

"Scleroscopic investigation of the structure of the welds shows only a very slight vein of hard cast iron at the line of the weld, shot through with fingers of gray cast iron, while behind this area there was no heat effect whatever. The metal thus deposited was easily workable with hammer and chisel, file or cutting tool. Another very important feature is that with the use of the low voltage and absolute automatic current control of the Wilson system, there is a minimum of heat transmitted to the parts to be welded, this being practically limited to a heat value absolutely necessary to bring the electrode and the face of the metal to be welded into a semi-plastic state, thus insuring a perfect physical union, and in accomplishing this result neither of the metals suffers from excessive heat, and there is absolutely no necessity for pre-heating. Neither are there any adverse results from shrinkage following the completed work owing to a minimum amount of heat being transmitted to the repair parts, thus avoiding the possibility of distortion of parts through uneven or excessive shrinkage strains that are very common where pre-heating is necessary or excessive heat is used for fusing metals."

A, Fig. 114, shows the damage done to the first intermediate cylinder of the U. S. S. "Pocahontas," formerly the "Prinzess Irene." The damage to this cylinder, it will be noted, was more destructive than to that of the "George Washington," rendering the repairs much more difficult.

B shows the steel section in place ready for welding, with the surfaces properly V'd out and with a staggering row of steel studs adjacent to the welding edge of the cylinder section.

C shows the complete job with the extra band or pad of metal completely covering the studs on the cast-iron section. These bands or pads of metal are peaned or worked over with a pneumatic hammer to insure protection against porosity of metal.

Had either or both of these cylinders been fractured on the lines shown of the cast-iron sections, and none of the parts removed, then the surfaces or edges of all lines of fracture would have been V'd out, and the weld made of the two cast-iron surfaces in the same manner that the cast steel was welded to the cast-iron cylinder proper.

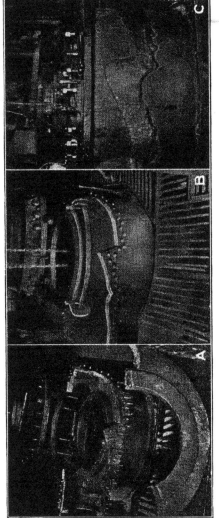

Fig. 114.—Break and Repair of First Intermediate Cylinder of the U. S. S. "Pocahontas"

OTHER SHIP WORK

In line with the foregoing J. O. Smith, writing in the *American Machinist*, Jan. 22, 1920, says: When the matter of welding in connection with ship-construction is considered, immense possibilities immediately suggest themselves. It has been definitely determined by exhaustive technical study and experiment that welding can be satisfactorily employed in ship construction, that ship plates joined by welding will be as strong or stronger than the original metal at the welded joint, and that welding can be employed for ship-construction work at a saving of 25 per cent. in time and 10 per cent. in material, as compared to riveting.

In actual figures, as determined by experiments of the Emergency Fleet Corporation's electric welding committee, it was determined that, by welding, in the case of a 9500-ton ship the saving in rivets and overlapped plates would amount in weight to 500 tons, making it possible for the ship to carry 500 tons more cargo on each trip than would be possible if the ship plates, etc., had been riveted, instead of welded.

An investigation by the same committee has definitely established the following points: That electric-welded ships can be built at least as strong as riveted ships; that plans for ships designed to be riveted can easily be modified so as to adapt them for extensive electric welding, and thus save considerably in cost and time for hull construction; that ships especially designed for electric welding can be built at a saving of 25 per cent. over present methods and in less time.

An electrically welded ship is credited with many advantages over a riveted ship. In a 5000-ton ship, about 450,000 rivets are used. A 9500-deadweight-ton ship requires 600,000 or 700,000 rivets. By the welding process the saving in labor on the minor parts of a ship is reckoned at from 60 to 70 per cent. on the hull, plating and other vital parts; the saving in labor, cost and time of construction by welding is conservatively placed at 25 per cent.

That electric welding will some day largely replace riveting is also the judgment of the electric-welding committee which is composed of many leading experts in both the electrical and metallurgical branches of the welding field.

Considerable investigation of the subject of welding instead of riveting has been made in England by Lloyd's Register of Shipping, particularly with regard to formulating rules for application to the electrical welding of ships. As a result of the investigations and experiments made by the technical staff, it was determined that the matter had assumed such importance as to warrant the formulation of provisional rules for electrically welded vessels, and these have been issued, for the guidance of shipbuilders, by Lloyd's Register.

The experiments conducted in England followed three well-defined lines of investigation: Determination of ultimate strength of welded joints, together with their ductile properties; capability of welded joints to withstand alternating tensile and compressive stresses, such as are regularly experienced by ships; and a microscopic and metallurgical analysis to determine if a sound fusion was effected between the original and added metal.

It was determined that the tensile strength of the welded joints was from 90 to 95 per cent. of the original plates, as against a strength of from 65 to 70 per cent. in riveted joints, showing a margin of 25 per cent. increased strength in favor of the welded joints.

The result of the tests of the elastic properties of welded joints determined that there was a slight difference in favor of the riveted joint, but the art of welding has made such great strides recently that it is now believed entirely possible to make a welded joint in ship plates that will stand as great a number of reversals of stresses as a riveted joint.

Microscopic and metallurgical analyses have determined that a good, solid, mechanically sound weld was made between the original and the added metal, the two having been fused together so perfectly that no line of demarcation could be seen.

The rules so far promulgated by Lloyd's (January, 1920), have been necessarily of a tentative nature and will no doubt be modified and enlarged from time to time in view of the experience that will be gained after welded ships have been in service for a time.

It does not require a great deal of imagination, however, to enable anyone to form the opinion that the shipbuilding industry is on the eve of great modifications in constructional lines, and the guidance given by the tests and comparisons so far made will undoubtedly lead to important, radical departures and developments.

In addition to the increased cost of riveting as compared to welding, it is practically always true that there is a certain percentage of imperfectly fitted rivets, that do nothing more than add weight to the ship. The main purpose of a rivet, of course, is to bind two or more thicknesses of material together, but if the rivet is bent, loses part of its head in the riveting process or otherwise fails in its proper purpose, there is no method by which such faults can be corrected after the rivet cools. If the importance of the riveted part requires a perfect joint, the faulty rivets must be removed entirely, and this is frequently a time-killing, expensive course to follow. When it is considered that a 5500-ton ship requires approximately 450,000 rivets to bind the various parts and plates and also that a certain percentage of these rivets is not fulfilling the purpose for which they were put into the ship, it is quite evident that practically every ship is burdened with a good-sized load of dead, useless weight. Such defective rivets are, in fact, more than a useless weight, in that they are a menace to the ship, for while they have been built into the ship for a purpose, and are supposed to be fulfilling that purpose, there is no telling how much the ship has been weakened structurally by their failure.

There are many reasons for defective rivets, and one of the greatest of them is the inaccessibility of the parts to **be** riveted and the consequent difficulty on the part of the riveter in putting the rivets properly in place. Another reason is that there is no certainty that rivets are at a proper, workable temperature; in consequence of which if they are too cold, the pneumatic hammer now generally used in riveting is unable to round off the end of the rivet properly, so as to insure a proper binding together of the plates the rivet is supposed to hold.

In many cases, when such faulty rivets are discovered, the present-day method is to weld such defective spots, which immediately brings up the natural question as to why the plates should not be welded in the first place.

The ability of a welder, using a direct-current, low-voltage arc with automatically regulated current to make sound mechanical welds in cramped, confined spaces, on overhead

Fig. 115.—Welded Parts for Ships.

or vertical walls, in fact, anywhere a man and a wire can go, naturally suggests that welding ship plates together should be the primary operation in shipbuilding; and from present in-

Fig. 116.—Welded Fuel-Oil Tanks.

dications and the trend of current events, it seems more than likely that this will be the outcome in the near future.

Examples of various ship parts welded by the metallic arc

arc shown in Fig. 115. In Fig. 116 is shown a welded tank and in Fig. 117 a welded steel-plate, 4×7 ft. condenser.

Reason for Successful Welds.—In connection with the work just described, the Wilson people claim that their success, and the uniformity of their welds, was made possible because their apparatus enables the welder to control his heat at the point of application. In welding there is a critical temperature at which steel can be worked to give the greatest tensile strength, and also ductility of metal. By raising the heat 15 or 20 amp. above this critical amperage a fracture of the

Fig. 117.—Welded Steel-Plate Condenser. No Rivets in Its Construction. Size 4 × 7 Ft.

weld will show segregation of carbon and slag pockets, which, of course, weakens the weld. If the amperage is decreased from the critical temperature, a fracture of the weld will show that the metal has been deposited in globules, with many voids, which proves that the weld has been made with insufficient heat. This shows, they claim, that with a fluctuating amperage or voltage, it is impossible to obtain uniformly high-grade welds.

In addition to their apparatus they use special electrodes for various jobs. One electrode is composed of a homogeneous alloy combined with such excess of manganese as will compensate for losses while passing through the electric arc, thus insuring a substantial amount of manganese in the welded joint which is essential to its toughness.   They also claim to have

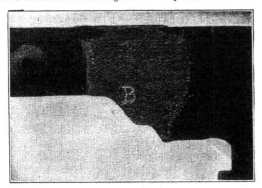

Fig. 118.—Welded Locomotive Frame.

Fig. 119.—Built Up Pedestal Jaw.

a manganese copper alloy welding metal electrode which is composed of iron homogeneously combined with such an excess of manganese and copper over the amount lost in the arc as will insure to the welded joint a substantial additional degree of toughness and ductility.

Their special electrodes run in grades, corresponding in sizes to the gage numbers of the American Steel and Wire Co.'s table. Grade 6 is for boiler work; grade 8 can be machined; grade 9 is for engine frames, etc.; grade 17 is for filling castings and grade 20 is for bronze alloys, bells, etc. The tensile strength of welds made with these electrodes is

FIG. 120.—At Work on a Locomotive Frame.

given as from 40,000 to 60,000 lb. The wire furnished is usually gage 9, approximately $^5/_{32}$ in. in diameter. This is shipped in coils of about 160 lb. No fluxes are used with any of these electrodes.

Locomotive Work.—The railroad shops of the United States were among the first to use arc welding to any extent. In fact, without the great amount of experimental work done in railroad shops, the use of the arc in the repair of the damaged ships by welding would have been practically impossible.

In some cases of locomotive repair there is a big question in the minds of engineers as to whether replacement is to be insisted upon or welding allowed. Rules have been drafted by a number of railroad associations, but at present no uniform rules covering all cases are in existence. However, on certain

Fig. 121.—Welding Cracked Driving Wheel Spokes.

classes of work there is no real question that welding is the quicker and better way.

In Fig. 118 is shown a repair on a steel locomotive frame, the size of the smaller section being 5×6 in. The broken ends were beveled off on each side and a piece of steel bar was welded in between the ends, thus saving considerable time and electrode material.

Fig. 119 shows how the worn face of a pedestal jaw was built up by means of the "plastic-arc" process.

FIG. 122.—Welding Locomotive Boiler Tubes to Back Sheet.

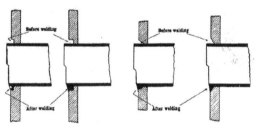

FIG. 123.—Method of Welding Boiler Tubes to Sheet.

Another frame-welding job is shown in Fig. 120. The weld was 3 in. high, 4½ in. wide and 4 in. deep. One man finished the job with a Westinghouse outfit in about 5 hours.

Fig. 121 shows the welding of a locomotive cast-steel drive wheel. Four spokes were cracked.

Fig. 122 shows the welding of locomotive boiler tubes to the back flue sheet. All of these jobs were done by the "plastic-arc" process, and represent a very small portion of the kinds of jobs that may be done in a railroad shop.

The method of welding flue ends to the sheets as suggested by Westinghouse is shown in Fig. 123.

H. A. Currie, assistant electrical engineer, New York Central R.R., writing in *Railway Age*, says:

The saving in our locomotive shop since electric welding was installed can hardly be calculated and the additional mileage that is obtained from locomotives is remarkable. This is mainly due to the following:

"A. Greater permanency of repairs.

"B. Shorter periods in the shop, giving additional use of equipment.

"C. Existing shop facilities permit taking care of a larger number of locomotives than originally expected. Shop congestion relieved.

"D. The use of worn and broken parts which without electric welding would be thrown in the scrap pile.

"E. The time required to make repairs is much less and requires fewer men.

"F. A smaller quantity of spare parts carried in stock.

"The following is a brief description of some of the work done on steam locomotives:

"Flue and Fire Box Welding.—The most important results are obtained by welding the boiler tubes to the back flue sheet. The average mileage between shopping on account of leaky flues on passenger locomotives was 100,000 miles. This has been raised to 200,000 miles with individual records of 275,000 miles. For freight this average has been raised from 45,000 to 100,000 miles. At the time of locomotive shortage this effect was of inestimable value.

"Good results have been obtained without the use of sandblast to prepare the tubes and sheets. The engine is either fired or an acetylene torch used to burn off the oil, after which the metal is cleaned off with a scraping tool. The ferrules are of course well seated and the tubes rolled back. The boiler is filled with water in order to cool the tubes, which having a much thinner cross-section than the sheets, would overheat sufficiently to spoil the weld or burn the tube. The metal is then laid on, beginning at the bottom of the bead and working to the top. Records show that the time to weld a Pacific type locomotive boiler complete is 12 hours.

"A variety of repair work is readily accomplished in locomotive fire-boxes such as the welding of crown-sheet patches, side-sheet cracks and the reinforcing and patching of mud rings. Smokebox studs are also welded on.

"Side Frames, Couplers and Wheels.—Cracked main members of side frames are restored and wearing parts built up and reinforced. Because of accessibility no special difficulties are encountered in this work. Formerly this work was chiefly done with oil welding and some acetylene and thermit work, but it was very much more expensive as the preparation required considerable effort and took a good deal of time.

"Fifty per cent of the engines passing through the shops have worn and broken coupler parts and pockets. By welding an average saving of about $15 per coupler is made. It costs about $30 in material and labor to replace a coupler and only $4 to repair the average broken coupler. The scrap value is about $5.

"Great success has resulted from various repairs to steel wheels and tires. Flat spots have been built up without removing the wheels from the locomotives, thus effecting a great saving in time and money. Building up sharp flanges saves about ⅜-in. cut off the tread, which when followed through means about $30 for a pair of wheels, a great increase in tire life and reduction in shop costs.

"Cylinders.—The most interesting feature developed by arc welding was the accomplishment of cast-iron welding. The difficulty in welding cast iron was that while the hot metal would weld into the casting, on cooling the strain would tear the welded portion away from the rest of the casting. Small studding was tried out with no success. Not until wrought-iron studs, proportioned to the sectional strength of the casting, were used did any satisfactory welds turn out. Studding of this large size was looked upon with distrust, as it was thought that the only weld was to the studding. This naturally meant that the original structure was considerably weakened due to the drilling. This, however, was not the case. The large studding was rigid enough to hold against the cooling strains and prevented the welds in the casting from pulling loose, thus adding the strength of all the welded portion to that of the studs. In most cases where external clearance will permit, sufficient reinforcing can be added to more than compensate for the metal removed in drilling for the studs.

"Perhaps more skill is required for this class of welding, but with a properly prepared casting success is certain. A concrete case of the economy effected in welding a badly damaged cylinder on a Pacific type engine is as follows:

WELDED JOB

Cost of welding broken cylinder, labor and material...........	$125.00
Length of time out of service, 5 days at $20 a day...........	100.00
Scrap value of old cylinder (8,440 lb. at 2.09 lb.).............	177.00
Total...	$402.00

REPLACED CYLINDER

Cost of new cylinder ready for locomotive...................	$1,000.00
Labor charge to replace it..................................	150.00
Locomotive out of service 18 days at $20 a day..............	360.00
	$1,510.00
Less cost of welding.....................................	402.00
Total saving...	$1,108.00

"Some twenty-five locomotives have been repaired in this way at one shop alone.

"Many axles are being reclaimed by building up the worn parts. These are tender and truck axles which are worn on the journals, wheel fits and collars. The saving is about $25 per tender axle and $20 for truck axles.

"The range of parts that may be repaired or brought back to standard size by welding is continually expanding. Wearing surfaces on all motion links and other motion work, crosshead guides, piston-rod crosshead fits, valves and valve seats, air, steam, sand and other pipes, keys, pins and journal boxes have all been successfully welded.

"A large saving is effected in welding broken parts of shop tools and machinery. During the war this was of untold value, as in some cases it was out of the question to get the broken parts replaced.

"**Training of Operators.**—The training of arc welders is most important. Success depends solely on the men doing the work. They must be instructed in the use of the arc, the type, size and composition of the electrode for various classes of work and the characteristics of the various machines they will be called upon to use. A properly equipped school for teaching these matters would be a valuable adjunct for every railroad. Manufacturers of equipment have recognized the importance of proper instruction and have equipped schools where men are taught free of charge.

"**Supervision.**—Co-ordinate with the actual welding is intelligent supervision. The scope of the supervisors should include preparation of the job for the welder and general oversight of the equipment in the shop.

"Thus the duties of the inspector might be summarized in the following points:

"1. To see that the work is properly prepared for the operator.

"2. The machines and wiring are kept in good condition.

"3. Proper electrodes are used.

"4. To inspect the welds in process of application, and when finished.

"5. To act as adviser and medium of interchange of welding practices from one shop to another.

"In work such as flue welding and industrial processes which repeat the same operation, piece-work rates may be fixed. For varying repair jobs this method cannot be used with justice either to the operator or the job.

"Bare electrodes are used almost exclusively, even for a.c. welds. Whenever a new lot of electrodes is received it is good practice to make up test-piece samples and subject them to careful tests and analysis.

"The sizes of electrodes and uses to which they are put are shown in the table.

Size	Type of Work
$1/8$ in.	Flue welding.
$6/32$ in.	For all repair work, broken frames, cylinders, etc.
$7/32$ in.	For building up wearing surfaces.

"**General Rules.**—In closing it will be well to point out a few general rules required to obtain satisfactory welds.

"**1.** The work must be arranged or chipped so that the electrode may be held approximately perpendicular to the plane of welding. When this cannot be accomplished the electrode must be bent so that the arc will be drawn from the point and not the side of the electrode. For cast iron the studding must be properly arranged and proportioned. The surfaces to be welded must be thoroughly clean and free from grease and grit.

"**2.** The proper electrode and current value must be selected for the work to be done.

"**3.** The arc should be maintained as constant as possible.

"**4.** For nearly all work the prepared surface should be evenly welded over and then the new surfaces welded together.

"**5.** Suitable shields or helmets must be used with proper color values for the lenses.

Fig. 124.—Built Up Cupped Rail Ends.

"For locomotive work a good operator will deposit an average of 1 to 1½ lb. of electrode per hour. The limits are from 1 to 2 lb. High current values give more ductile welds, in proportion to deposited metal. For locomotive welding the great advantage of the arc over thermit, oil or acetylene welding is that preparation at the weld is all that is necessary. No secondary preparation for expansion of the members is necessary. This is the great advantage in welding side frames."

Considerable welding work is done in building up worn track parts. Fig. 124 shows the building up of cupped rail ends and Fig. 125 shows manganese-steel cross-over points built up by arc welding. Such repairs have stood long and hard service.

Other Welding Work.—In the steel mills a great deal of welding is required to build up worn roll or pinion pods. Fig. 126 shows a welder at work building up worn pods with a carbon arc and filler. Fig. 127 shows a finished job with the

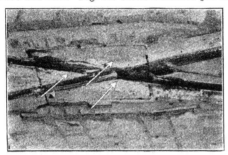

FIG. 125.—Built Up Manganese Steel Cross-Over Points.

FIG. 126.—Building Up Worn Roll Pods.

worn part outlined in white. The cost of repairing four ends (two pinions) was $170. The pinions cost $1,000 each.

The way a five-ton roll housing was repaired is shown in Fig. 128. In this case a heavy steel plate was bolted over the crack and welded as indicated. It might have been all

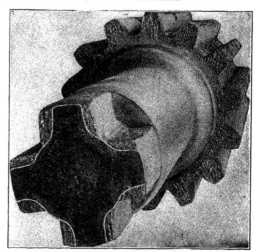

FIG. 127.—Finish-Welded Pinion Pods.

FIG. 128.—Repaired 5-Ton Roll Housing.

FIG. 129.—Welded Blowholes and Machined Pulley.

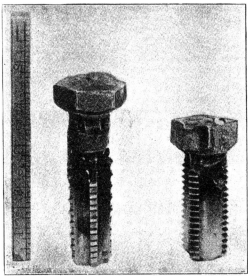

FIG. 130.—Method of Welding Taps Broken Off in the Hole.

right to weld direct, but in this case, owing to the heavy duty required, it was thought best to play safe and use the steel plate.

Welded blowholes in the rim of a large pulley are shown at the left in Fig. 129. At the right the pulley is shown after machining.

Broken taps may be removed if a nut is welded on as shown in Fig. 130. In doing work of this kind, the arc is struck on top of the tap and kept there until the metal is built up above the top of the hole. An ordinary nut is then laid over it and welded fast. If the arc is kept on the tap the metal may run against the sides of the hole but will not adhere, but care must be exercised so as to not let the arc strike the sides of the hole.

ELECTRIC CAR EQUIPMENT MAINTENANCE

The growing possibilities of electric welding processes in connection with the maintenance of rolling stock and other railway equipment have been a source of amazement to every electric railway man who has come into contact with the practice, says the *Electric Railway Journal*. This began with the repair of broken members of the various parts of electric car equipment and has led to its use in a still larger field, which includes the building up of worn surfaces of steel parts which previously would have been headed for the scrap heap. The accompanying illustrations show some parts of electric car equipment which have been reclaimed by electric welding in the shops of several electric railways. This work was begun at a time when it was very difficult to obtain railway equipment parts and it has resulted in large savings and has enabled the equipment to be returned to service so quickly, that the work is being extended and used for defective-part repair which previously would not have been considered.

The United Traction Company, Albany, N. Y., constructed a special concrete building for its electrical repair work a year ago. A separate room was built at one end of this building and arranged particularly for electric welding, and all important details were incorporated in the design to fit this room for the purpose to which it was to be put. The building is a concrete structure throughout and the floor of the welding room is also of concrete. In dimensions this room is about 10 ft.×30 ft. and it is entirely inclosed and separated from the rest of the building.

As a safety precaution no one is allowed to enter the welding room while work is in progress. Two observation windows are provided on either side of the entrance door, in which colored glass has been installed as a protection to the eyes of the observer. Any one having business in the welding room

Fig. 131.—G. E. Portable Arc Welding Outfit.

can see when welding work is being done and thus avoid the danger of any harmful effect from the light of the arc.

The equipment at present in use in the welding room consists of a General Electric motor-generator set and an oxy-acetylene welding outfit, a welding table, convenient holders, masks and other welding equipment, and a chain hoist which travels on an I-beam the length of the room and also outside the entrance to pick up heavy work and facilitate the handling of heavy parts. Since the installation of this equipment the General Electric Company has developed a self regulating welding generator which constitutes a part of its single-operator

metallic electric arc welding equipment. This can be either
stationary or portable and as it is self-contained it makes a
very desirable combination. The generator has a two-pole
armature, in a four-pole frame, with commutating poles, and
generates sixty volts, open circuit. Bucking the shunt field
is a series field, with taps brought out for different welding
currents. As current flows from the main brushes through
the series field windings it reduces the generator voltage to

Fig. 132.—G. E. Generator Direct Connected to Motor, with Control
Panel and Starter.

the proper welding value. Figs. 131 and 132 show two types
of G. E. equipment.

One of the most important operations and one which shows
far reaching economies in the work undertaken by the United
Traction Company is the building up of worn armature shafts,
as shown in Figs. 133 and 134. The pinion ends of the shafts
were "chewed up" due to the wear of the keyways for the
pinions. The defective ends of the shafts which were to be
repaired were carefully cleaned of all oil and dirt and sufficient
metal was welded on so that the shafts could be re-machined

and re-threaded. A large number of these armatures were all right except for the damage to the keyways, so that they were returned to service as soon as the shafts were re-machined

Fig. 133.—Worn Armature Shafts Before Welding.

Fig. 134.—Armature Shafts After Welding.

and fitted. Others had damaged coils or grounded insulation and where it was necessary to re-wind an armature this was stripped before the welding operations took place. For welding operations of this character where a large amount of work is to be done which is similar in character the General Electric Company has developed an automatic welding machine described elsewhere. Its chief advantage lies in the increase

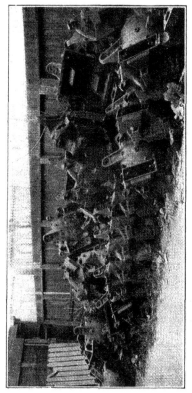

FIG. 135.—Motor Shells Which Were Reclaimed by Welding.

in speed which is possible and the uniformity of welds which results. In the work done at Albany the building up and re-machining of the shafts cost from $3 to $4 each, which was only about one-tenth of the cost of a new shaft. As local conditions as to labor costs as well as the cost of energy vary to quite an extent detailed costs for the various operations are not included, but on roads which are performing this work and which have actual data regarding the purchase cost of the various parts, the savings which result offer convincing proof of the economics which can be effected with the use of electric arc welding.

Fig. 135 shows a pile of motor cases in the yards of the United Traction Company. Before the advent of the welding equipment many of these motor shells were intended for scrap

Fig. 136.—Repaired Gear-Case Suspension Arm.

due to various breakages and excessively worn parts. By the use of the welding equipment a large proportion of these have already been reclaimed.

The method employed in welding broken lugs or broken ends of motor shells consists first in fitting the broken parts together and lining them up in their correct position. The pieces are then welded at a few points so as to hold the broken parts in position and, where necessary, the fracture is cut out "V" shape to provide additional space for the welding metal. Much of the success which has been obtained in this class of work at Albany is attributed to the use of studs for interlocking the metal which is added to the broken parts. Holes for the ⅜-in. studs are drilled and tapped at several points adjacent to the break and the studs are so inserted as to extend above the motor shell to about the same height as the thickness of the additional metal to be added. The deposited

FIG. 137.—Broken Cast-Iron Motor Shell and Axle Housings Repaired by Electric Welding (Case Broken in Twelve Pieces).

metal is then allowed to bridge over these studs in welding and so obtains additional support which helps to strengthen the weld. In the illustration Fig. 136 showing repairs made to a broken gear-case suspension arm, one of these studs can be seen projecting from the casting.

As an example of what can be accomplished, in repairing broken shells, the illustration Fig. 137 showing a welded end of a motor shell alongside a lathe, is an extreme case. This motor shell was broken in twelve pieces and from the illustration it will be seen that nearly the entire end was welded.

Another record job made in the shop of the United Traction Company was the welding of a truck bolster. The car, under which was a truck with a broken bolster, was brought to the shop and placed on a track adjacent to the welding room.

FIG. 138.   FIG. 139.

FIG. 138.—Wheel Turned Down Ready for Welding. Note
Thinness of Flange.

FIG. 139.—Flange Built Up Ready to Be Shaped in Wheel Lathe.

The car body was jacked up and the bolster was repaired in approximately eight hours. The work was started at 9 o'clock after the morning rush hour and the car was ready for service again at 5.15 P.M.

In addition to the class of work illustrated as being done by the United Traction Company other interesting work is reported from various electric railways showing what has been accomplished. The Spokane & Inland Empire Railroad has done some work in reclaiming wheels with sharp flanges. Three views are given to illustrate the methods used. The first of these, Fig. 138, shows a wheel with the flange turned down ready to receive new metal. The second Fig. 139 shows the flange with a new layer of welded metal. The third, Fig. 140, shows the finished wheel after it has been machined. After the new metal has been added the flange is merely shaped up with a forming tool. It is left quite rough in some cases, but as the practice has always been to put on new brake shoes when the wheels are repaired, the company has had no difficulty in wearing down the tread to a smooth contour.

A number of steam railways are at present reclaiming all of their cold rolled steel wheels which are slid flat or have

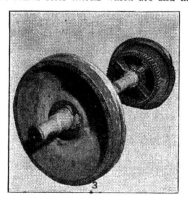

FIG. 140.—Finished Wheel Ready for Service.

flaked-out places, as well as those with sharp flanges. This operation creates quite a saving in itself as often the car is merely placed over the drop pit and the work can then be taken care of with the car fully equipped. By this method the car is withheld from service but a short period. In the welding of sharp flanges it is not contended by those who have had extended experience that the metal deposited will give the life of the parent material, but they agree that savings are created as a result of maintaining the car in service until such time as it is necessary to shop it for major repairs.

Another example of reclaiming electric car equipment is shown in the repairs to gear cases, Fig. 141. These are a fair sample of the repairs that are frequently found necessary. In this case patches are made of No. 10 sheet iron. In welding these patches on, the operator first determines the size of the patch and outlines it with chalk on the old case. He then builds up a layer of metal just outside the chalk mark. The patch is then laid on and welded to a layer of metal. In this way a tight and secure joint is made. As gear cases are frequently covered with oil when they are brought in for repairs, they should be cleaned off as much as possible. In making a patch that requires a bend, as in the case illustrated, the operator first welds the patch to the bottom of the case, then heats the patch and bends it into shape.

Split Gears Made Solid.—Some electric railways which have

FIG. 141.—Gear Cases with Patches Welded On.

split gears have found it advisable to change these to solid gears by welding and then to press them on the axles. Fig. 142 shows a gear which is being welded in this manner and Fig. 143 an axle which has been built up so as to increase the gear seat. The method employed in welding the gears consists, first, of cutting a "V" along the joint of the gear down to the bolts with a carbon electrode. The operator then builds up with new metal and welds each bolt and fills up the old keyways. This bore is then re-machined and a new keyway is cut. Broken teeth in gears are also easily repaired by welding.

Another use of welding which has been of benefit to electric railways is in the maintenance of housings for the bearings of railway motors. Constant vibration and heavy jarring causes the fit in the motor frame to become badly worn and many railways have used shims to take up this wear. A small layer of metal deposited by the electric arc and then machined to the desired dimensions provides a more serviceable job than

FIG. 142.   FIG. 143.

FIG. 142.—Welding Split Gear to Make a Solid One.
FIG. 143.—Axle Enlarged by Welding.

that of the shims, and when a tight fit is once secured, the wear is eliminated.

The filling in of bolt holes in various parts of the car equipment is another use which is showing far-reaching results. Heavy duty and constant vibration cause the holes to become worn, and the bolts then readily become loose and often fall out. The filling in of these holes and their re-drilling takes very little time and the cost is extremely low.

Some other welding operations which have been carried out with success are these: side bearings which have become

Fig. 144.—Crankshaft with Break Cut away for Welding.

Fig. 145.—Completed Weld Before Trimming.

badly worn have been built up, brakeshoe heads and hangers have been welded and truck side frames have been repaired in numerous cases. A large number of uses for electric welding are constantly presenting themselves to all railways. Enough instances have been cited to demonstrate the fact that the art

of welding has greatly increased the resources available for
lengthening the life of equipment.

ELECTRIC WELDING A SIX-TON CRANKSHAFT

A six-ton crankshaft in the plant of the Houston Ice Co.,
Houston, Tex., broke through at one of the webs. As there
was no means at hand to repair the break, the crankshaft
was shipped to the Vulcan Iron Works, Jersey City, N. J.,
where it was electrically welded by the Wilson plastic-arc
process.

The broken web, cut away preparatory to welding, is shown
in Fig. 144, and the finished weld in Fig. 145. Owing to the
size of the shaft, great care had to be exercised in keeping
it in proper alignment. Fig. 146 shows it leveled and clamped
to a large surface plate. A straight-edge is shown laid across
the webs to assist the operator in judging and keeping the
alignment.

A big feature in electric welding of this kind is that owing
to the intense heat of the arc, no preheating is required as in
using other methods. This, of course, greatly reduces the time
required to complete a repair of this kind.

ARC-WELDING HIGH-SPEED TOOL TIPS

One large manufacturer has installed a Westinghouse arc-
welding equipment for the sole purpose of making tools for
turning heavy work. Ordinarily these tools are made from
high-speed steel, and cost about $12 each. This manufacturer
uses high-speed steel for the tip of the tool only, welding
it to a shank of carbon or machine-steel, as shown in Fig. 147,
and in this manner the tools are produced at a cost of $2
to $4.

For several weeks this plant has been turning out 240
welded tools a day, the men working in shifts of four, which
is the capacity of this outfit.

The equipment consists of a 500-amp. arc-welding motor
generator with standard control panel, and three outlet panels
for metal-electrode welding, and one special outlet panel for
the use of either metal or graphite electrodes. The special
panel is intended to take care of special filling or cutting

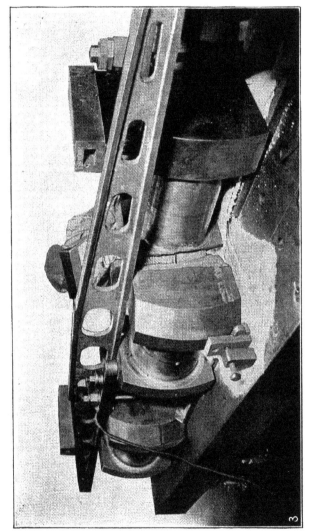

Fig. 146.—Method of Lining Up and Holding the Work.

processes that may be necessary, but ordinarily it is used in the same manner as other panels for making tools. These panels are distributed about the shops at advantageous points.

For toolmaking, which involves the hardest grades of steel, a preheating oven is used, not because it is necessary for making a perfect weld, but because otherwise the hard steel is likely to crack from unequal cooling and also because pre-

Fig. 147.—Welding High-Speed Tips Onto Mild Steel Shanks.

heating makes it easier to finish the tool after the welding process has been completed. For ordinary arc welding operations the preheating oven is never used.

ELECTRICALLY WELDED MILL BUILDING.

A small all-welded mill building was erected in Brooklyn in 1920 for the Electric Welding Co., of America, by T. Leonard MacBean, engineer and contractor. The structure is about 60 × 40 ft., and has four roof trusses of 40-ft. span supported on 88-in. H-beam columns fitted with brackets for a five-ton traveling crane. In its general arrangement the structure follows regular practice, but the detailing is such as to suit the use of welding, and all connections throughout are made by this process. A considerable advantage in cost and time is claimed for the welded connections, but in the present instance the determinative feature was not cost economy so much as the fact that the fabricated work could be obtained more quickly by buying the plain steel members and cutting and welding them at the site instead of waiting for bridge shop deliveries.

The roof was designed for a total load of 45 lb. per sq. ft., of which about 30 lb. represents live load. Each truss weighs 1,400 lb. The chords are $4 \times 5 \times \frac{3}{8}$-in. tees, while the web members are single $3 \times 2 \times \frac{3}{8}$-in. angles. On the trusses rest 10-in. 15-lb. channel purlins spanning the 20-ft. width of bay. The columns are 8×8-in. H-beams, 19 ft. high, and the crane bracket on the inner face of the column is built up of a pair of rear connection angles, a pair of girder seat angles, and a triangular web plate, as one of the views herewith shows. Base and cap of the columns are made by simple plates.

All material was received on the job cut to length. A wooden platform large enough to take a whole truss was built as a working floor and the chord members were laid down on it in proper relative position to form a truss when connected. The top chord was made of a single length of tee, bent at the peak point after a triangular piece was cut out of the stem. At the heel points of the truss the stem of the top-chord tee was lapped past the stem of the bottom chord tee, and when the two members were clamped together the contact seams were welded; the seam of the stem at the peak was also welded shut. Then the web members were placed in position and clamped, and their connections to the chord welded. The metallic-electrode arc process was used and various welded parts are shown in Fig. 148.

Loading Tests.—When the plans for the building were submitted to the Department of Buildings, Borough of Brooklyn, the proposal to weld the connections was approved only with the stipulation of a successful load test before erection. This test was carried out March 20. Two trusses were set up at 20-ft. spacing and braced together, purlins were bolted in place, and by means of bags of gravel a load of 48 tons was applied. This was sufficient to load the trusses approximately to their elastic limit. No straining or other change was observable at the joints, and the test was considered in every respect successful. The deflection of the peak, 0.0425 ft., did not

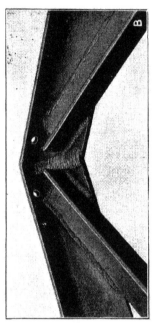

Fig. 148.—Some Details of All-welded Mill Building. *A*, Heel Joint of 40-ft. Truss. *B* and *C*, Front and Back Sides of Peak and Joint Truss. *D*, Column Base. *E*, Crane Bracket. Parts of Bracket were First Welded Together, and then

change during 48 hours, and upon removal of the load at the end of that period a set of less than 0.01 ft. was measured.

Speed of Arc Welding.—In a paper read before the American Institute of Electrical Engineers, New York, Feb. 20, 1919, H. M. Hobart says:

All sorts of values are given for the speed, in feet per hour, with which various types of joints can be welded. Operators making equally good welds have widely varying degrees of proficiency as regards speed. Any quantitative statement must consequently be of so guarded a character as to be of relatively small use. In general, and within reasonable limits, the speed of welding will increase considerably when larger currents are employed. It appears reasonable to estimate that this increase in speed will probably be about 25 to 35 per cent for high values of current. This increase is not directly proportional to the current employed because a greater proportion of time is taken to insert new electrodes and the operator is working under more strenuous conditions. Incidentally, the operator who employs the larger current will not only weld quicker but the weld will have also better strength and ductility.

On this point Mr. Wagner writes as follows:

I would not say that speed in arc welding was proportional to the current used. Up to a certain point ductility and strength improve with increased current, but when these conditions are met, we do not obtain the best speed due to increased heating zone and size of weld puddle. Speed may fall off when current is carried beyond certain points.

In a research made by William Spraragen for the Welding Research Sub-Committee on several tons of half-inch-thick ship plate, the average rate of welding was only two feet per hour. Highly skilled welders were employed, but they were required to do the best possible work, and the kinds of joints and the particular matters under comparison were very varied and often novel.

However, in the researches carried on by Mr. Spraragen it was found that about 1.9 lb. of metal was deposited per hour using a $\frac{5}{32}$-in. bare electrode and with the plates in a flat position. The amount of electrodes used up was about 2.7 lb. per hour, of which approximately 16.5 per cent was wasted as short ends and 13 per cent burnt or vaporized, the remainder being deposited at the speed of 1.9 lb. per hour mentioned above.

For a 12-ft.-cube tank of $\frac{1}{4}$-in. thick steel welded at Pittsfield, the speed of welding was 3 ft. per hour. The weight of the steel in this tank was 16,000 lb. and the weight of electrode used up was 334 lb. of which 299 lb. was deposited in the welds. The total welding time was 165 hours corresponding to using up electrodes at the rate of just 2 lb. per hour. The total length of weld was 501 ft., the weight of electrode used up per foot of weld thus being 0.60 lb. The design of this tank comprised eighteen different types of welded joint. Several different operators worked on this job and the average current per operator was 150 amp.

For the British 125-ft.-long Cross-Channel Barge for which the shell plating was composed of ¹/₄-in. and ⁵/₁₆-in. thick plates, described in H. Jasper Cox's paper read before the Society of Naval Architects on Nov. 15, 1918, and entitled "The Application of Electric Welding to Ship Construction," it is stated that: "After a few initial difficulties had been overcome, an average speed of welding of 7 ft. per hour was maintained including overhead work which averaged from 3 to 6 ft. per hour."

In a report appearing on page 67 of the minutes and records of the Welding Research Sub-Committee for June 28, 1918, O. A. Payne, of the British Admiralty, states: "A good welder could weld on about one pound of metal in one hour with the No. 10 Quasi-Arc electrode, using direct current at 100 volts. An electrode containing about 1½ oz. of metal is used up in about 3 minutes, but this rate cannot be kept up continously."

The makers of the Quasi-Arc electrode publish the following data for the speed of arc welding in flat position with butt joints, a 60-deg. angle and a free distance of ⅛-in.

Thickness of Plates	Speed in Feet per Hour
⅛ in.	30
¼ in.	18
½ in.	6
1 in.	1.3

I cannot, however, reconcile the high speed of welding ½-in. plate published in this report as 6 ft. per hour, with the report given above by the British Admiralty that a good welder deposits 1 lb. of metal per hour with the Quasi-Arc electrode. If the rate given by the manufacturer is correct, it would mean that about four pounds of metal were deposited per hour. On this basis the rate must have been computed on the time taken to melt a single electrode and not the rate at which a welder could operate continuously, allowing for his endurance and for the time taken to insert fresh electrodes in the electrode holder and the time taken for cleaning the surface of each layer before commencing the next layer. From his observations I am of the opinion that a representative rate for a good welder lies about midway between these values given respectively by Mr. Payne, and by the makers of the Quasi-Arc electrode, say for ½-in. plates some 2 lb. per hour. This, it will be observed, agrees with Mr. Spraragen's experience in welding up some 6 tons of ½-in. ship plate with a dozen or more varieties of butt joint and Mr. Wagner's results with an 8-ton tank. Even this rate of 2 lb. per hour is only the actual time of the welding operator after his plates are clamped in position. This preliminary work and the preparation of the edges which is quite an undertaking, and requires other kinds of artisans, accounts for a large amount of time and should not be under-estimated.

The practice heretofore customary of stating the speed of welding in feet per hour has led to endless confusion as it depends on type of joint, height of weld and various details. A much better basis is to express the speed of welding in pounds of metal deposited per hour. Data for the pounds of metal deposited per hour are gradually becoming quite definite. The pounds of metal per foot of weld required to be deposited can be readily calculated from the drawings or specifications. With the further available knowledge of the average waste in electrode ends and from other causes, the required amount of the electrode material for a given job can be estimated.

Suitable Current for Given Cases.—For a given type of weld, for example, a double V-weld in a $\frac{1}{2}$-in. thick ship plate, it was found that in the summer of 1918, while some operators employed as low as 100 amp., others worked with over 150 amp. Some, in making such a weld, employed electrodes of only $\frac{1}{8}$-in. diameter and others preferred electrodes of twice as great cross-section. For the particular size and design of weld above mentioned, the Welding Research Sub-Committee had welds made with 200 to 300 amp. The conclusion appears justified that the preferable current for such a weld is at least 200 amp. If the weld of the $\frac{1}{2}$-in.-thick plate is of the double-bevel type, some 50 amp. less current should be used for the bottom layer than is used for the second layer, if two layers are used. For $\frac{3}{4}$-in.-thick plates, the most suitable welding current is some 300 amp. This is of the order of twice the current heretofore usually employed for such a weld.

Mr. Wagner writes:

We have made a number of tests to determine the effect of varying current on the strength of the weld. Tests were made on a $\frac{1}{2}$-in. plate with current values as follows: 80, 125, 150, 180, 220, 275 and 300 amp. These tests show improvement in the tensile strength and bending qualities of welds as the current increases. The speed of welding increases up to a certain point and then decreases.

Effect on Arc Welding of Voltage Employed.—We have made a number of tests to determine the influence of variable voltages on the strength and character of electric welds. The experiments were made welding $\frac{1}{2}$-in. plate with 150 amp. held constant and voltage varying as follows: 40, 75, 100, 125, 150, 200 and 225 volts. This test demonstrates that there is no material difference in the tensile strength, bending qualities or the appearance of the welded-in material. There is this advantage, however, in the higher voltage, that variations in the strength of the arc do not materially affect the value of the current. A curve-drawing ammeter was installed on the welding circuit which showed variations in current at 75 volts, but at 150 volts the current curve was practically a straight line.

Preferable Size of Electrode.—On certain railways, a single diameter of electrode is employed independently of the size or shape of the plates or parts being welded. The experience of other people leads them to make use of several different sizes of electrodes according to the size of the job and the type of joint. Present British practice appears to be to use such a size of electrode as to have a current density of some 4,000 to 6,000 amp. per square inch. The investigations of the Welding Research Sub-Committee indicate that at least 10,000 to 12,000 amp. per square inch is suitable for electrodes of $\frac{1}{4}$-in. and $\frac{5}{32}$-in. diameter and well up toward 10,000 amp. per square inch for electrodes of $\frac{3}{16}$-in. and $\frac{3}{4}$-in. diameter.

CHAPTER IX

PHYSICAL PROPERTIES OF ARC-FUSED STEEL

The work of the Bureau of Standards in investigating the physical properties of arc-fused steel, was described in Chemical and Metallurgical Engineering, by Henry S. Rowdon, Edward Groesbeck and Louis Jordan. This was by special permission of Director Stratton. The article was substantially as follows:

During the year 1918 at the request of and with the co-operation of the welding research sub-committee of the Emergency Fleet Corporation an extensive program was outlined by the Bureau of Standards for the study of arc-welding. Due to changed conditions, however, at the close of the year 1918, the original program was modified and shortened very considerably. In drawing up the modified program, it was decided to make the study of the characteristic properties of the fused-in metal the primary object of the investigation, the study of the merits of the different types of electrodes being a secondary one. Since the metal of any weld produced by the electric-arc fusion method is essentially a casting, as there is no refinement possible as in some of the other methods, it is apparent that the efficiency of the weld is dependent upon the properties of this arc-fused metal. Hence a knowledge of its properties is of fundamental importance in the study of electric-arc welds.

Preliminary Examinations of Electric-Arc Welds.—Numerous articles have appeared in technical literature bearing on the subject of electric-arc welding. Most of these, however, are devoted to the technique and comparative merits of the method, manipulations, equipment, etc., rather than to the study of the characteristics of the metal of the weld itself. The information on this phrase of the subject is rather meager.

A considerable number of examinations were made of welds prepared by means of the electric-arc process and representative of different conditions of welding.

Most of these were of a general miscellaneous nature and the results do not warrant including a description of the different specimens here. One series of particular interest, however, may well be referred to in detail. As part of this study the welding research sub-committee submitted to the Bureau of Standards a number of welds of ship-plate representative of English practice for examination, some of which were considered as very superior examples of welding as well as others of a decidedly inferior grade. In Tables VII and VIII are given the results obtained by the mechanical tests made upon these specimens. The welding was done by skilled operators by means of special brands of electrodes (welding pencils), the trade names of which, however, have been omitted from the tables. The specimens were examined microscopically very carefully, in addition to the mechanical tests made. The results are not included, however, as the structural features of the material did not differ from those to be discussed in another chapter. The results of the mechanical tests given are of value in that they are indicative of the average mechanical properties which should be expected in electric-arc welds of satisfactory grade for the shape and size of those examined.

Method of Building Specimens.—The specimens required for the study of the mechanical properties of the arc-fused metal were prepared for the most part at the Bureau of Standards, direct current being used in the operation. The apparatus used is shown diagrammatically in Fig. 149. By means of the adjustable water rheostat the current could be increased progressively from 110 to 300 amp. By the use of automatic recording instruments the voltage and current were measured and records were taken at intervals during the preparation of a specimen. The values of current given in the tables are those which were desired and were aimed at. The average deviation from this value as recorded by the curves was approximately 5 amp. The value of the current at the instant "the arc was struck" was of course many times the normal working value used during the fusion.

Since the investigation was concerned primarily with the properties of the arc-fused metal, regular welds were not made. Instead the metal was deposited in a block large enough to

Table VII—Mechanical Properties of Twelve Good Welds*

No.	Average Voltage	Average Amperage	Type of Weld†	Thickness of Plate In.	Ult. Str. Tension, Lb./Sq.In.	Elong., Per Cent	Fracture
1	d.c. 60	120	Vertical	⅜	51,450	7 in 8 in.	In weld: fine crystalline, some holes
2	d.c. 60	120	Vertical		53,200	11 in 8 in.	In weld: fine crystalline, some holes
3	a.c. 75	110	Flat		52,430	12 in 8 in.	Outside weld; few holes
4	a.c. 75	110	Flat		54,210	14 in 8 in.	Outside weld; few holes
5	a.c. 110	70	Flat		60,610	5 5 in 6 in.	Outside weld; few holes
6	d.c. 110	125	Flat		59,000	6 in 6 in.	In weld: crystalline, fine to coarse, few holes
7	d.c. 110	150	Flat		52,570	6 in 6 in.	In weld: very fine crystalline, few holes
8	d.c. 110	100	Overhead		59,470	4 in 6 in.	In weld: fine crystalline, many holes
9	d.c. 110	120	Flat		55,460	6 in 6 in.	In weld: crystalline, fine to coarse, few holes
10	d.c. 110	120	Vertical		49,030	3.7 in 6 in.	In weld: coarse crystalline, few holes

					Cold Bend‡ Load at Yield (f.lb.)	Load at Break (f.lb.)	Angle of Bend, Deg.
11	d.c. 110	70	Flat		850	1,010	105
12	d.c. 110	150	Flat		13,530	17,450	20 In weld: fine crystalline, few holes

* All the welds were made in steel plate of the thickness shown. Electrodes of the covered type were used, the welds were of 60 deg., V type, except the over-head welds in which a 90 deg. V was used.
† Refers to the position of the plates which were welded together.
‡ The bend tests were made with the apex of V in tension with a 2-in. span over a pin of 2-in. radius except the 1-in. plate for which a pin of 1-in. radius was used

Table VIII—Mechanical Properties of Twelve Inferior Welds*

No.	Average Voltage	Average Amperage	Type of Weld*	Thickness of Plate, In.	Ult. Str. Tension, Lb./Sq.In.	Elong., Per Cent	Fracture
13	d.c. 110	120	Flat		32,460	Nil	In weld: fine crystalline, many holes
14	d.c. 95	105	Vertical		19,890	Nil	In weld: spongy metal, poor junction with metal of plate
15	d.c. 95	105	Flat		31,700	Nil	In weld: spongy metal, poor junction with metal of plate
16	d.c. 60	120	Flat		37,290	2 in 6 in.	In weld: very fine grained with many holes
17	d.c. 60	110	Vertical		38,820	2 in 6 in.	In weld: coarse, crystalline, many holes
18	a.c. 75	110	Vertical		31,360		In weld: fine to coarse crystalline, many holes
19		110	Vertical		27,090	1 4 in 8 in.	In weld: coarse crystalline, many holes
20	d.c. 110	120	Vertical		39,400	3 5 in 6 in.	In weld, very fine crystalline with crystalline areas: many holes
21	d.c. 110	120	Flat		34,650	Nil	In weld: very fine grained, very many holes
22	d.c. 110	120	Flat		35,120	Nil	In weld: very fine to coarse crystalline, many holes

					Cold Bend Test* Load at Yield	Load at Break	Angle of Bond, Deg.
23	d.c. 95	105	Flat		4,930	4,930	Nil In weld: very many laps and holes
24	d.c. 95	105	Vertical		4,120	4,610	1 In weld: very many laps and holes

* See corresponding notes, Table VII.

permit a tension specimen (0.505 in. diameter, 2 in. gage length)
to be machined out of it. Although the opinion is held by
some welders that the properties of the metal of an arc-weld
are affected materially by the adjacent metal by reason of
the interpenetration of the two, it was decided that the change
of properties of the added metal induced by the fusion alone
was of fundamental importance and should form the basis
of any study of arc-welding. The method adopted also permitted the use of larger specimens with much less machining

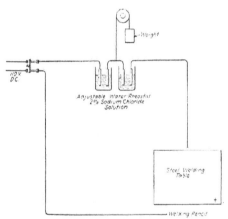

Fig. 149.—Arrangement of Apparatus for Welding.

than would have been possible had the metal been deposited
in the usual form of a weld.

In the first few specimens prepared (ten in number) the
metal was deposited by a series of "beadings" inside a 1½-in.
angle iron. The tension specimens cut from the deposited
metal were found to be very inferior and entirely unsuitable
for the study. This was largely on account of the excessive
overheating which occurred as well as the fact that a relatively
"long arc" was necessary for the fusion in this form. Because
of the very evident inferiority of these specimens, the results
of the mechanical tests made are not given in the tables.
The method of deposition of the metal was then changed to

that shown in Fig. 150. This method also had the advantage
in that the amount of necessary machining for shaping the
specimens for test was materially reduced. The block of arc-

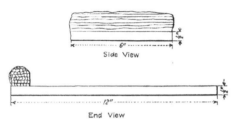

Side View

End View

Fig. 150.—Method of Formation of the Blocks of Arc-Fused Metal.

fused metal was built up on the end of a section of $\frac{1}{2}$-in.
plate of mild steel (ship plate) as shown. When a block of
sufficient size had been formed, it, together with the portion

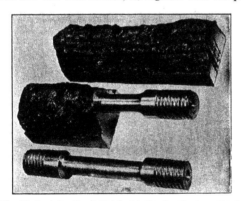

Fig. 151.—Block of Arc-Fused Metal with Tension Specimen Cut from It.
Approximately Half Natural Size.

of the steel plate immediately beneath, was sawed off from
the remainder of the steel plate. The tension specimen was
turned entirely out of the arc-fused metal. No difficulty whatever was experienced in machining the specimens. Fig. 151

shows the general appearance of the block of fused metal as well as the tension specimen turned out of it.

In general in forming the blocks, the fused metal was deposited as a series of "beads" so arranged that they were parallel to the axis of the tension specimen which was cut later from the block. In two cases, for purposes of comparison, the metal was deposited in "beads" at right angles to the length of the specimen. In all the specimens, after the deposition of each layer, the surface was very carefully and vigorously brushed with a stiff wire brush to remove the layer of oxide and slag which formed during the fusion. There was found to be but little need to use the chisel for removing this layer.

Two types of electrodes were used as material to be fused. These differed considerably in composition as shown in Table IX, and were chosen as representative of a "pure" iron and a low-carbon steel. The two types will be referred to as "A" and "B" respectively in the tables. They were obtained in the following sizes: $1/8$, $5/32$, $3/16$ and $1/4$ in. ("A" electrode $5/16$ in.). It was planned to use the different sizes with the following currents: $1/4$ in.—75, 110 and 145 amp.; $5/32$ in.—145, 185 and 225 amp.; $3/16$ in.—185, 225 and 260 amp.; $1/4$ in. ($5/16$ in.)—300 amp. The electrodes were used both in the bare condition and after being slightly coated with an oxidizing and refractory mixture. For coating, a "paste" of the following composition was used: 15 g. graphite, 7.5 g. magnesium, 4 g. aluminium, 65 g. magnesium oxide, 60 g. calcium oxide. To this mixture was added 120 c.c. of sodium silicate (40 deg. Bé.) and 150 c.c. of water. The electrodes were painted on one side only with the paste. The quantity given above was found to be sufficient for coating 500 electrodes. The purpose of the coating was to prevent excessive oxidation of the metal of the electrode during fusion and to form also a thin protective coating of slag upon the fused metal.

Tension specimens only were prepared from the arc-fused metal. It is quite generally recognized that the tension test falls very short in completely defining the mechanical properties of any metal; it is believed, however, that the behavior of this material when stressed in tension is so characteristic that its general behavior under other conditions of stress,

TABLE IX—Composition of Electrodes Before and After Fusion *

Electrode Size, Type In	Carbon Before	Carbon After	Silicon Before	Silicon After	Manganese Before	Manganese After	Phosphorus Before	Phosphorus After	Sulphur Before	Sulphur After	Copper Before	Copper After	Nitrogen§ Before	Nitrogen After
A ¼	0.058	{0.046, 0.051‡}	0.33	{0.007, 0.007‡}	0.042	{tr, tr}	0.002	{0.005, 0.005‡}	0.057	{0.036, 0.033‡}	...	...	0.0030	{0.156 / 0.127, 0.149‡ / 0.140‡, 0.121‡}
A	0.022	{0.010, 0.010‡, 0.033}	0.16	{0.012, 0.014‡, 0.006}	0.038	{tr, tr‡, 0.069}	-0.002	{0.003, 0.002‡, 0.012}	0.040	{0.033, 0.035‡, 0.043}	...	0.058	0.0040	{0.140 / 0.123, 0.124 / 0.126, 0.119‡ / 0.113‡, 0.127‡}
A, R	0.15	0.050, 0.027, 0.024‡	0.06	0.11, 0.008, 0.010‡	0.47	0.014, tr, tr‡	0.018	0.011, 0.002, 0.004‡	0.021	0.026, 0.035, 0.035‡	...	0.063	0.0037, 0.0032	0.131, 0.133, 0.117, 0.152, 0.132 / 0.131‡, 0.134‡, 0.111‡, 0.141‡, 0.135‡
B	0.15		0.001		0.46		0.014		0.017		...		0.0035	0.124, 0.121, 0.117, 0.119, 0.112 / 0.122‡, 0.132‡, 0.123‡, 0.106‡, 0.108‡, 0.094‡
B													0.0022, 0.0025	
B ¼													0.0014, 0.0022	
C														{0.133, 0.098}

* The electrodes which furnished the specimens used for analysis after fusion were not the identical ones used before fusion but were the same stock.
† Determinations for copper were not carried out upon the unfused electrodes.
‡ Results were obtained from the fusion of coated electrodes.
§ Each of the results reported in the "after" fusion columns is the average of two determinations, excepting as noted below, made on one separate specimen.
¶ Average of nine determinations.

Credit is due to J. R. Cain, chemist, Bureau of Standards for this method, details to be published later.

particularly when subjected to the so-called dynamic tests—i.e., vibration and shock—can be safely predicted from the results obtained. In order to supplement the specimens made at the Bureau a series of six were also prepared by one of the large manufacturers of equipment for electric welding to be included in the investigation. These are designated as "C" in the tables.

In Table IX it will be noted that the general effect of the fusion is to render the two materials used for welding pencils more nearly the same in composition. The loss of carbon and of silicon is very marked in each case where these elements exist in considerable amounts. A similar tendency may be noted for manganese. The coating with which the electrodes were covered appears to have but little influence, if any, in preventing the oxidation of the carbon and other elements.

TABLE X—RELATION BETWEEN NITROGEN-CONTENT AND CURRENT DENSITY *

Size of Elec.-trode. In.	Amperes (Approx)	Current Density	Nitrogen Content (Per Cent†) "A" Spec.	"B" Spec.	"C" Spec.	Average
⅛	110	9,000	0.156 / 0 149§	0.152 / 0.141§	....	0.138
⅜	145	11,800	0 127 / 0.140‡	0 132 / 0 135§	.....	0.126
⁵⁄₃₂	145	7,600	0.140 / 0 121§	0 124 / 0 122§	.....	0.127
⁵⁄₃₂	185	9,650	0 123 / 0 119§	0 121 / 0 133§ / 0 132‡	.....	0.131
³⁄₁₆	225	11,700	0 124 / 0 113§	0.117 / 0 123§	.....	‡
³⁄₁₆	175	9,100	.....	.....	0.133 / 0 098	b
³⁄₁₆	185	6,700	0.126 / 0.127§	0.119 / 0.106§	.....	0.120
¼	225	8,150	0.131 / 0.131§	0.111 / 0.108§	.....	0.120
¼	260	9,400	0.133 / 0.134§	0.112 / 0.094	.....	0.118
¼	300	3,900	0.117 / 0 111§	.....	.....	0.114

* Credit due J. R. Cain.
† Average of two determinations.
‡ Included in average for C-D 11,800.
§ Coated electrodes.
b Included in average for C-D 9,000.
a Average of 9 determinations.

The most noticeable change in composition is the increase in the nitrogen content of the metal. In general the increase was rather uniform for all specimens. In Table X are summarized the results of the nitrogen determinations together

TABLE XI—TENSILE PROPERTIES OF ELECTRODES

Electrode	Size, In.	Ulto. Strength, Lb. Sq.In.	Propor. Limit, Lb. Sq.In.	Elong. in 2 In. Per Cent	Reduct. Area, Per Cent
A	$\frac{3}{8}$	65,800	39,000	16.5	69.2
A	$\frac{5}{16}$	62,100	48,000	9.0	69.3
A	$\frac{7}{32}$	60,100	34,500	14.0	66.4
A	$\frac{3}{16}$	57,300	......	15.5	67.6
B	$\frac{5}{32}$	88,600	67,000	4.5	51.5
B	$\frac{5}{16}$	84,700	58,500	7.0	59.8
B	$\frac{1}{4}$	66,300	37,500	15.0	61.4
B	$\frac{1}{8}$	67,900	......	15.5	62.4

with the corresponding current density used for the fusion of the metal. In Fig. 152 the average nitrogen contents found for the different conditions of fusion are given and plotted against the corresponding current density. Though no definite conclusion seems to be warranted, it may be said that, in

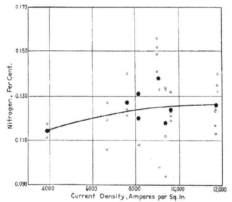

FIG. 152.—Relation of Current Density to Nitrogen Content in Arc-Fused Iron.

Black dots represent averages.

general, the percentage of nitrogen taken up by the fused iron increases somewhat as the current density increases. With the lowest current densities used the amount of nitrogen was found to decrease appreciably.

Mechanical Properties of the Arc-Fused Metal.—The mechanical properties of the two types of electrodes used as determined by the tension test are summarized in Table XI.

TABLE XII—TENSILE PROPERTIES AND HARDNESS OF FIFTY SPECIMENS OF WELD-METAL AT THE BUREAU. (0.505-IN. DIAM. STANDARD TENSION BAR USED)

Sample No.	Size Electrode, In.	Amp., D.C.	Ult. Strength	Yield Pt.	Proportional Limit	Elong. in 2 In., per Cent	Reduc. Area, per Cent	Brinell Hardness
			Bare Electrodes					
A2		110	49,850	36,600	25,000	6.0	6.5	108
A3		145	51,950	36,250	30,000	8.0	13.0	114
A7		145	47,550	.....	.....	6.0	7.4	108
A8		185	48,100	.....	.....	8.0	8.7	104
A9		225	45,500	.....	.....	8.0	9.6	104
A4		185	50,600	33,750	29,500	5.5	13.5	105
A5		225	49,150	36,250	22,000	7.0	10.0	102
A6		260	50,950	33,750	28,800	10.5	12.0	107
A10		300	46,670	.....	.....	12.0	11.9	104
			Covered Electrodes					
AD2		110	51,250	35,000	25,600	9.5	11.0	103
AD2-D		110	43,000	.....	25,000	5.0	9.0	...
AD3		145	51,100	33,750	25,000	8.5	10.5	110
AD3-D		145	46,250	.....	24,250	7.0	12.0	...
AD7		145	41,750	.....	.....	6.0	6.6	99
AD7-D		145	46,950	.....	25,500	8.0	9.4	...
AD8		185	44,620	.....	.....	6.5	5.8	103
AD8-D		185	43,600	.....	23,250	6.5	9.0	...
AD9		225	46,900	.....	.....	9.5	10.1	96
AD9-D		225	41,550	.....	25,500	5.0	6.5	...
AD4		185	51,200	35,000	30,000	10.5	10.5	101
AD4-D		185	45,700	.....	25,500	8.5	11.5	...
AD5		225	48,600	35,000	30,000	7.0	10.0	96
AD5-D		225	46,250	.....	23,750	11.5	12.0	...
AD6		260	47,500	34,500	31,500	9.0	9.0	97
AD6-D		260	50,700	.....	.....	8.0	2.8	105
AD10		300	45,900	.....	.....	8.5	11.5	98
			Bare Electrodes					
B2		110	52,650	37,000	27,000	7.5	7.5	114
B3		145	54,500	36,000	27,000	12.5	12.0	106
B4		145	46,450	33,500	26,000	5.0	7.0	102
B5		185	49,600	34,250	27,000	7.5	9.0	108
B6		225	49,500	30,500	28,000	9.0	5.0	110
B7		185	47,550	.....	28,500	7.5	11.5	95
B8		225	42,900	.....	18,750	7.5	16.2	101
B9		260	47,500	.....	21,500	12.0	13.5	102
			Covered Electrodes					
BD2		110	49,050	33,750	27,500	9.0	12.0	100
BD2-D		110	44,400	.....	20,000	6.5	9.4	...
BD3		145	52,100	34,300	30,500	12.5	16.0	116
BD3-D		145	50,850	.....	23,500	13.0	17.5	...
BD4		145	48,130	31,000	30,500	8.0	10.0	101
BD4-D		145	41,750	.....	21,000	6.0	9.5	...
BD5		185	49,086	31,730	29,000	12.5	13.0	97
BD5-D		185	47,100	.....	22,500	11.0	12.5	...
BD6		225	45,500	30,500	25,000	8.5	10.5	95
BD7		185	49,950	.....	24,500	11.5	21.5	98
BD7-D		185	51,150	.....	23,750	14.5	19.5	...
BD8		225	41,500	.....	17,850	6.0	12.7	99
BD8-D(?)	(?)	225(?)	48,750	.....	21,250	12.5	16.0	...
BD9		260	46,350	.....	24,000	10.0	15.0	99
			Bare Electrodes					
C1		175	48,650	32,650	23,000	12.0	19.1	...
C2		175	45,200	32,400	23,000	7.5	16.6	...
C3		175	49,720	32,650	25,000	9.0	13.6	...
C4		175	54,500	32,500	25,000	11.0	17.5	118
C5		175	50,900	32,500	24,000	15.0	23.0	109
C6		175	50,500	33,500	23,000	12.0	16.0	...

TABLE XIII—TENSILE PROPERTIES AND HARDNESS OF FIFTY SPECIMENS OF WELD-METAL PREPARED BY THE BUREAU—ARRANGED IN ORDER OF AMPERAGE USED

Amperage Used Amps.†	Ultimate Strength lb. Sq.In.				Tensile Properties Yield Point lb. Sq.In.				Elongation in 2 In. per Cent				Reduction of Area per Cent				Brinell Hardness			
	A*		B*		A		B		A		B		A		B		A		B	
	Bare	Cov-ered	Bare	Cov-ered	Bare	Cov-ered	Bare	Cov-ered	Bare	Cov-ered	Bare	Cov-ered	Bare	Cov-ered	Bare	Cov-ered	Bare Brin.	Cov-ered Brin.	Bare Brin.	Cov-ered Brin.
110	49,850	51,250; 52,650	36,600	49,050; 44,060‡	35,000; 37,000		36,600	33,750	6.	9.5; 5.5‡	7.5	9.0; 6.5‡	6.5	11.0; 9.0‡	7.5	12.0; 9.4‡	108	103	103	100
145	51,950	43,000; 54,500 51,000‡	36,250	44,060‡ 52,100‡ 50,850‡	33,750	33,750	36,000	34,300		8.0; 8.0‡	12.5	13.5; 13.0‡	13.0	10.5; 12.0‡	12.0	16.5‡; 17.0‡	114	110	114	116
	47,550	46,250; 46,450 41,750‡		48,130‡ 41,750‡ 49,086‡			35,500	31,000	6.0	6.0; 6.0	5.0	8.0; 6.0‡	7.0	6.6; 5.8	7.0	10.0; 6.0‡	108	99	106	101
185	48,100	43,000; 49,600 44,620	33,750	47,100‡ 49,950‡	35,000			31,730‡	8.0	6.5‡; 9.0‡	7.5	12.0‡; 14.5‡	9.0	9.4‡; 9.0‡	9.0	9.5‡; 13.5‡	104	103	102	97
	50,600	51,200; 47,550 45,200‡		49,950‡ 51,150‡ 45,500			30,500	30,500‡	5.5	9.5‡; 10.5‡	9.0	11.5‡	11.5	10.5; 12.5‡	11.5	12.5‡; 19.5‡	105	101	108	98
225	45,500	41,550; 42,900 45,250‡	36,250	41,550‡	35,000				8.0	5.0‡; 9.0‡	9.0	14.5‡	7.5	10.1‡; 10.0‡	7.5	19.5‡; 10.5	101	96	95	95
	49,150	47,500; 47,500	33,750	45,250‡	34,500				7.0	9.0; 12.0	7.5	6.0	9.6	6.5‡; 10.0‡	8.5	10.5	102	97	101	99
260	50,950	46,350		47,500‡					10.5	11.5‡; 8.0‡	12.0	10.0	10.0	2.8‡	16.2	12.7	107		102	99
300	46,670	45,940		30,700‡					12.9	8.5	8.5		11.9	9.0‡	13.5	15.0	104	100	105	101
Average	48,900	46,600; 48,800	35,300	47,450	34,650	34,250	34,250	32,250	12.9	8.5	8.5	9.9	10.3	9.2	10.5	13.8	106	100	105	101

Av. 47,400   Av. 47,980   Av. 35,000   Av. 33,250   Av. 7.9   Av. 9.0   Av. 7.9   Av. 12.5   Av. 9.6   Av. 103   Av. 103

* A and B refer to the two types of electrodes used (Table III).
† Size of electrode used: ⅛ in. diam. = 110 amps. and 145 (1) amps. ³⁄₁₆ in. diam. — 145 (2) amp. — 185 (1) amp. and 225 (1) amp., and 225 (2) amp., 225 (2) amp., 260 amp. ³⁄₁₆ in. diam.—300 amp.
‡ Duplicate specimen.

In Table XII are given the results of the mechanical tests made upon the tension specimens which were turned out of the blocks of metal resulting from the fusion of the electrodes.

The specimens listed, C_1, C_2....C_6 are the six which were prepared outside the Bureau and submitted for purposes of comparison. It was stated that they were prepared from bare electrodes $^5/_{32}$ in. diameter of type "B," containing 0.17 per cent carbon and 0.5 per cent manganese.

As an aid for more readily comparing the mechanical properties of the two types of arc-fused metal "A" and "B," the results have been grouped as given in Table XIII.

The characteristic appearance of specimens after testing, illustrating their behavior when stressed in tension till rupture occurs is shown in Fig. 153. These represent two views of the face of the fracture, one in which the line of vision is perpendicular to the face, the other at an angle of 45 deg., together with a side view of the cylindrical surface of the specimen. The features shown are characteristic of all the specimens tested, though in some they were much more pronounced than those shown. The fracture of the specimen in all cases reveals interior flaws. In some of the specimens, however, these are microscopic and of the character to be discussed in a subsequent chapter on Metallography. Although many of the specimens (from the results of Table XII) appear to have a considerable elongation, it is seen from Fig. 153 that the measured elongation does not truly represent a property of the metal itself. It is due rather to interior defects which indicate lack of perfect union of succeeding additions of metal during the process of fusion. The surface markings of the specimen after stressing to rupture are very similar to those seen in the familiar "flaky steel."

Resulting Physical Properties Depend Essentially on Soundness.—It appears from the results above that, as far as the mechanical properties are concerned, nothing was gained by coating the electrodes. The results show no decided superiority for either of the two types of electrodes used. This may be expected, however, when one considers that the two are rendered practically the same in composition during fusion by the burning out of the carbon and other elements.

The results of the tension tests upon the "C" series of

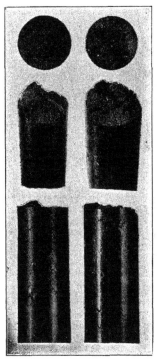

FIG. 153.—Characteristic Appearance of Tension Specimen After Test.

At top, face of fracture, viewed normally. Middle, fractured end of specimen, viewed at an angle of 45 deg. At bottom, cylindrical surface of specimen. Magnification, × 2.

specimens which were made outside of the Bureau and submitted to be included in the investigation, show no marked difference between these samples and those prepared by the Bureau. In all cases the results obtained in the tension test are determined by the soundness of the metal and do not necessarily indicate the real mechanical properties of the material.

The results of the hardness determinations do not appear to have any particular or unusual significance. The variations are of the same general nature and relative magnitude as the variations observed in the results of the tension test. In general the higher hardness number accompanies the higher tensile values, though this was not invariably so. As previously noted, specimens were prepared for the purpose of showing the relation between the direction in which the stress is applied and the manner of deposition of the metal. The metal was deposited in the form shown in Fig. 151, except that the "beads" extended across the piece rather than lengthwise, hence the "beads" of fused metal were at right angles to the direction in which the tensional stress was applied. The results of the tension tests show that these two specimens (AW_1 and AW_2) were decidedly inferior to those prepared in the other manner as shown in Table XIV.

TABLE XIV.—MECHANICAL PROPERTIES OF ARC-FUSED METAL DEPOSITED AT RIGHT ANGLES TO LENGTH OF SPECIMEN

Specimen	Ult: Strength, Lb. Sq. In.	Proportional Limit, Lb. Sq. In.	Elongation in 2 in. (per Cent)	Red. of Area, per Cent
AW^1	40,450	22,500	6.5	8.5
AW^2	39,500	22,500	4.0	3.0

Macrostructure.—The general condition of the metal resulting from the arc-fusion is shown in Figs. 154 and 155, which show longitudinal median sections of a series of the tension bars adjacent to the fractured end. The metal in all of these specimens was found to contain a considerable number of cavities and oxide inclusions, these are best seen after the surfaces are etched with a 10 per cent aqueous solution of copper-ammonium chloride. In many of the specimens the successive additions of metal are outlined by a series of very fine inclusions (probably oxide) which are revealed by the etching. There appears to be no definite relation between the soundness of the metal and the conditions of deposition—i.e., for the range of current density used—nor does either type

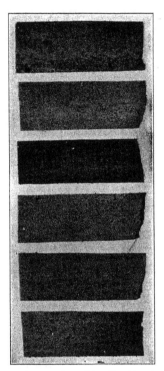

FIG. 154.—Macrostructure of Arc-Fused Metal, Type A.

Medial Longitudinal sections of the tension bars indicated were used (Table XII); etching, 10 per cent aqueous solution of copper-ammonium chloride. Magnification, × 2. From top to bottom in order:

AD6—A electrode; ³⁄₁₆ in., covered, 260 amp.
A5—A electrode; ³⁄₁₆ in., bare, 225 amp.
A6—A electrode; ³⁄₁₆ in., bare, 260 amp.
A3—A electrode; ⅛ in., bare, 145 amp.
A4—A electrode; ³⁄₁₆ in., bare, 185 amp.
AD2—A electrode; ⅛ in., covered, 110 amp.

of electrode used show any decided superiority over the other with respect to porosity of the resulting fusion. In Fig. 156

Fig. 155.—Macrostructure of Arc-Fused Metal, Type B.

Medial longitudinal sections of the tension bars indicated were used (Table XII); etching, 10 per cent aqueous solution of copper-ammonium chloride. Magnification, × 2. From top to bottom in order:

B4—B electrode; ⁵⁄₃₂ in., bare, 145 amp.
B5—B electrode; ⁵⁄₃₂ in., bare, 185 amp.
B2—B electrode; ⅛ in., bare, 110 amp.
B3—B electrode; ⅛ in., bare, 145 amp.
BD6—B electrode; ⁵⁄₃₂ in., covered, 225 amp.
BD4—B electrode; ⁵⁄₃₂ in., covered, 145 amp.

is shown the appearance of a cross-section of one of the blocks of arc-fused metal prepared outside of the Bureau by skilled welding operators. The condition of this material is quite similar to that prepared by the Bureau.

The microscopic study of the material to be discussed in a subsequent chapter also revealed further evidence of unsoundness in all three types, "A," "B" and "C."

Discussion of Results.—In any consideration of electric-arc welding it should constantly be borne in mind that the weld-

Fig. 156.—Macrostructure of Arc-Fused Metal, Type C.

Specimen C1 (Table XII), cross-section of the block of arc-fused metal from which the tension bar was turned; etched with 5 per cent alcoholic solution of picric acid. Magnification, × 1.7.

metal is simply metal which has been melted and has then solidified in situ. The weld is essentially a casting, though the conditions for its production are very different from those ordinarily employed in the making of steel castings. The metal loses many of the properties it possesses when in the wrought form and hence it is not to be expected that a fusion weld made by any process whatever, will have all the properties that metal of the same composition would have when in the forged or rolled condition. A knowledge of the characteristic properties of the arc-fused iron is then of fundamental importance in the study of the electric-arc weld.

The peculiar conditions under which the fusion takes place also render the metal of the weld quite different from similar metal melted and cast in the usual manner. It is seemingly impossible to fuse the metal without serious imperfections. The mechanical properties of the metal are dependent therefore to an astonishing degree upon the skill, care and patience of the welding operator. The very low ductility shown by specimens when stressed in tension is the most striking feature observed in the mechanical properties of the material as revealed by the tension test. As explained above, the measured elongation of the tension specimen does not truly indicate a property of the metal. Due to the unsoundness, already described in the discussion of the structure, the true properties of the metal are not revealed by the tension test to any extent. The test measures, largely for each particular specimen, the adhesion between the successively added layers which value varies considerably in different specimens due to the unsoundness caused by imperfect fusion, oxide and other inclusions, tiny enclosed cavities and similar undesirable features. The elongation measured for any particular specimen is due largely, if not entirely, to the increase of length due to the combined effect of the numerous tiny imperfections which exist throughout the sample.

That the metal is inherently ductile, however, is shown by the behavior upon bending (later to be discussed) in the microstructure of bent specimens. The formation of slip-bands within the ferrite grains to the extent which was observed is evidence of a high degree of ductility. It appears, however, that the grosser imperfections are sufficient to prevent any accurate measurement of the real mechanical properties of the metal from being made. The conclusion appears to be warranted therefore that the changes of composition which the fusion entails, together with the unusual features of microstructure which accompany the composition change are of minor importance in determining the strength, durability and other properties of the arc weld.

In arc-fusion welds in general, the mass of weld-metal is in intimate contact with the parts which are being welded so that it is claimed by many that because of the diffusion and intermingling of the metal under repair with that of the weld, properties of the latter are considerably improved. The comparison shown in Table XV somewhat supports this claim. The nearest comparison found available with the Bureau's specimen are some of those of the welds designated as the "Wirt-Jones" series reported by H. M. Hobart. These welds were of the 45 deg. double-V type made in ½-in. ship plate; the specimens for test were of uniform cross-section 1×½ in., the projecting metal at the joint having been planed off even with the surface of the plates and the test bars were so taken that the weld extended transversely across the specimen near the center of its length. The electrodes used were similar to those designated as type "B" in the Bureau's investigation.

TABLE XV.—COMPARISON OF WELDS WITH TESTS OF ARC-FUSED METAL PREPARED UNDER SIMILAR CONDITIONS.

Bureau of Standards				Wirt-Jones			
Size Electrode, In.	D.C. Amp.	Ult. Strength, Lb./Sq.In.	Elong. Per Cent per 2 In.	Size Electrode,* In.	D.C. Amp.	Ult. Strength, Lb./Sq.In.	Elong. Per Cent In 2 In.
1/8	110	52,650	7.5	1/8	110	45,800	8.0
1/8†	110	49,050	9.0	1/8	115	58,200	14.0
1/8†	110	44,400	6.5	1/8	115	59,400	13.5
Average		48,700	7.7	1/8	120	53,700	7.0
5/32	145	46,450	5.0	1/8	120	57,600	8.5
5/32†	145	48,130	8.0	Average		54,940	10.2
5/32†	145	41,750		11/64	150	60,900	8.0
Average		45,440	6.3	5/32	155	62,600	11.5
5/32	185	49,600	7.5	Average		61,750	9.8
5/32	185	49,086	12.5	11/64	175	59,800	9.0
5/32	185	47,100	11.0				
Average		48,395	10.3				

* Electrodes were used in bare condition.

† Electrodes were coated as previously described, those not so designated in this column were used bare.

Since the specimens used in work described in the foregoing sections were prepared in a manner quite different from the usual practice of arc-welding, no definite recommendations applicable to the latter can be made. It appears, however, from the results obtained that the two types of electrodes used —i.e., "pure" iron and low-carbon steel—should give very similar results in practical welding. This is due to the changes which occur during the melting so that the resulting fusions are essentially of the same composition. The use of a slight coating on the electrodes does not appear to be of any material advantage so far as the properties of the resulting fused metal are concerned. Since the program of work as carried out did not include the use of any of the covered electrodes which are highly recommended by many for use in arc welding, particularly so, for "overhead work," no data are available as to the effect of such coatings upon the properties of the metal resulting from fusion. Although all of the specimens used in the examinations were made by the use of direct current, it appears from the results obtained with a considerable number of welds representing the use of both kinds of current, submitted for the preliminary examinations which were made, that the properties of the fused metal are independent of the kind of current and are influenced primarily by the heat of fusion. Any difference in results obtained by welding with alternating current as compared with those obtained with direct current apparently depends upon the relative ease of manipulation during welding rather than to any intrinsic effect of the current upon properties of the metal.

CHAPTER X

METALLOGRAPHY OF ARC-FUSED STEEL

The same authors responsible for the description of the investigations at the Bureau of Standards, given in the previous chapter, also furnished the data given in this chapter:

Fusion welds evidently are fundamentally different from other types of joints in that the metal at the weld is essentially a casting. A preliminary study of a considerable number of specimens welded under different conditions confirmed the impression that the arc-fusion weld has characteristics quite different from other fusion welds.

In the present study, of which both the previous chapter and this one form a part, two types of electrodes, a "pure" iron called "A" and a mild steel called "B," were used, in the bare condition, and also after receiving a slight coating. With these were included a set of similar specimens prepared outside of the Bureau by expert welding operators. During the fusion the composition of the metal of the two types of electrodes is changed considerably by the "burning-out" of the carbon and other elements, the two becoming very much alike in composition. A very considerable increase in the nitrogen content occurs at the same time, as shown by chemical analysis.

The mechanical properties of the arc-fused metal as measured by the tension test are essentially those of an inferior casting. The most striking feature is the low ductility of the metal. All of the specimens showed evidence of unsoundness in their structure, tiny inclosed cavities, oxide inclusions, lack of intimate union, etc. These features of unsoundness are, seemingly, a necessary consequence of the method of fusion as now practiced. They determine almost entirely the mechanical properties of the arc-fused metal. The observed elongation of the specimen under tension is due to the combined action of the numerous unsound spots rather than to the ductility of the metal. That the metal is inherently ductile, however, will be shown by the changes in the microstructure, produced by cold-bending. By taking extreme precautions during the fusion, a great deal of the unsoundness may be avoided and the mechanical properties of the metal be considerably improved. The specimens described, however, are more representative of actual present practice in welding.

General Features of Microstructure.—For purposes of comparison the microstructure of the electrodes before fusion is shown in (1) and (2), Fig. 157. The "A" electrodes have the appearance of steel of a very low carbon content; in some cases they were in the cold-rolled state; all showed a considerable number of inclusions. The "B" electrodes have the structure of a mild steel and are much freer from inclusions than are those of the other type. It is, undoubtedly true, however, that the condition of the arc-fused metal with respect to the number of inclusions is a result of the fusion rather than of the initial state of the metal.

It is to be expected that the microstructure of the material after fusion will be very considerably changed, since the metal is then essentially the same as a casting. It has some features, however, which are not to be found in steel as ordinarily cast. The general type of microstructure was found to vary in the different specimens and to range from a condition which will be designated as "columnar" to that of a uniform fine equiaxed crystalline arrangement as shown at 3 and 4, Fig. 157A. This observation held true for both types of electrodes, whether bare or covered. In the examination of cross-sections of the blocks of arc-fused metal, it was noticed that the equi-axed type of structure is prevalent throughout the interior of the piece and the columnar is to be found generally nearer the surface—i.e., in the metal deposited last. It may be inferred from this that the metal of the layers which were deposited during the early part of the preparation of the specimen is refined considerably by the successive heatings to which it is subjected as additional layers of metal are deposited. The general type of structure of the tension bars cut from the blocks of arc fused metal will vary considerably according to the amount of refining which has taken place as well as the relative position of the tension specimen within the block. In addition it was noticed that the columnar and coarse equi-axed crystalline condition appears to predominate with fusion at high-current densities.

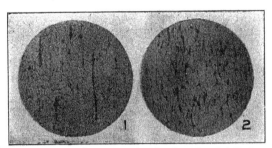

Fig. 157.—(1) "A" Electrode, ⁵/₃₂-in. Diameter. Annealed As Received. (2) "B" Electrode, ³/₁₆-in. Diameter. Cold-Drawn. Both×100. Picric Acid Etching.

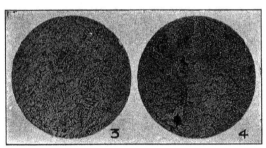

Fig. 157A.—(3) Columnar Structure of B₂. ×66. Five Per Cent Picric Acid Etching. (4) Equi-axed Structure of AD₂. ×200. Two per Cent Alcoholic HNO₃ Etching.

Microscopic Evidence of Unsoundness.—In all of the speci-mens of arc-fused metal examined microscopically there ap-pear to be numerous tiny globules of oxide as shown in Figs. 158 to 160. A magnification of 500 diameters is usually neces-sary to show these inclusions. In general they appear to have

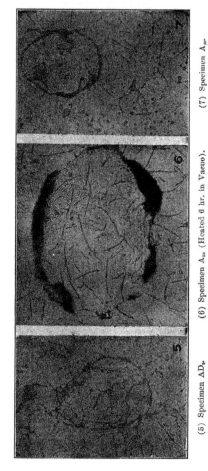

(5) Specimen AD_{2v}.   (6) Specimen A_{1v} (Heated 6 hr. in Vacuo).   (7) Specimen A_{2v}.

FIG. 158.

"Metallic-globule" Inclusions in Arc-Fused Iron. (5) and (7) etched with 2 per cent alcoholic solution of HNO_2. (6) With 5 per cent picric acid. × 450.

no definite arrangement, but occur indiscriminately throughout the crystals of iron.

A type of unsoundness frequently found is that shown in (5), (6) and (7), Fig. 158; this will be referred to as "metallic-globule inclusions." In general these globules possess a microstructure similar to that of the surrounding metal, but are enveloped by a film, presumably of oxide. It seems probable that they are small metallic particles which were formed as a sort of spray at the tip of the electrode and which were deposited on the solidified crust surrounding the pool of molten metal directly under the arc. These solidified particles apparently are not fused in with the metal which is subsequently deposited over them—i.e., during the formation of this same layer and before any brushing of the surface occurs. By taking extreme precautions during the fusion, a great deal of this unsoundness may be avoided and the mechanical properties of the metal may be considerably improved.

Characteristic "Needles" or "Plates."—The most characteristic feature of the steel after fusion is the presence of numerous lines or needles within the crystals. The general appearance of this feature of the structure is shown in (8) to (11), Fig. 159, inclusive. The number and the distribution of these needles were found to vary greatly in the different specimens. In general, they are most abundant in the columnar and in the coarse equi-axed crystals; the finer equi-axed crystals in some specimens were found to be quite free from them, although exceptions were found to this rule. In general, a needle lies entirely within the bounds of an individual crystal. Some instances were found, however, where a needle appeared to lie across the boundary and so lie within two adjacent crystals. Several instances of this tendency have been noted in the literature on this subject. The needles have an appreciable width, and when the specimen is etched with 2 per cent alcoholic nitric acid they appear much the same as cementite—i.e., they remain uncolored, although they may appear to widen and darken if the etching is prolonged considerably. The apparent widening is evidently due to the attack of the adjacent ferrite along the boundary line between the two. The tendency of the lines to darken when etched with a hot alkaline solution of sodium picrate, as reported

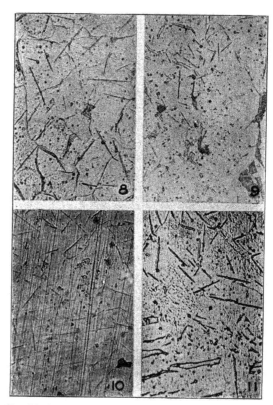

Fig. 159 (8 to 11).—Characteristic "Needles" or "Plates" × 375.

(8) BDs etched with 5 per cent picric acid in alcohol.

(9) Specimen BDs after using for thermal analysis, re-heated in vacuo to 900 deg. C. four times. Picric acid etching.

(10) Same as (9) except etched in hot alkaline sodium picrate solution.

(11) Specimen of welded joint between slip-plate. Additional very small needles are noted. Etching: 2 per cent HNO_3 in alcohol.

by Comstock, was confirmed; (10) illustrates the appearance when etched in this manner. The needles are sometimes found in a rectangular grouping—i.e., they form angles of 90 deg. with one another. In other cases they appear to be arranged along the octahedral planes of the crystal—i.e., at 60 deg. to one another. This is best seen in specimens which have been heated, as explained below:

In some of the specimens certain crystals showed groups of very fine short needles as in (11). The needles comprising any one group or family are usually arranged parallel to one another, but the various groups are often arranged definitely with respect to one another in the same manner as described above. Similar needles have been reported in articles by S. W. Miller.

An attempt was made by Dr. P. D. Merica to determine whether the so-called lines or needles were really of the shape of needles or of tiny plates or scales. An area was carefully located on a specimen prepared for microscopic examination, which was then ground down slightly and repolished several times. It was possible to measure the amount of metal removed during the slight grinding by observing the gradual disappearance of certain of the spherical oxide inclusions the diameter of which could be accurately measured. By slightly etching the specimen after polishing anew it was possible to follow the gradual disappearance of some of the most prominent needles and to measure the maximum "depth" of such needles. It was concluded from the series of examinations that the term "plate" is more correctly descriptive of this feature of the structure than "line" or "needle." The thickness of the plate —i.e., the width of the needle—varies from 0.0005 to 0.001 mm. and the width of the plate ("depth") may be as great as 0.005 mm. The persistence of the plates after a regrinding of the surface used for microscopical examination may be noted in some of the micrographs given by Miller. The authors are not aware, however, of any other attempt to determine the shape of these plates by actual measurements of their dimensions.

Plates Probably Due to Nitrates.—The usual explanation of the nature of these plates is that they are due to the nitrogen which is taken up by the iron during its fusion. Other suggestions which have been offered previously attribute them to oxide of iron and to carbide. The suggestion concerning oxide may be dismissed with a few words. The plates are distinctly different from oxide in their form and their behavior upon heating. It is shown later that the tiny oxide globules coalesce into larger ones upon prolonged heating in vacuo; the plates also increase in size and become much more distinct (see (32), (34) and (36), Fig. 166). In no case, however, was any inter-mediate stage between the globular form and the plate pro-

Fig. 160.—(12) Specimen AD₃, Etched with 2 Per Cent Alcoholic Nitric Acid. Shows Pearlite Islands, "Needles" and Oxide Inclusions. × 750.

duced such as would be expected if both were of the same chemical nature.

Regarding the assumption that they are cementite plates, it may be said that the tendency during fusion is for the carbon to be "burned out," thus leaving an iron of low carbon content. In all the specimens, islands of pearlite (usually with cementite borders) are to be found and may easily be distinguished with certainty. The number of such islands in any specimen appears to be sufficient to account for the carbon content of the material as revealed by chemical analysis. In some cases the pearlite islands are associated with a certain type of "lines" or "needles" such as are shown in (12), Fig. 160. These needles, however, appear distinctly different from those of the prevailing type and are usually easily distinguished from them.

The fact that the plates found in the arc-fused metal are identical in appearance and in behavior (e.g., etching) as those found in iron which has been nitrogenized is strong evidence that both are of the same nature. (13) Fig. 161 shows the appearance of the plates produced in electrolytic iron by heating it for some time in pure ammonia gas. These plates behave in the same characteristic manner when etched with hot sodium picrate as do those occurring in arc-fused

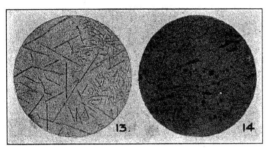

Fig. 161.—(13) Characteristic Structure of Electrolytic Iron Heated in NH_3 at 650 Deg. C. Two Types of Nitride Plates. Etched with 2 Per Cent Alcoholic HNO_3. $\times$ 375.

Fig. 161.—(14) Arc-Fused Iron Produced in CO_2 Atmosphere. Type "A," $^5/_{32}$-in. Electrodes, 150 Amperes. Etched with 5 Per Cent Picric Acid in Alcohol. $\times$ 375.

iron—i.e., they darken slightly and appear as finest rulings across the bright ferrite. The fact that the nitrogen content of the steel as shown by chemical analysis is increased by the arc-fusion also supports the view that the change which occurs in the structure is due to the nitrogen. The statement has been made by Ruder that metal fused in the absence of nitrogen —i.e., in an atmosphere of carbon dioxide or of hydrogen— does not contain any plates and hence the view that the plates are due to the nitrogen is very much strengthened. In (15), Fig. 162, the appearance of specimens prepared at the Bureau by arc fusion of electrodes of type "A" in an atmosphere of

(15) Specimen B₄. (16) Specimen B₅. (17) Specimen B₆.

FIG. 162.—Electrolytic Copper Deposit for Protection During Polishing. Etching: 2 Per Cent HNO₂ in Alcohol. × 280.

carbon dioxide is shown. The microscopic examination of the fused metal shows unmistakable evidence of the presence of some plates, although they differ somewhat from those found in nitrogenized iron and in metal fused in the air by the electric arc. Evidently they are due to a different cause from the majority of those formed in the iron fused in air. For convenience, in the remainder of the discussion the "plates" will be referred to as "nitride plates."

Relation of Microstructure to the Path of Rupture.—The faces of the fracture of several of the tension specimens after testing were heavily plated electrolytically with copper so as to preserve the edges of the specimens during the polishing of the section and examined microscopically to see if the course of the path of rupture had been influenced to an appreciable extent by the microstructural features. In general, the fracture appears to be intercrystalline in type. Along the path of rupture in all of the specimens were smooth-edged hollows, many of which had evidently been occupied by the "metallic globules" referred to above, while others were gas-holes or pores. Portions of the fracture were intracrystalline and presented a jagged outline, but it cannot be stated with certainty whether the needles have influenced the break at such points or not. (16) shows the appearance of some of the fractures and illustrates that, in general, the "nitride plates" do not appear to determine to any appreciable extent the course of the path of rupture.

The behavior of the plates under deformation can best be seen in thin specimens of the metal which were bent through a considerable angle. Results of examination of welds treated in this manner have been described by Miller. Small rectangular plates of the arc-fused metal, approximately $^3/_{32}$ in. thick, were polished and etched for microscopic examination and were then bent in the vise through an angle of 20 deg. (approximate).

In (18) to (21), Fig. 163, inclusive are given micrographs illustrating the characteristic behavior of the material when subjected to bending. For moderate distortion the nitride plates influence the course of the slip-bands in much the same way that grain boundaries do—i.e., the slip-bands terminate usually on meeting one of the plates with a change of direction so that they form a sharper angle with the plate than does the portion of the slip-band which is at some distance away (18). When the deformation is greater the slip-bands occur on both sides of the nitride plate, but usually show a slight variation in direction on the two sides of the nitride plate (19); this is often quite pronounced at the point where the plate is crossed by the slip-band. In a few cases evidence

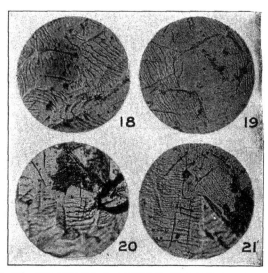

Fig. 163.—(18 to 21) Behavior of "Nitride Plates" During Plastic Deformation of the Iron. Specimen RD$_9$, Etched with 2 Per Cent Alcoholic, Nitric Acid Before Bending. $\times$ 500.

of the "faulting" of the plate as a result of severe distortion was noted (20). This was a rare appearance, however, because of the nature of the metal, and is not shown in (21). On account of the inclusions and other features of unsoundness of the metal, rupture occurs at such points before the sound crystals have been sufficiently strained to show the characteristic behavior of the plates. Other micrographs show the beginning of a fracture around one of the "metallic globule" inclusions before the surrounding metal has been very severely strained. For this reason the influence of the plates on the mechanical properties of the crystals cannot be stated with certainty. It would appear, however, that on account of the apparently unavoidable unsoundness of the metal, any possible influence of the nitride plates upon the mechanical properties of the material is quite negligible.

Some of the same specimens used for cold bending were torn partially in two after localizing the tear by means of a saw cut in the edge of the plate. The specimen was then copper plated and prepared for microscopic examination, the surface having been ground away sufficiently to reveal the weld-metal with the tear in it. The nitride plates did not appear to have determined to any extent the path taken in the rupture produced in this manner.

Effect of Heat Treatment Upon Structure.—With the view of possibly gaining further information as to the nature of the plates (assumed to be nitride), which constitute such a characteristic feature of the microstructure, a series of heat treatments were carried out upon several specimens of arc-fused electrodes of both types. Briefly stated, the treatment consisted in quenching the specimens in cold water after heating them for a period of ten or fifteen minutes at a temperature considerable above that of the Ac_3 transformation; 925, 950 and 1,000 deg. C. were the temperatures used. After microscopical examination of the different quenched specimens they were tempered at different temperatures which varied from 600 to 925 deg. C. for periods of ten and twenty minutes. The samples which were used were rather small in size, being only $\frac{1}{8}$ in. thick, in order that the effect of the treatment should be very thorough, were taken from test bars A_2, A_3, AD_{10}, B_2, B_6 and B_9. These represented metal which had been deposited under different conditions of current density, as shown in Table X. No plates were found to be present in any of the specimens after quenching. (22) Fig. 164 shows the appearance of one of the quenched bars, a condition which is typical of all. The structure indicates that the material comprising the plates had dissolved in the matrix of iron and had been retained in this condition upon quenching. The needle-like striations within the individual grains are char-

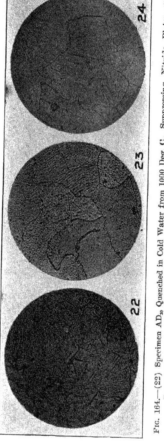

FIG. 164.—(22) Specimen AD₂₀ Quenched in Cold Water from 1000 Deg. C., Suppressing Nitride Plates and Developing Martensitic Structure. Etched with 5 Per Cent Alcoholic Picric Acid. × 500.

FIG. 164.—(23) "A" Electrode Quenched in Cold Water from 1000 Deg. C. Faint Martensitic Markings, Especially Near Surface. Etched with 2 Per Cent HNO₃ in Alcohol. × 500.

FIG. 164.—(24) Same as (23), but Showing Interior Markings Suggestive of "Plates" of Arc-Fused Metal. Etched with 2 Per Cent HNO₃. ×500.

acteristic of the condition resulting from the severe quenching and are to be observed at times in steel of a very low carbon content. (23) shows the appearance of one of the "A" electrodes ($^5/_{32}$ in.) quenched in cold water from 1,000 deg. C. Some of the crystals of the quenched iron also show interior markings somewhat similar in appearance to the nitride plates (24). These are, however, probably of the same nature as the interior tree-like network sometimes seen in ferrite which has been heated to a high temperature. The striations were found to be most pronounced in the specimens of arc-fused metal which were quenched from the highest temperatures, as might be expected. Braune states that nitride of iron in quenched metal is retained in solution in the martensite. The same may be inferred from the statement by Giesen that "in hardened steel, it (nitrogen) occurs in martensite." Ruder has also shown that nitrogenized electrolytic iron (3 hr. at 700 deg. C. in ammonia) after being quenched in water from temperatures 600 to 950 deg. C. shows none of the plates which were present before the specimen was heated.

The sets of specimens (A_2, A_6, AD_{10}, B_2, B_6 and B_9) quenched from above the temperature of the Ac_3 transformation were heated to various temperatures, 600, 700, 800 and 925 deg. C. In all cases the specimens were maintained at the maximum temperature for approximately ten to fifteen minutes and then cooled in the furnace. (25) to (30), Fig. 165, inclusive summarize the resulting effects upon the structure. Heating to 650 deg. C. is not sufficient to allow the plates to redevelop, but in the specimens heated to 700 deg. C. a few small ones were found. The effect is progressively more pronounced with the increased temperature of tempering, and in the material heated to 925 deg. C. they are as large and as numerous as in any of the arc-fused specimens. The heating also develops the islands of pearlite which are not always to be distinguished very clearly in the simple fused metal. The work of Ruder shows that nitrogenized iron which has been quenched and so rendered free from the nitride plates behaves in a similar manner upon heating to temperatures varying from 700 to 950 deg. C.; the plates reappear after a heating for fifteen minutes at 700 deg. C. (or above), followed by a slow cooling. The similarity in behavior of the two is a

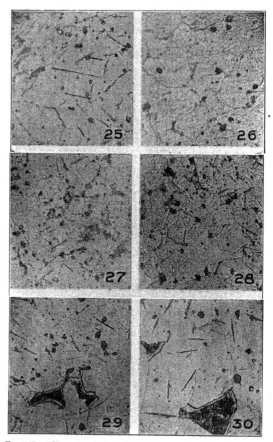

FIG. 165.—(25 to 30) Effect of Heat-Treatment of Arc-Fused Iron.
All etched with 2 per cent alcoholic HNO₃. × 450.
(25) Specimen AD₁₀ as deposited.
(26) Same after quenching from above HC₃ and reheating to 650 deg. C. No "plates" have formed.
(27) Specimen AD₁₀ after quenching from above HC₃ and reheating to 700 deg. C. "Plates beginning to reform.
(28) Specimen B₉ after quenching from above AC₃ and reheating to 800 deg. C.
(29) Specimen B₃ after quenching from above AC₃ and reheating to 925 deg. C.
(30) Specimen A₂ after quenching from above AC₃ and reheating to 925 deg. C.

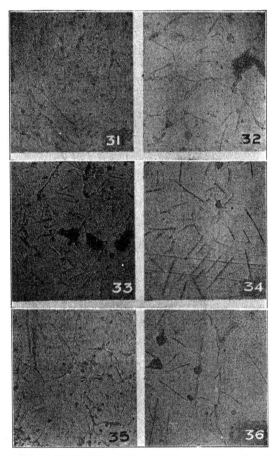

FIG. 166.—(31 to 36) Effect of 6-hr. Heating at 1000 Deg. C. in Vacuo.
All etched with 2 per cent alcoholic HNO_3. × 450.

(31) Initial structure of AD_2.
(32) AD_2 after heating.
(33) Initial structure of B_4.
(34) B_4 after heating.
(35) Initial structure of A_{10}.
(36) A_{10} after heating.

further line of evidence that the arc-fused metal contains more or less nitrogenized iron throughout its mass.

Plates Remain After Long Annealing.—The persistence of the nitride plates was also studied in specimens heated at 1,000 deg. C. *in vacuo* for a period of 6 hr. A set of specimens (one each of test-bars AD_2, A_3, AD_6, A_{10}, B_2, B_4, B_3 and BD_3) was packed in a Usalite crucible, and covered with alundum "sand"; this crucible was surrounded by a protecting alundum tube and the whole heated in an Arsem furnace. A vacuum,

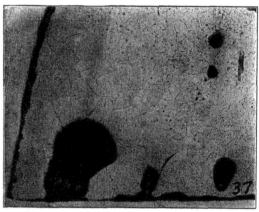

FIG. 167.—(37) Effect of Pronounced Heating Upon the Structure of Arc-Fused Iron.

Specimen AD_{10} was heated for 6 hr. in vacuo at 1000 deg. C. The micrograph represents a section of the specimen at one corner. The oxide and "nitride plates" have been removed in the exposed tip of the thread. Etching, 2 per cent alcoholic solution of nitric acid. × 150.

equivalent to 0.2 mm. mercury, was maintained for the greater part of the 6-hr. heating period; for the remainder of the time the vacuum was equivalent to 0.1 to 0.2 mm. mercury. The specimens were allowed to cool in the furnace. Ruder has stated that 1 hr., heating *in vacuo* at 1,000 deg. C. was sufficient to cause a marked diminution in the number of plates in both arc-weld material and nitrogenized iron and that at 1,200 deg. C. they disappeared entirely.

The results obtained are shown in (31) to (36), Fig. 166,

inclusive. In contradistinction to Ruder's work the plates are more conspicuous and larger than before, the oxide specks are larger and fewer in number. Many of the "plates" appear to have been influenced in their position by an oxide globule. It would appear that the conditions of the experiment are favorable for a migration of the oxide through an appreciable distance and for a coalescing into larger masses. (32), (34) and (36) all show some cementite at the grain boundaries which resulted from the "divorcing" of pearlite. The oxide is eliminated entirely in a surface layer averaging approximately 0.15 mm. in depth. Only in projections (right-angled corners, sections of threads of the tension bar, etc.), was there any removal of the nitride plates by the action of the continued heating *in vacuo*. This is shown in (37), Fig. 167, which illustrates the removal of the oxide inclusions also. No evidence was found that the small amount of carbon present in the arc-fused metal is eliminated, particularly beneath the surface.

(6) Fig. 158 illustrates an interesting exception to the rule that the nitride plates are flat. In the metallic and globular inclusion shown the plates have a very pronounced curve. The general appearance suggests that the "metallic globules" solidified under a condition of "constraint" and that this condition still persists even after the 6-hr. heating at 1,000 deg. C. which the specimen received.

Several of the specimens which were heated *in vacuo* (6 hr. at 1,000 deg. C.) were analyzed for nitrogen. The results are given in Table XVI.

TABLE XVI.—CHANGE IN NITROGEN CONTENT UPON HEATING

Specimen	Wt. of Sample in Gr.	Average Nitrogen Content, per Cent		Loss per Cent
		Before Heating	After Heating in Vacuo.	
A₃	1.39	0.127	0.062	51
B₄	6.0	0.124	0.078	37
BD₅	1.62	0.140	0.059	57
B₅	1.16	0.121	0.054	55

The fact that the specimens lose nitrogen upon heating (although the amount remaining is still many times the nitrogen-content of the metal before fusion), coupled with the fact that the "nitride plates" are larger and more conspicuous after heating than before, suggests very strongly that these plates are not simple nitride of iron. The method used for the determination of nitrogen gives only the "nitride" nitrogen, hence a possible explanation for the change in nitrogen content is that it has been converted into another form than nitride and may not have been eliminated from the specimen.

Thermal Analysis of Arc-Fused Steel.—In order to throw further light on the nature of the plates (nitride) found in the metal after fusion in the arc, the thermal characteristics of the electrode material before and after fusion as revealed by heating and cooling curves were determined. Samples of a $3/16$-in. electrode of type "A" and of the specimen A, which resulted from the fusion were used as material (composition in Tables IX and XII.)

TABLE XVII.—THE THERMAL CHARACTERISTICS OF ARC-FUSED IRON

Rate of Heating and Cooling, Deg. C., Sec.	Ac₂, Maximum Deg. C.	Ac₃			Maximum Temp. Deg. C.	Time Above A₃, Min.	Ar₃			Ar₂ Maximum, Deg. C.
		Beginning	Maximum, Deg. C.	End			Beginning	Maximum, Deg. C.	End	
				Unfused Electrode						
0.15*	768	892	910	918	960	..	896	893	879	766
	765	897	911	916	960	..	895	891	879	766
				Arc-Fused Metal †						
0.14	764	....	847	874	960	28	847	838	820	764
0.13	764	....	849	876	985	42	847	836	822	764
0.13	764	..	844	870	960	29	847	837	821	765
0.13	766	..	850	874	1.035	256	848	835	816	764

* Heated at rate of 0.16 deg. C. per sec., cooled 0.15 deg. C. per sec. for other specimens, the rate of cooling equaled the rate of heating.
† The same specimen was heated four times in succession, as shown. (Fig. 38)

In Fig. 168 are given the curves obtained which show the characteristic behavior of the arc-fused metal upon heating. The commonly used inverse-rate method was employed in plotting the data; the details of manipulation and the precautions necessary for the thermal analysis have already been described. In Table XVII are summarized the data shown graphically in the last cut.

The principal change to be noted which has resulted from

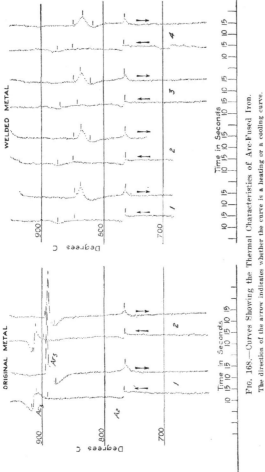

Fig. 168.—Curves Showing the Thermal Characteristics of Arc-Fused Iron. The direction of the arrow indicates whether the curve is a heating or a cooling curve.

the arc-fusion of the iron is in the A_3 transformation. This is now very similar to the corresponding change observed in a very mild steel (e.g., approximately 0.15 per cent carbon). That the difference in the A_3 transformation of the arc-fused metal as compared with that of the original electrode is not due to an increase in the carbon content is evident from the lack of the sharp inflection of the A_1 transformation ("pearlite point") which would, of necessity, be found in a low carbon steel. No evidence of the A_1 change was observed for the arc-fused iron within the range of temperature, 150 to 950 deg C. The change in the character of the A_3 transformation is without doubt to be attributed to the influence of the increased nitrogen-content of the iron.

The specimen was maintained above the temperature of the A_3 transformation for a total period (four heatings) of 6 hr., the maximum temperature being 1,035 deg. C. The transformation apparently is unaffected by the long-continued heating, thus confirming the results described in the preceding section.

In discussing the properties of steel nitrogenized by melting it in nitrogen under pressure, Andrews states that it was found possible to extract almost entirely the small quantities of nitrogen by heating a specimen at 1,000 deg. C. *in vacuo* for periods of 1 to 6 hr. The metal used contained 0.16 per cent carbon and 0.3 per cent nitrogen. Thermal curves are given to show that there are no critical transformations in the material; the nitrogen suppresses them. They gradually reappear, however, as the nitrogen is removed by heating the material *in vacuo* at 1,000 deg. C. Several days' heating was required, however, to obtain an entirely degasified product, the carbon being removed also. A further statement is made that a steel of 0.6 per cent carbon content containing 0.25 per cent nitrogen can be brought back to the normal state of a pure steel only by several weeks' heating *in vacuo*.

The results of the thermal analysis add considerable confirmatory evidence to support the view that the plates existing in the arc-fused metal are due to the nitrogen rather than to carbon.

Summary.—Microscopic examination of bent pieces of arc-fused metal show that the metallic grains are inherently ductile, even to a high degree. Grosser imperfections, however, are entirely sufficient to mask this excellence.

The view that the characteristic features observed in the structure of the arc-fused iron are due to the increased nitrogen content is supported by several different lines of evidence. These include the likeness of the structure of the material to that of pure iron which has been "nitrogenized," the similarity in the behavior of both arc-fused and nitrogenized iron upon heating, the evidence shown by thermal analysis of the arc-fused metal, together with the fact that, as shown by chemical analysis, the nitrogen content increases during fusion, while the other elements, aside from oxygen, decrease in amount. The characteristic form in which oxide occurs in iron, together with its behavior upon heating, renders the assumption that the oxide is responsible for the plates observed in the material a very improbable one.

Judged from the results obtained, neither type of electrode appears to have a marked advantage over the other. The use of a slight protective coating on the electrodes does not appear to affect the mechanical properties of the arc-fused metal materially in any way. The specimens were prepared in a manner quite different from that used ordinarily in electric-arc welding and the results do not justify any specific recommendations concerning methods of practice in welding.

CHAPTER XI

AUTOMATIC ARC WELDING

The automatic arc welding machine, made by the General Electric Co., Schenectady, N. Y., is a device for automatically feeding metallic electrode wire into the welding arc at the rate required to hold a constant arc length, says H. L. Unland in a paper read before the American Welding Society. Under these circumstances the electrical conditions are kept constant and the resulting weld is uniform and its quality is thereby improved. It is possible with this device to weld at a speed of from two to six times the rate attained by skilled operators welding by hand. This is partly due to the stability of the welding conditions and partly due to the fact that the electrode is fed from a continuous reel, thus eliminating the changing of electrodes. The automatic welding machine is adaptable to practically any form of weld from butt welding of plates to the depositing of metal on worn surfaces such as shafts, wheels, etc.

Everyone who has made any investigation of electric arc welding has noted the wide variation in results obtained by different welders operating, as nearly as can be determined, under identical conditions. This also applies to the operations of a single welder at different times under identical conditions. These variations affect practically all factors of welding such as speed of welding, amount of electrode consumed, etc. When indicating instruments are connected to an electric welding circuit, continual variations of considerable magnitude in the current and voltage of the arc are at once noticed. Considerable variation was found some years ago in the cutting of steel plates by the gas process and when an equipment was devised to mechanically travel the cutting torch over the plate a series of tests to determine the maximum economical speed, gas pressure, etc., for the various thickness of plate were made.

The result was that the speed of cutting was increased to as much as four or five times the rate possible when operating under the unsteady conditions incident to hand manipulation of the torch. Further, the gas consumption for a given cut was found to be decreased very greatly.

As a result of many experiences an investigation was started to determine what could be done in controlling the feed of the electrode to the electric arc in a metallic electrode welding circuit. An electric arc is inherently unstable, the fluctuations taking place with extreme rapidity. In any regulating device the sensitiveness depends on the percentage of variation from normal rather than on the actual magnitude of the values, since these are always reduced to approximately a common factor by the use of shunts, current transformers, or series resistances. The characteristics of practically all electric welding circuits are such that the current and voltage are inter-related, an increase in one causing a corresponding decrease in the other. Where this is the case it will generally be found that the percentage variation of the voltage from normal when taken at the customary arc voltage of 20, will be approximately twice the percentage variation in current. Further, an increase in arc voltage, other conditions remaining the same, indicates that the arc has been lengthened, thus giving the metal a greater opportunity to oxidize in the arc with a probability of reduction in quality of the weld. The automatic arc welding machine utilizes the arc voltage as the basis for regulating the equipment. The rate of feeding the wire varies over a wide range, due to the use of electrodes of different diameters, the use of different current values, etc., caused by details of the particular weld to be made. The simplest and most reliable method of electrically obtaining variations in speed is by means of a separately excited direct current motor. Thus the operation of this equipment is limited to direct current arc welding circuits, but these may be of any established type, the variations in characteristics of the welding circuits being taken care of by proper selection of resistors, coils, etc., in the control.

The Welding Head.—The welding head consists essentially of a set of rollers for gripping the wire and feeding it to the arc. These rollers are suitably connected through gearing to a small direct-current motor, the armature of which is connected across the terminals of the welding arc. This connection causes the motor to increase in speed as the voltage across the arc increases due to an increase in the length of the arc and to decrease in speed as the voltage decreases, due to a shortened arc. A small relay operating on the principle of a generator voltage regulator is connected in the field circuit of the motor which assists in the speed control of the motor as the arc voltage varies. Rheostats, for regulating and adjusting the arc voltage, are provided by means of which the equipment can be made to maintain steadily an arc of the desired length and this value may be varied from over twenty to as low as nine volts. No provision is made in the machine for adjustment of the welding current since the automatic operation is in no way dependent on it. The welding current adjustment is taken care of by the control panel of the welding set. This may be either of the variable voltage or constant potential type but it is necessary to have a source of constant potential to excite the fields of feed motor. It may be possible to obtain this excitation from the welding circuit, but this is not essential. The voltage of both the welding and constant potential circuits· is immaterial, provided it is not too high, but these voltages must be known before the proper rheostats can be supplied.

On account of the great variation in conditions under which this welding equipment may be used it is provided with a base which may be bolted to any form of support. It may be held stationary and the work traveled past the arc or welding head may be movable and the work held stationary. These points will be dictated by the relative size of the work and the head and the equipment which may be available. Provision must be made for traveling one or the other at a uniform speed in order to carry the arc along the weld. In the case of straight seams a lathe or planer bed may be utilized for this purpose and for circular seams a lathe or boring mill may be used. In many cases it will be found desirable to use clamping jigs for securely holding the work in shape and also to facilitate placing in position and removing from the feeding mechanism.

In Fig. 169, the welding head is shown mounted on a special

device for making circular welds. The work table is driven
through a worm and worm gear by means of a separate motor.

Fig. 169.—Special Set-Up of Machine for Circular Welding.

The welding head may be led along the arm by means of
the handwheel, and it may be tilted at an angle of 45 deg.

both at right angles to the line of weld and also parallel
to the line of weld. Fig. 170 shows the building up of a shaft,
the work being mounted on lathe centers and the welding
head placed on a bracket clamped to saddle.

Fig. 171 shows a simplified diagram of the control of the
feed motor. In this cut A is the regulating rheostat in the
motor field circuit controlled by the arc voltage regulator G;
B is the adjusting rheostat in the motor field circuit; F

Fig. 170.—Set-Up for Building up a Shaft.

indicates the feed motor field winding; M the feed motor winding; D is the resistance in the motor armature circuit to adjust
the speed when starting the feed motor before the arc is struck.
The open-circuit voltage of the welding circuit is ordinarily
considerably higher than the arc voltage. This resistance D
is short circuited by contactor X when the arc is struck. The
arc voltage regulator G maintains constant arc voltage by
varying the motor field strength through resistor A. The
regulator is adjusted to hold the desired voltage by the rheostat

C. Permanent resistance *E* is in series with the over-voltage relay *H*, to compensate for the voltage of the welding circuit. Over voltage relay *H* holds open the coil circuit of the regulator *G* until the electrode makes contact in order to protect the coil from burning out.

Observation of indicating meters on the control panel show that the current and voltage are practically constant, but it should be remembered that all indicating meters have a certain amount of damping which prevents observation of the variations which are extremely rapid or of small magnitude. The resultant value as read on the instrument is the average value. Oscillographs taken with short arcs show that notwithstanding the fact that the indicating meters show a constant value, a

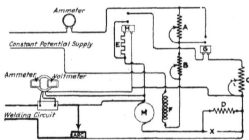

Fig. 171.—Simplified Diagram of Control of Feed Motor.

succession of rapid short circuits is continually taking place, apparently due to particles of the molten wire practically short-circuiting the arc in passing from the electrode to the work. This is indicated by the fact that the voltage curve fell to zero each time, and accompanying each such fluctuation there was an increase in the current. It was found that with the shorter arc the frequency of occurrence of these short-circuits was considerably higher than was the case when the arc was increased in length. To all appearances the arc was absolutely steady and continuous and there was no indication either by observation of the arc itself or of the instruments that these phenomena were occurring.

Some Work Performed By the Machine.—The principal field for an automatic arc welding machine is where a consider-

able amount of welding is required, the operations being a
continuous repetition of duplicate welds. Under these conditions one can economically provide jigs and fixtures for
facilitating the handling of the work and the clamping. Thus
can be reaped the benefit of the increased speed in the actual
welding which would be lost if each individual piece had to
be clamped and handled separately.

Examples of different jobs done with this machine, using
various feeding and holding methods, are shown in the accompanying cuts. Fig. 172 is a worn pulley seat on an electric
motor shaft built up and ready to be re-turned to size.

It is possible to build up pulley and pinion seats, also worn
bearings, without removing the armature or rotor from the

Fig. 172.—Worn Motor Shaft Built Up.

shaft and in practically all cases without removing the windings due to the concentration of the heat at the point of the
weld. On shafts of this kind, 3 to 4 in. in diameter, the figures
are: current 115 amp.; arc voltage 14; electrode $^3/_{32}$ in. in
diameter; travel, 6 in. per min.; rate of deposit about 2.1 lb.
per hour.

Similar work on a 14-in. shaft where the flywheel seat
21 in. long was turned undersize, was as follows: metal about
$^5/_{16}$ in. deep was deposited over the undersize surface, using
current, 190 amp.; arc voltage 18; electrode $\frac{1}{8}$ in. diameter;
travel 4 in. per min.; rate of deposit, about 2 lb. per hour;
welding time, 16 hr.; machining time, 4 hr.

Fig. 173 shows worn and repaired crane wheel flanges.
These are easily handled by mounting on a mandrel in a lathe,

and placing the welding machine on a bracket bolted to the cross-slide or the saddle. On wheels of this type 22 in. in diameter, the time taken to weld by hand would be about 12 hr. and by machine 2 hr.; machining time **4 hr.**; approximate cost by hand welding $9; by machine **$4.**

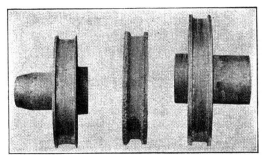

Fig. 173.—Worn and Repaired Crane Wheels.

Fig. 174.—Welded Automobile Hub Stampings.

Fig. 174 is an automobile **wire wheel** hub stamping, to which a dust cover was welded as shown. Joint was between metal $1/16$ and $3/16$ in. thick. Current 100 amp.; arc voltage, 14; travel 10 in. per min.; electrode $3/32$ in. diameter.

Fig. 175, welded automobile rear-axle housing, $^3/_{16}$ in. thick; current 120 amp.; arc voltage 14; travel 6 in. per min.; electrode diameter $^3/_{32}$ in.

Fig. 176, welded tank seam; metal $\frac{1}{8}$ in. thick; current 140 amp.; arc voltage 14; travel, 6 in. per min.; time for welding ten tanks by hand, 4 hrs. 40 min.; by machine, 2 hrs.

FIG. 175.—Welded Rear-Axle Housing.

Tables XVIII and XIX give an idea of the speed of welding which may be expected, but it should be borne in mind that these figures are actual welding speeds. It is necessary to have the material properly clamped and supported and to have it travel past the arc at a uniform speed. In some cases the

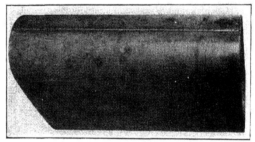

FIG. 176—Welded Straight Tank Seam.

figures given have been exceeded and under certain special conditions it may be desirable to use lower values than those given.

TABLE XVIII.—SEAM WELDING

Thickness in Inches	Amperes	Speed, Inches Per Minute
0.040	45 to 50	20 to 30
1/16	50 to 80	15 to 25
1/8	80 to 120	6 to 12
3/16	100 to 150	4 to 6

TABLE XIX—BUILDING UP (WHEELS OR SHAFTS)

Diameter or Thick., In.	Electrodes, Dia., In.	Amperes	Speed, In. per Min.	Lb. Deposit Per Hour
Up to 1"	$^{1}/_{16}$	60 to 90	11 to 13	1.04–1.56
Up to 3"	$^{5}/_{32}$	90 to 120	6 to 8	1.59–2.1
Over 3"	$^{1}/_{8}$	120 to 200	4 to 6	2.5 –4.5

A SEMI-AUTOMATIC ARC-WELDING MACHINE

A paper on "Welding Mild Steel," by H. W. Hobart, was read at the New York meeting of the American Institute of Mining and Metallurgical Engineers in 1919. In discussing this paper Harry D. Morton, of the Automatic Arc Welding Co., Detroit, brought out some interesting things relating to Automatic Arc Welding:

"The generally accepted theory of the electric arc is that part of the electrode material is vaporized, and that this vaporous tube or column forms a path for the electric current. As a result of the vaporous character of the current path, all arcs are inherently unstable; and the maximum of instability is no doubt found in that form of arc employed for metallic-electrode welding purposes. We here have, in conjunction with the natural instability characteristic of all arcs rapidly fusing electrode materials and the disturbing effect of the constant passage through the arc of a large quantity of molten metal to form the weld. This molten metal must pass through the arc so rapidly that it will not be injured or materially contaminated; otherwise the weld will be useless. Prima facie, the combination of these unfavorable conditions would seem to justify fully the skepticism of most electrical engineers as to the possibility of affecting such control of the metallic arc as to permit of uniformity and continuity in welding results. In addition, there is another and more important factor, and one that seriously mitigates against this desired uniformity and continuity; namely, the personal equation of the operator. The consensus of opinion, so far as is known to the writer, seems to be that about 95 per cent. of the welding result is dependent on the skill of the operator and that at least six months' practice is necessary to acquire reasonably satisfactory proficiency.

"As the result of thousands of observations of welds produced automatically (wherein the personal equation is entirely eliminated), the writer inclines toward the theory that the molten electrode material passes through the arc in the form of globules; and that where $\frac{1}{8}$-in. electrode material is employed with a current of about 150 amp. these globules are deposited at the rate of approximately two per second. The passage through the arc of each globule apparently constitutes a specific cause of instability in addition to those existent with slowly consumed electrodes. This hypothesis seems to be borne out by ammeter records, typical specimens of which appear in Fig. 177, together with the fact that the electrode fuses at the rate of about 0.20 in. per sec. Moreover, the globules appear to be approximately equal in volume to a piece of wire 0.125 in. in diameter and 0.10 in. long.

"Assuming this theory to be correct, to maintain a uniform arc length in manual welding, the operator must feed the electrode toward the work

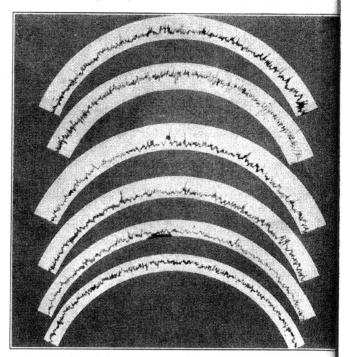

Fig. 177.—Typical Ammeter Charts of Operation of Morton Automatic, Metallic-Electrode Arc-Welding Machine.

Average Time about 1 Min. 45 Sec.

at the rate of 0.10 in. upon the deposition of each globule; in other words, 0.10 in. twice per second, a synchronism beyond human attainment. Simultaneously with such feeding, the arc must be moved over the work to melt the work material, distribute the molten electrode material, and form the weld. Inasmuch as the effect of the arc is highly localized, it is reasonable to suppose that different parts of the welding area present relatively wide variations in respect to temperature, fluidity, and conductivity of the molten mass—controlling factors not within the ken of the human mind. The situation is further complicated by the facts that neither the welding wire nor the work material is uniform in fusibility or in conductivity, and that the contour of the work varies continually as its surface is fused and the molten metal is caused to flow. The belief is general that a very short arc is productive of the best welding results; but it is an arc of this character that makes the greatest demands on the skill of the operator, for there is always the danger that the electrode will actually contact with the work and destroy the arc.

"As the fusing energy of the arc varies widely with fluctuations in the arc length and as the uniformity of the weld depends on the constancy and correctness of this fusing energy, it seems remarkable that operators are able ever to acquire such a degree of skill as to enable them to produce welds that are even commercially satisfactory. Further, so far as the writer is informed, there is no means, other than such as would be destructive, for determining whether a completed weld is good or bad. The logical solution appeared to be the elimination of the personal equation and the substitution therefor of means whereby tendencies toward variations in the arc would be caused automatically to correct themselves, just as a steam engine, through the action of its governor, is caused to control its own speed.

Methods of Mechanically Stabilizing and Controlling the Arc.—Our efforts for a number of years have been directed toward stabilizing and controlling the metallic arc, and applying such stabilizing and controlling means to two general lines of welding machinery: (1) Machines for automatically feeding the electrode wire, with reference to the work, and producing simultaneously therewith relative movement between the wire and the work, and (2) what, for lack of a better term, might be called a semi-automatic machine, in which the feeding of the electrode and the control of the arc are accomplished automatically but the traversing of the electrode with reference to the work is manually effected by the operator, permitting him the exercise of judgment with reference to the quantity of metal to be deposited in various parts of the groove. The automatic machine has been in successful operation for a long period and the semi-automatic machine for about five months. While the goal was not attained without many difficulties and a great expenditure of time and money, the results have been surprisingly successful.

"Because of the lack of any definite data as to what actually occurs in this form of arc, or why it occurs, due, no doubt, to the impossibility of differentiating between phenomena that are characteristic of the arc and phenomena due to the personal equation of the welder, it seemed logical that the initial step should be to so environ the arc that it would not be subject to erratic extraneous influences, to the end that reasonably definite determinations might be substituted for scientific speculation. In the design and construction of the machines, great care was exercised to minimize the possibility of mechanical defects that might lead to erroneous conclusions. Starting with the assumption that the work could only be based on open-minded observation of the behavior of the arc under machine control, an automatic welding machine was built in which was incorporated the greatest possible number of adjustable features, in order that, if necessary, it might be possible to wander far afield in the investigations. This adjustability has proved invaluable in that it has permitted logical, consistent, and sequential experimenting over a very wide range of conditions. Working under these favorable circumstances, there were soon segregated a few clearly demonstrable facts to serve as a foundation for the structure, which has since been added to, brick by brick, as it were.

"Efforts have been directed toward the practical rather than the scientific aspect of the subject. The operation of the automatic machines has brought to light many curious and interesting phenomena, some of which appear to negative conclusions heretofore formed which have been predicated upon observations made in connection with manual welding. It is hoped that these and other phenomena, which can thus be identified as purely arc characteristics, will be the subject of profitable scientific investigation when time is available for this purpose.

"In the five forms of machines made in the course of the development, the welding wire is automatically fed to the arc; and, in the first four machines, the relative movement between the work and the welding wire is automatically and simultaneously effected. Early in his investigations, the writer concluded that a substantial equilibrium must be maintained between the fusing energy of the arc and the feeding rate of the welding strip; and it soon became evident that if the welding strip is mechanically fed forward at a uniform rate equal to the average rate of consumption with the selected arc energy, this equilibrium is actually maintained by the arc itself, which seems to have, within certain circumscribed limits, a compensatory action as follows: When the arc shortens, the resistance decreases and the current rises. This rise in current causes the welding strip to fuse more rapidly than it is fed, thereby causing the arc to lengthen. Conversely, when the arc lengthens, the resistance increases, the current falls, the welding strip is fused more slowly than it is fed, and the moving strip restores the arc to its normal length.

"While this compensatory action of the arc will maintain the necessary equilibrium between the fusing energy and the feeding rate under very carefully adjusted conditions, this takes place only within relatively narrow limits. It was very apparent that, due to variations in the contour of the work, and, perhaps, to differences in the fusibility or conductivity of the welding strip or of the work, the range of this self-compensatory action of the arc was frequently insufficient to prevent either contacting of the welding strip with the work or a rupture of the arc due to its becoming too long. The problem that arose was to devise means whereby the natural self-compensatory action of the arc could be so greatly accentuated as to preclude, within wide limits, the occurrence of marked arc abnormalities. There was ultimately evolved, by experiment, such a relation between the fusing energy of the arc and the feeding rate of the welding strip as to give the desired arc length under normal conditions; and tendencies toward abnormalities in arc conditions, no matter how produced, were caused to

FIG. 178.—Piloted Cup Automatically Welded by Metallic-Electrode Arc Process to Tube to Form 75-MM. Shrapnel Shell.

Analysis of Electrode Material: Silicon, 0.02 Per Cent; Sulphur, 0.013 Per Cent; Phosphorus, 0.07 Per Cent; Manganese, Trace; Carbon, 0.07 Per Cent; Aluminum, 0.038 Per Cent.

FIG. 179.—Piloted Cup Automatically Welded by Metallic-Electrode Arc Process to Tube to Form 75-MM. Shrapnel Shell.

Analysis of Electrode Material: Silicon, 0.03 Per Cent; Sulphur, 0.049 Per Cent; Phosphorus, 0.008 Per Cent; Manganese, 0.31 Per Cent; Carbon, 0.28 Per Cent.

bring into operation compensatory means for automatically, progressively, and correctively varying this relation between fusing energy and feeding rate, such compensatory means being under the control of a dominant characteristic of the arc. In their ultimate forms, the devices for effecting the control of the arc are simple and entirely positive in action, making discrepancies between fusing energy and feeding rate self-compensatory throughout widely varying welding conditions. For instance, the shrapnel shell shown in Fig. 178 was automatically welded with wire differing greatly in chemical constitution from that used on the shell shown in Fig. 179 (see analyses), yet no change was made in either the mechanical or the electrical adjustments. The radically different welding conditions were compensated for solely by the operation of the automatic control. The electrode materials used for the shells shown in Figs. 180 and 181

Fig. 180.—Piloted Cup Automatically Welded by Metallic-Electrode Arc Process to Tube to Form 75-MM. Shrapnel Shell.

Analysis of Electrode Material: Silicon, 0.02 Per Cent; Sulphur, 0.032 Per Cent; Phosphorus, 0.008 Per Cent; Manganese, 0.20 Per Cent; Carbon, 0.18 Per Cent.

differed so greatly from those employed respectively in welding the shells shown in Figs. 178 and 179 that a change in the relation between fusing energy and feeding rate had to be made manually. After this adjustment was made, the shells were welded with their respective electrodes, which varied widely in their chemical constitution, without further manually changing either the mechanical or the electrical conditions.

"In a recent test of the semi-automatic machine, shown in Fig. 182, successful welds were made under the condition that the impressed voltage of the welding generator was changed throughout a range of from 50 to 65 volts, without necessitating any manual adjustment. The only observable effects of the wide variations in the supply voltage were slight differences in the arc length. In short, the compensatory action of the control has proved effective over a wide range of welding conditions, not only as to the electrical supply and chemical constitution of both electrode and work materials, but also as to extensive variations in the contour of the work and in many other particulars. This makes it seem apparent that the machines do not represent merely successful laboratory experiments but are suited to the requirements of actual commercial welding.

"One particularly interesting observation resulting from the experiments is that the angle of inclination of the electrode with reference to the work is very important. An angular variation of 5 deg. will sometimes determine the difference between success and failure in a weld. About 15 deg. from the perpendicular works well in many cases. In welding some materials, the electrode should drag, that is, point toward the part already welded rather than toward the unwelded part of the seam.

Fig. 181.—Piloted Cup Automatically Welded by Metallic-Electrode Arc Process to Tube to Form 75-MM. Shrapnel Shell.

Analysis of Electrode Material: Silicon, 0.04 Per Cent; Sulphur, 0.016 Per Cent; Phosphorus, 0.058 Per Cent; Manganese, None; Carbon, 0.24 Per Cent.

"While it has been customary in some welding systems to provide means whereby extra resistance is inserted in series with the arc at the instant of the initial contact which starts the flow of current, the resistance being automatically cut out upon the striking of the arc, experience with the automatic machines indicates that this is quite unnecessary.

"Early in the experiments, it was noted that in many cases there was a decidedly marked affinity between particular electrode materials and particular work materials. A slight change in either element affects the degree of this affinity. While it has invariably been possible to control and maintain the arc and weld continuously, in some instances incompatibility between electrode material and work material has been productive of interesting phenomena. For instance, the combination of work material (steel of about 0.45 per cent. carbon content) and the particular electrode material used in Fig. 178 produced an arc that was remarkably quiet and free from sputtering. Throughout the weld, this arc was suggestive of the quiet flame of a candle or lamp, the erratic behavior that we are accustomed to associate with the ordinary metallic arc being absent. The effect is reflected in the uniform deposition of the welding material.

"On some classes of work material Bessemer wire, which some authorities claim cannot be used in metallic-electrode arc welding, produces an arc

FIG. 182.—Morton Semi-Automatic Metallic-Electrode Arc-Welding Machine.

The Electrode is automatically fed to the arc, which is automatically maintained while the machine is manually moved along the groove to be welded.

and a weld very satisfactory in appearance. On other work material, the Bessemer wire arc is violently explosive. These explosions are accompanied by quite sharp reports and the scattering over some considerable distance of globules of molten metal frequently $^1/_{32}$ in. or more in diameter. Under certain other conditions, apparently growing out of incompatibility between the work material and the electrode material, the oxygen flame accompanying the arc gyrates very rapidly about the arc, producing an effect suggestive of the 'whirling dervish.'

"From both the practical and the scientific points of view, the writer has experimented quite extensively with varying combinations of work material and electrode material. Throughout all the differences in arc conditions, many of which palpably accentuate the natural inclination toward instability, the control has so operated as to justify the expression 'the arc persists.'

"Generally speaking, the Swedish and Norway iron wires seem to produce more quiet arcs and, possibly, a more uniform deposition of electrode material, than do wires of other classes. These welds may perhaps be found to be slightly more ductile than those made with wires of other chemical composition. On the other hand, these soft wires, although undoubtedly of relatively high fusibility, do not, for some reason, seem to produce an arc that cuts into some work material as deeply as might be desired, nor as deeply as do the arcs formed with certain other kinds of wire. Considered from every angle, the writer is disposed to regard the Roebling welding wire as the best he has thus far tested for use on mild steel. The wire produces a reasonably quiet arc which seems to cut into the work to more than the ordinary depth, while, at the same time, the electrode material is fused with more than average rapidity—thus increasing the welding rate.

" While scientists will no doubt ultimately arrive at the correct hypothesis for solving the problem of why one combination of electrode material and work material is productive of better results than can be obtained with another combination, the writer's conclusion is that, with the data at present available, the determinations must be made by actual experimenting —having in mind the qualities desired in the particular weld, such as ductility, tensile strength, elongation, and elastic limit. Inasmuch as it is possible, with the automatic machine, to maintain arc uniformity with practically any kind of electrode material and to produce welds which, under low magnification, at least, appear to be perfect, and which respond favorably to ordinary tests such as bending, cutting and filing, it is reasonable to conclude that proper selection of electrode material will be productive of perfect welds on any kind of work material. To date, no steel has been tested on which apparently satisfactory welds could not be made. High-speed tungsten steel has been successfully welded to cold-rolled shafting, using Bessemer wire as electrode material, as is shown in Fig 183. Ordinary steels varying in carbon content from perhaps 0.10 to 0.55 per cent. have been welded with entire success.

"Because of the fact that the complete welding operation has been automatic and may be continued for a considerable length of time, say 5 min., an exceptional opportunity has been afforded for close concentration upon the study of the appearance of the arc. What seems to occur is that the molten metal in the crater is in a state of violent surging, suggestive of a small lake lashed by a terrific storm. The waves are dashed against the sides of the crater, where the molten metal of which they are composed quickly solidifies. The surgings do not seem to synchronize with nor to be caused by the falling of the globules of molten metal into the crater, but seem rather to be continuous. They give the impression that the molten metal is subjected to an action arising from the disturbance of some powerful force associated with the arc—such, for instance, as might result from the violent distortion of a strong magnetic field. Altogether, the crater phenomena are very impressive; and the writer hopes ere long to be able to have motion pictures made which, when enlarged, should not only afford material for most fascinating study, but also throw light upon some of the mysterious happenings in the arc.

So far, electrode wires ⅛ in. in diameter have been chiefly used in the machines. Successful welds have been made with current values ranging from below 90 to above 200 amp., at impressed voltages of 40, 45, 50,

Fig. 183.—Tungsten High-Speed Ring Automatically Welded by Metallic-Electrode to Cold-Rolled Core to Form Milling-Cutter Blank.

55, 60, 65 and 80. Under these varying conditions, the voltage across the arc has been roughly from 16 to 22. The machines have thus far been run only on direct current. Inasmuch as it is possible, by electrical and mechanical adjustments, to establish nearly any arc length that may be found to be most desirable for a particular class of work, and as the control system will maintain substantially that arc length indefinitely, the fully automatic type of machine is nearly as certain in operation as a lathe, drilling machine, or any other machine tool.

"The tool shown in Fig. 182 weighs about 10¼ lb. The operator draws the tool along the groove to be welded at such a rate as will result in the deposition of the quantity of metal required to satisfactorily effect the weld. This tool is intended for use in the many restricted spaces encountered in ship welding, which would be relatively inaccessible to a fully automatic machine. In its use, the skill required by the operator is reduced to a minimum. After one man had practised with the welding tool for not more than 2 hr., the opinion was expressed that it would require six months to train a welder to such a degree of proficiency as to enable him to make a weld equally good in appearance.

"Mr. Hobart, says 'There is always a matter of a 0.10 in. or more between the end of the welding rod and the work.' While undoubtedly it is difficult, if not impossible, to maintain in manual welding an arc shorter than this, the writer has frequently, with the automatic machines, made continuous and strikingly good welds with arcs of much less length. In fact, in some cases there has been continuously maintained an arc so short that there hardly seemed to be any actual separation. The writer

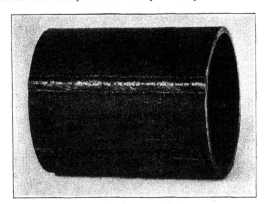

FIG. 184.—No. 11 Gage Steel Tubing Automatically Welded by Metallic-Electrode Arc Process at the Rate of One Foot per Minute.

has even wondered whether, under these conditions, there was not a close approach to casting with a continuous stream of fluid metal acting as the current conveyor in lieu of or in parallel with the usually assumed vapor path. The work that has been done indicates that under automatic control much shorter arcs can be utilized than have hitherto been deemed possible, and with probable marked gain in quality of work in some instances; also, that there is much to be learned as to the mode of current action and current conduction in such an arc.

"With the automatic machine, black drawing steel 0.109 in. thick has been welded at the rate of 22 in. per minute. A Detroit manufacturer welded manually with oxy-acetylene at the rate of four per hour a large number of mine floats 10 in. in diameter, made of this material. The automatic machine made the welds at the rate of forty per hour. Liberty motor valve cages 2¾ in. in diameter have been welded to cylinders in 36 sec., as against about 5 min. required for manual welding. No. 11 gage steel tubing, shown in Fig. 184, has been welded, with an unnecessarily

Fig. 185.—Two ½-in. Ship Plates Automatically Welded by Metallic-Electrode Arc Process to Form Lap Joint.

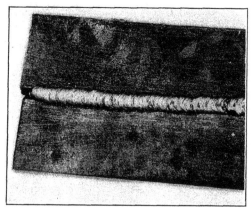

Fig. 186.—Two ½-in. Ship Plates Automatically Welded by Metallic-Electrode Process to Form Butt Joint.

heavy deposit of metal, at the rate of 1 ft. per minute. The productive capacity of the machines so far made has been from three to ten times that of manual welding methods, depending on the thickness of the work material; the difference in favor of automatic welding varies inversely as such thickness. The writer is now designing an improved type of machine for use especially on heavy work. with which machine it is expected to be able automatically to lapweld ½-in. ship plates, in the manner shown in Fig. 185, at the rate of 15 ft. per hour. One of the largest shipbuilding concerns in the United States reports that the general average of all its manual welders on this class of work is from 1 ft. to 18 in. per hour. Other specimens of automatic welding on ship plates are shown in Figs. 186 and 187.

"Bare wire only has been used in the automatic machines; and the results obtained seem to indicate that the covering of the electrodes is an expensive superfluity. If the chief advantage of the covered electrode lies in the ability of the operator to maintain a very short arc, an arc equally short and possibly shorter can be continuously maintained by the automatic machine using bare electrodes.

"No attempt has thus far been made to use the automatic machines

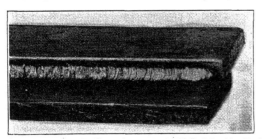

FIG. 187.—Two ½-in. Ship Plates Automatically Welded by Metallic-Electrode Arc Process, Showing First of Three Layers to Form Lap Joint.

on overhead work. The welds made with the fully automatic machine have been of three kinds. the usual longitudinal form, annular about a horizontal axis, and annular about a vertical axis.

"As far as the maintenance of arc uniformity and the apparent character of the welds are concerned, the writer has repeatedly welded with wire showing evidence of pipes and seams, as well as with rusty wire and with wire covered with dirt and grease. In this connection it may be said that no pains is ever taken to remove rust, scale, or slag from the work material—even where welds are superimposed. Apparently under uniform conditions of work traverse, arc length, and electrode angle of inclination, such as are possible in the automatic machine, impurities vanish before the portion of the work on which they occur reaches the welding area of the arc.

"The writer is fully convinced that with the use of the automatic machine, ductility, like other physical properties in the weld, can be controlled by proper selection of electrode wire. in conjunction with electrical

and mechanical adjustments best suited to the particular purpose in view. Automatic welds have repeatedly been made on $5/16$-in. mild steel which, when subjected to a 90-deg. bend, showed a marked extrusion of the welded material but no sign of fracture. When the welded pieces are cut with a hacksaw, it is very unusual to be able to note any difference in cutting qualities between the unwelded and the welded parts.

"While the automatic machine has not been used on metal less than 0.109 in. thick, it is fair to presume that, with proper adjustments, entirely satisfactory results can be obtained on much thinner work—particularly if the nature of the work is such as to permit of the use of a chill. The best method in welding very light metal seems to be to use a small electrode, a relatively low current, and a high rate of work traverse. In this way welding conditions may be controlled to almost any desired extent, because

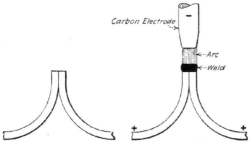

FIG. 189.—How the Metal Edges Are Welded.

the heating action of the arc can be modified, its effect intensely localized, and the edges to be welded subjected to the fusing action for as brief a time as might be found necessary to prevent burning of the metal. These conditions, which seem to be requisite in order to successfully weld very thin material, cannot be met by the manual welder. It is here that the deficiencies incident to the personal equation become most apparent. A very slight variation in arc length or the least hesitancy in moving the arc over the work will almost certainly result in its being burned through. In short, this class of welding calls for a coördination of faculties and a delicacy of manipulation beyond the capabilities of the most skillful manual electric welder. Therefore this work is usually done with the oxy-acetylene flame, wherein fusing conditions are far more easily controlled than is possible in manual metallic electrode arc welding."

SHEET METAL ARC-WELDING MACHINE

The machine shown in Fig. 188 is used by the General Electric Co., Schenectady, N. Y., for arc-welding corrugated steel tank work. The seams are 116 in. long, and the arc is applied by means of a tapered carbon pencil 6 in. long, $\frac{1}{2}$ in. in diameter at the large end and $\frac{1}{5}$ in. at the arc end. This concentrates heat where wanted. No metal is supplied to the weld, as the arc is employed simply to fuse the upturned edges as shown in Fig. 189. The metal welded is $\frac{1}{16}$ and $\frac{3}{32}$ in. thick.

The speed on $\frac{1}{16}$-in stock is $5\frac{1}{2}$ in. per minute with a d.c. current of 45 amp., and 75 volts. On $\frac{3}{32}$-in. stock the speed is the same but 70 amp. and 75 volts d.c. current is used.

CHAPTER XII

BUTT-WELDING MACHINES AND WORK

Aside from arc-welding machines, which have already been described, electric welding machines may be all included under one head—Resistance Welding Machines. These may be divided into butt-, spot-, seam-, mash- and percussive-welding classes. The first three are sometimes, for manufacturing purposes, used in combinations in the same machine, such as a spot-and-seam machine or a butt-and-spot-welding machine, and so on. This does not mean that these different methods of welding are carried on at the same time, but that a welder can do work on the same machine by simply shifting the work, or a part of the fixture.

In butt-welding, alternating current, single phase, of any commercial frequency such as 220, 440 or 550 volts, 60 cycles, is commonly used. Lower voltages and lower frequencies can be used, but they add to the cost of the machine. The machine can be used on one phase of a two-phase or a three-phase system, but cannot be connected to more than one phase of a three-phase circuit. Direct current is not used because there is no way of reducing the voltage without interposing resistance, which wastes the power. As an example, a d.c. plating dynamo will give approximately 5 volts, which will do for certain kinds of welding, but for lighter work, less current is needed. If resistance is used to reduce the current this resistance is using up power just as if it were doing useful work. The voltage at the weld will run from 1 to 15 volts, depending on the size of the welder and work. To obtain this low voltage, a special transformer inside the machine reduces the power line voltage down to the amount required at the weld. The transformer is placed within the frame of the machine, as shown in Fig. 190. The secondary winding of the transformer is connected to the platens by means of flexible copper leads.

239

From the platens the welding current travels to the work clamps and through them to the pieces to be welded. As the parts to be welded are brought into contact a switch is thrown in and the current traveling across heats the ends of the work and when the proper welding heat is reached the operator

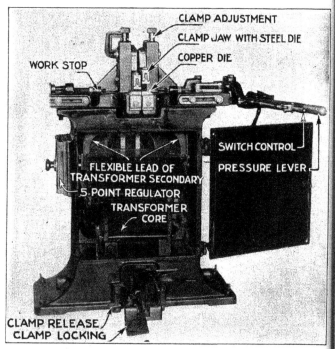

FIG. 190.—Principal Parts of a Butt-Welding Machine.

pushes the two parts together and the weld is completed. Since the current value rises as the potential falls in the secondary circuit, and since the heating effect across the work is directly proportional to the current value it will be easily seen why a transformer is necessary to produce a heavy current by lowering the line potential. Due to the intermittent character of the load, there is no standard rating for welding transformers, and different makers frequently give entirely different ratings for their machines. However, regardless of the rating capacity in kilowatts, there can be very little difference in the actual amount of current consumed unless an especially bad

FIG. 191.—Butt-Welding Machine with Work in Jaws.

transformer design is used. To heat a given size stock to welding temperature in a given time requires an approximately invariable amount of current.

The machine just illustrated, is shown at a slightly different angle and with two pieces of rod in the jaws, in Fig. 191. This is the Thomson regular No. 3, butt-welding machine. It

FIG. 192.—Details of Foot-Operated Clamping Mechanism.

FIG. 193.—A Hand-Operated Clamp.

FIG. 194.—Toggle-Lever Clamp for Round Stock.

has a capacity of rod from $\frac{1}{8}$ to $\frac{3}{4}$ in. in diameter or flat stock
up to $\frac{1}{4}\times2$ in., in two separate pieces, or rings of $\frac{5}{16}$-in.
stock and not less than 2 in. in diameter. Hoops and bands
up to $\frac{1}{16}\times1\frac{3}{4}$ in. and not less than $9\frac{1}{2}$ in. diameter when
held below the line of welding, may also be welded. With
jaws specially made to hold the work above the line of welding
a minimum diameter of $4\frac{1}{2}$ in. is necessary. This machine will
produce from 150 to 200 separate pieces, 150 to 300 hoops,
or 300 to 400 rings per hour. The lower dies are of hard
drawn copper with contact surfaces $1\frac{1}{8}\times2$ in.$\times2\frac{1}{16}$ in. thick.

Fɪɢ. 195.—Clamping Device for Heavy Flat Stock.

Standard transformer windings are for 220, 440 and 550 volts,
60 cycle current. Current variation for different sizes of stock
is effected through a five-point switch shown at the left.
Standard ratings are 15 kw. or 22 kva., with 60 per cent power
factor. The dies are air cooled but the clamps to which the
dies are bolted are water cooled. This type of machine occupies
a floor space 40×33 in., and is 53 in. high. The weight is
1,750 lb. A close-up view of the treadle-operated clamping
jaw mechanism is given in Fig. 192.

The method of operating the clamping jaws differs according to the size of the machine and the work that is to be done. On some of the smaller machines the type of hand-operated clamp shown in Fig. 193 is used. On other machines, intended to handle round stock principally, the toggle lever clamp shown in Fig. 194 is used. For very heavy flat stock, the hand-lever clamping mechanism, shown in Fig. 195, is used. On some of the machines used on small repetition work the clamps and switch are automatically cam-operated as shown in Figs. 196 and 197. The first machine is a bench type used

Fig. 196.—A Cam-Operated Machine.

for welding on twist drill shanks, and the second machine is used for welding harness rings. These jobs are, of course, merely examples as the machines are adapted for all sorts of the smaller welding jobs. Spring pressure, toggle-lever or hydraulic pressure are used to give the final "shove-up" according to the machine used or weight of stock being welded.

In welding hard steel wire of over 35 per cent carbon content, it is necessary to anneal the work for a distance of about 1 in. on each side of the weld. This is due to the fact that the wire on each side is rendered brittle by the cooling effect of the clamping jaws. To accomplish this annealing, all the small Thomson machines used for this work are equipped with a set of V-jaws outside of the clamping jaws, as shown in front in Fig. 198. The wire is laid in these V's with the

Fig. 197.—Automatic-Operated Machine Welding Harness Rings.

weld half way between and the current is thrown on intermittently by means of a push button until the wire has become heated to the desired color, when it is removed and allowed to cool. The annealing of a small drill is shown in Fig. 199. The process of welding and annealing 12 gage, hard steel wire,

FIG. 198.—Machine Equipped with Annealing Device.

FIG. 199.—Annealing a Small Drill.

requires about 30 sec. when done by an experienced operator.
Copper and brass wire are easily welded in these same machines.
The machine shown will weld iron and steel wire from No.
21 B. & S. to $\frac{1}{8}$ in. in diameter and flat stock up to No. 25
B. & S.$\times\frac{1}{2}$ in. wide. Production is from 150 to 250 welds per
hour, the actual welding time being $1\frac{1}{2}$ sec. on $\frac{1}{8}$-in. steel wire.
The clamps are spring-pressure, with adjustable tension
released by hand lever. The standard windings are furnished
for 110, 220, 440 and 550 volts, 60 cycles. Five variations are
made possible by the switch. The ratings are $1\frac{1}{4}$ kw. or 3
kva., with 60 per cent power factor. The weight is 120 pounds.

For use in wire mills where it is desired to weld a new
reel of wire to the end of a run-out reel on the twisting or
braiding machines, it has been found convenient to mount the
machine on a truck or small bench on large casters. This
enables one to move the welder from one winding machine to
another very easily, to splice on new reels of small wire, the
electrical connection to the welder being made by flexible cord,
which is plugged into taps arranged at convenient points near
each winding machine. It is also desirable to mount on this
same bench a small vise in which to grip the wire to file off
the burr resulting from the push-up of the metal in the weld.
The average time required to weld, anneal and file up a 16-gage
steel wire with this bench arrangement is only about one
minute. The only preparation necessary for welding wire is
that the stock be clean and the ends be filed fairly square so
that they will not push by one another when the pressure
is applied.

In connection with welding wires and rods up to $\frac{3}{8}$ in.
in diameter, Table XX will be found very handy. For sizes
from $\frac{1}{4}$ to $2\frac{1}{4}$ in. the reader is referred to Table XXVI.

Examples of Butt-Welding Jobs.—while, as a rule, it is
only necessary to have clean and fairly square ends for butt-
welding in some cases where small welding is to be done it
has been found best to bevel or V the abutting ends. This is
more apt to be the case with non-ferrous metals, however, than
with iron or steel. A notable example in the larger work is
in the scarfing of the ends of boiler tubes when butt-welding
is done. This phase of the question has apparently not been
given the attention it deserves, and some cases where welding

TABLE XX.—APPROXIMATE CURRENT CONSUMPTION FOR WELDING UP TO ⅞ IN. ROD

| Dia. of rod in inches | | Wire gauge | | Dia. of rod in millimeters | Area of section in square in. | Current consumption per 1000 welds in K.W.H. | Cost per 1000 welds at 1 c. per K.W.H.* |
Frac.	Dec.	B. & S.	Birm.				
	.03196	20			.00079	2	$0.02
	.035		20		.00095	2	.02
	.0394			1	.00121	2	.02
	.0403	18			.00127	2	.02
	.049		18		.00189	2	.02
	.0508	16			.00205	2.5	.025
1/16	.0625		16		.00307	2.5	.025
	.0641	14			.00326	2.5	.025
	.065				.00332	2.5	.025
	.0787			2	.00486	2.5	.025
	.0808	12			.00513	2.5	.025
	.083		14		.00541	3	.03
	.1019	10			.00817	3	.03
	.109		12		.00934	3.5	.035
	.1181			3	.01096	4	.04
1/8	.125				.01227	4	.04
	.128	8			.01287	4	.04
	.134		10		.01411	4.5	.045
	.1575			4	.01948	5	.05
	.162	6			.02061	5.5	.055
	.165		8		.02139	5.5	.055
3/16	.1875				.02761	6	.06
	.1968			5	.03043	6.5	.065
	.203		6		.0327	7	.07
	.2043	4			.03277	7	$0.07
	.2362			6	.0438	8	.08
	.238		4		.0448	9	.09
1/4	.25				.04909	10	.10
	.2576	2			.0521	11	.11
	.2755			7	.0596	11	.11
	.284		2		.0633	12	.12
5/16	.3125				.0767	12	.12
	.3149			8	.0779	12	.12
	.3249	0			.0829	13	.13
	.34		0		.0908	14	.14
	.3543			9	.0987	15	.15
3/8	.375				.11045	16	.16
	.3937			10	.1217	19	.19
	.4724			12	.1753	20	.20
1/2	.5				.19635	26	.26
	.5612			14	.2472	30	.30
5/8	.625				.3068	34	.34
	.6299			16	.3115	45	.45
	.7087			18	.3946	52	.52
3/4	.75				.44179	60	.60
	.7874			20	.487	80	.80
	.8661			22	.585	85	.85
7/8	.875				.60132		

*Multiply these values by the rate you are paying per K. W. Hour for current, to determine what the cost per 1000 welds for any size would be at your plant.

has been declared a failure in manufacturing may be laid to the fact that the parts to be welded were not scarfed and consequently would not stand the required tests after being welded. As a general rule, a properly executed butt-weld should, when reduced to the size of the original section, have practically the same strength.

Although copper and brass rod and strip can be welded

FIG. 200.—Typical Copper Welds.

with perfect success, owing to the nature of the metal it requires a specially constructed machine to secure the best results. Since copper has a very low specific resistance as compared to iron or steel, it requires much more current to melt it on a given size rod. A longer time is required also to heat a given size of rod as compared to steel, but when

FIG. 201.—Welded Aluminum Ring.

the plastic stage is reached the metal flows so rapidly that it must be pushed up with tremendous speed or the molten copper will flow out between the abutting ends. To effect this rapid push-up of stock the platen on which the movable right-hand clamp is mounted must move very freely indeed, necessitating roller bearings on the larger sizes of machines. The

pressure spring on the smaller machines must also be capable
of maintaining its tension through a longer distance than on

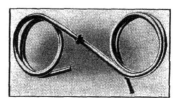

FIG. 202.—A Steel Wire Weld.

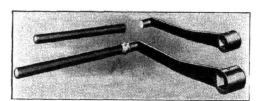

FIG. 203.—Welded Hoisting Drum Crank Forging.

FIG. 204.—Large Welded Pinion Blank.

a machine for iron and steel, since more metal is pushed up
on a given size of copper rod than would be on steel or iron.
The properties of brass and also aluminum are practically

Fig. 205.—Welding a Band Saw.

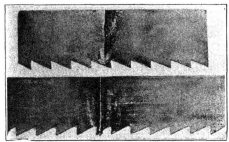

Fig. 206.—Bandsaw Weld before and after Removing Flash.

the same as those of copper and therefore this special type
of machine is just as well adapted for these metals.

Typical copper welds are shown in Fig. 200. The one at
the left shows it just as it came from the machine, and the
one at the right with the flash partly removed. Fig. 201
shows an aluminum ring immediately after welding. A steel
wire weld is shown in Fig. 202, and a welded hoisting drum
crank in Fig. 203. This last illustration shows how some
drop forgings may be simplified and the cost of dies and
production lessened. A large pinion gear blank is shown in
Fig. 204. Made in this way, a large amount of time and metal
is saved. The way to weld pieces of large and small cross
section is described in the article on tool welding.

Band saws may be butt-welded as shown in Fig. 205. The
way a band saw looks after welding and after the flash is
removed is shown in Fig. 206.

T-WELDING

T-welding, which is a special form of butt-welding, is, as
its name implies, the process of making a weld in the shape
of the letter "T". Where it is desired to weld a piece of
iron to the middle of another bar of equal size or larger, it
becomes necessary to heat the top bar of the "T" to a bright
red; then bring the lower bar to the preheated one and again
turn on the current, when a weld can quickly be made. The
reason for doing this is as follows: The pieces are of unequal
area in cross-section at the junction of the two pieces. As
it takes longer to heat the upper part, the end of the lower
part of the "T" would burn before the upper piece would
reach the welding temperature. Preheating will equalize and
overcome this difficulty. Special machines known as "T"
welders are built for this class of work to facilitate the preheating, when the highest possible production on this form
of weld is desired.

Automobile Rim Work.—One of the largest applications of
butt-welding today is to be found in the automobile-rim industry. The special form of clamp shown in Fig. 195 was
especially designed to handle rims of all kinds and sizes. It
is not adaptable for any type of work other than flat stock,

as the amount of jaw-opening is much smaller than the diameter of equivalent section of round stock.

No backing-up stops of any kind are built for these machines with rim-clamps, as stops are unnecessary for this class of work. In order to secure sufficient gripping effect of the stock to prevent it slipping in the clamp-jaws, the upper dies are made of self-hardening steel with the gripping surface corrugated. The lower dies, which carry all the current to the work, are made of copper with Tobin-bronze shoes on which the work rests, so as to give good conductivity and yet present a hard wearing surface to the steel rim. These lower dies must not only bear the gripping effort exerted by the steel dies above, but also the weight of the rim, which, in large sizes, amounts to considerable.

The method employed in welding automobile rims is the "flash-weld" principle, wherein the current is first turned on with the edges to be welded pulled apart. The pressure is then applied gently to bring the abutting ends slowly together. As uneven projections come into contact across from opposite edges they are burned or "flashed" off, which is evidenced by flying particles of burning iron. The pressure is gradually increased, bringing more of the length of the opposite edges into contact and when the "flash" throws out for the full width of the rim which indicates the abutting ends are touching all the way across, the final pressure is quickly applied as the current is turned off, thereby completing the weld. It has been found that experienced operators on this kind of work do not look at the weld itself but govern their actions by the appearance of the amount of flash or sparks thrown out. When this assumes the shape of a complete fan they know it is the right moment to cut off the current and apply the final pressure.

The burr or fin thrown up in this type of weld is very short and very brittle, making its removal much easier than would be the case with the heavy burr resulting from a slow butt-weld. It is the common practice in rim plants to remove the burr while it is still hot and with a pneumatic chisel or a sprue cutter. The slight amount of burr then remaining is ground off with a coarse abrasive wheel and the rim is ready for the forming process. In most rim plants the operations of rolling, welding, chiseling burr, grinding burr, forming, shaping, etc., fit in so closely to one another that a rim is practically kept moving continuously from the time the flat stock is put into the rolls until a finished rim emerges. The welding operation itself on a rim blank for $30 \times 3\frac{1}{2}$ tire size, for instance, has an average production rate of 60 rims per hour, some concerns doing even better than this. On large

Fig. 207.—Truck Rim Welding Machine.

truck rims for solid tires, having a section of $16 \times \frac{3}{4}$ in. thick, a production of 10 rims per hour is considered very good, although there are concerns doing even better than this on such heavy work.

The machine shown in Fig. 207 was specially designed for handling heavy truck rims only. The lower jaws on this welder are placed very low in order that the machine can be set in a comparatively shallow pit to bring the line of weld on a level with the floor. This makes it possible, with proper tracking arrangements, to roll heavy rims right onto the lower dies without any lifting, the rim being rolled out again after welding. The double oil-transformers used in this welder hang below the base line, which necessitates a small pit directly under the center of machine. Owing to this and also the weight to be supported, a concrete foundation only should be employed.

This machine has a capacity for stock $\frac{3}{4} \times 8$ to $\frac{3}{8} \times 16$ in., or a maximum thickness of 1 in. with a cross-sectional area of not over 7 sq. in. Rims with a minimum diameter of 30 in. can be welded. The pressure is effected by twin hydraulic

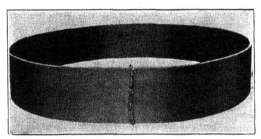

Fig. 208.—A Heavy Welded Rim.

cylinders operated from an external accumulator giving a maximum pressure of 24 to 37 tons on the work. The voltage windings are of the same capacity as for other machines. The transformer is of the oil cooled type, and the ratings are 160 kw. or 266 kva., with 60 per cent power factor. Primary windings of transformers are submerged in cooling oil contained in casings. Platens on which the clamps are mounted and the bodies of the lower jaws to which the contact shoes are bolted, are water cooled. This machine is 66×101 in. and 66 in. high. The net weight is 14,000 pounds.

A heavy rim after welding is shown in Fig. 208.

Welding Pipe.—In order to weld pipe and tubing in the form of coils for condenser systems cooling tubes, heating coils, etc., as shown in Fig. 209, it was found necessary to employ a special form of clamp wherein the jaws could be set up high to give clearance above the pressure-device. The thickness of the die and die-block to which it is bolted also had to be reduced to a minimum so as to insert the jaws between coils, since the pipe is coiled through each length and then another length is welded on, which in turn is coiled, and so on. In order to secure the best gripping effect with a comparatively light die, it is necessary to make this form of die considerably longer than those used in the other types

Fig. 209.—Welding Pipe Coils.

of horizontal-acting clamps. Moreover, since there is not enough space in the narrow block to which the die is bolted to permit water circulation, the die itself must be water-cooled to prevent softening of the copper from continued contact with the hot pipe just in back of the weld.

This type of clamp, Fig. 210, is designed for welding of pipe and tubing only, which requires a much lighter pressure to push up than solid stock of the same cross-sectional area, and since the line of weld is considerably above the line of pressure, the slides will be quickly worn on the movable platen if heavy pressure is used continually. For this reason the

FIG. 210.—Clamp Used for Pipe Welding.

FIG. 211.—Winfield Portable Butt-Welding Machine.

TABLE XXI.—APPROXIMATE CURRENT CONSUMPTION FOR WELDING PIPE UP TO 4½ IN.

Ordinary Sizes — Diameters				Extra Heavy — Diameters				Double Extra Heavy — Diameters				Miscellaneous Data			
Nominal Internal	Actual Internal	Actual External	Pipe Wall Thickness	Nominal Internal	Actual Internal	Actual External	Pipe Wall Thickness	Nominal Internal	Actual Internal	Actual External	Pipe Wall Thickness	Square Inch Cross-section	Weight in Lbs. per Foot	Current Consumption per 1000 Welds	Cost per 1000 Welds at 1 c. per K.W.H.*
⅛	.27	.405	.068	⅛	.205	.405	.1					.0717	.241	12	$0.12
¼	.364	.54	.088	¼	.294	.54	.123					.096	.29	13	.13
⅜	.494	.675	.091	⅜	.421	.675	.127					.1240	.42	16	.16
½	.623	.84	.109	½	.542	.84	.149					.161	.54	18	.18
¾	.824	1.05	.113	¾	.736	1.05	.157	¾	.244	.84	.298	.1063	.559	19	.19
1	1.048	1.315	.134	1	.951	1.315	.182	¾	.432	1.05	.314	.219	.74	21	.21
1¼	1.38	1.66	.14	1¼	1.272	1.66	.194	1	.587	1.315	.361	.2492	.837	25	.26
1½	1.611	1.9	.145	1½	1.494	1.9	.203	1¼	.885	1.66	.388	.323	1.00	35	.35
2	2.067	2.375	.154	2	1.933	2.375	.221	1½	1.088	1.9	.406	.3327	1.115	37	.37
2½	2.468	2.875	.204	2½	2.315	2.875	.28	2	1.491	2.375	.442	.414	1.39	50	.50
3	3.067	3.5	.217	3	2.892	3.5		2½	1.736	2.875	.56	.4954	1.668	60	.60
3½	3.548	4.	.226	3½	3.358	4						.307	1.7	70	.70
4	4.026	4.5	.237									.648	2.17	90	.90
4½	4.508	5.	.246									.727	2.44	100	1.00
												.797	2.678	110	1.10
												.893	3.609	130	1.30
												1.074	3.63	160	1.60
												1.082	3.65	210	2.10
												1.087	5.02	220	2.20
												.495	5.739	230	2.30
												1.549	6.1	340	3.40
												.708	7.536	360	3.60
												1.903	7.67	410	4.10
												.4	9.001	460	4.60
												2.243	9.02	570	5.70
												2.283	10.25	590	5.90
												.679	10.665	740	7.40
												.686	12.35	760	7.60
												3.052	12.47	850	8.50
												3.174	13.68	940	9.40
												3.674		1150	11.50
												3.71		1190	11.90
												4.073		1300	13.00

* Multiply these values by the rate you are paying per K.W. hour for current, to determine what the cost per 1000 welds for any size would be at your plant.

welding of any solid stock with this class of machine is not advisable.

The machine shown will weld iron and steel pipe from $\frac{3}{4}$ to 2 in. in diameter, ordinary pipe sizes and $1\frac{1}{2}$ in. extra heavy pipe, or double heavy 1 in. in diameter. Standard steel tubing

FIG. 212.—A General Purpose Butt-Welding Machine.

from 1 to $2\frac{1}{4}$ in. diameter may be welded. Pressure is supplied by a hydraulic oil jack exerting a maximum of 5 tons. The standard ratings are 30 kw. or 50 kva., with power factor of 60 per cent. The machine will weigh about 2,500 pounds.

For welding pipe, Table XXI will be found useful for

reference purposes. This table was compiled by the Thomson Electric Welding Co., with special reference to their machines.

Winfield Butt-Welding Machines.—The Winfield Electric Welding Machine Co., Winfield, Ohio, makes a complete line of butt-welding machines but only a few representative of their line, will be shown. A very convenient portable or bench type is shown in Fig. 211. This is especially useful for light manufacturing work. It has a capacity of 18 to 6 gage wire. It is equipped with a 1 kw. transformer, hand clamping levers and a 3-step self-contained regulator for controlling the current. It occupies a floor space of $13\frac{1}{2} \times 16$ in., is 35 in. high from floor to center of welding dies, and weighs about 130 lb. complete.

The machine shown in Fig. 212 is for general all-round shop work. It has a capacity of from $\frac{1}{4}$ to 1 in. round, or $\frac{3}{4} \times 2$ in. flat stock. It has a 25-kw. transformer, water-cooled welding jaws, enclosed non-automatic switch on upsetting lever, stop for regulating amount of take-up on each weld, ten-step self-contained regulator for controlling the current, occupies a floor space of 44×25 in., is 42 in. high to center of jaws and weighs about 1,800 lb. The jaws overhang as shown, for welding hoops, rings, rims, etc.

The machine shown in Fig. 213 is for toolroom work and was especially designed for handling large cross-sections. It will weld up to $2\frac{1}{4}$ in. round. All clamping and upsetting operations are accomplished by means of air or hydraulic pressure. The clamping cylinders are operated independently of each other by means of separate valves, which enable the operator to clamp each piece before the current is turned on. The small air cylinder on the right-hand end of the machine keeps the work in close contact during the heating operation. The final pressure is applied by the hydraulic ram after the proper welding heat has been attained. The table at the left is equipped with adjustments for moving it up or down, back and forth, tilting or twisting. This feature is especially valuable in experimental work and often saves buying a special machine for unusual manufacturing jobs. The terminals are cooled by a stream of water which flows from one to the other. The dies are held in place by slotted clamps which permit easy removal. Work stops and stops to regulate the amount of upset are provided. The movable table is fitted with roller bearings to insure easy operation. The transformer is a Winfield 125 kw. The machine has a ten-step current regulator, and the current for welding is controlled by a Cutler-Hammer magnetic switch which in turn is operated by means of a small auxiliary switch placed on the valve lever controlling the hydraulic ram. The floor space occupied is 60×90 in., and the approximate weight, ready for shipment, is 8,000 lb.

Fig. 213.—Winfield Toolroom Machine.

Table XXII compiled by this concern contains some useful data not given in the other tables.

Federal Butt-Welding Machines.—The machines built by the Federal Machine and Welder Co., Warren, Ohio, do not differ in the principles of operation from the machines already described. The form of the one shown in Fig. 214, however, differs considerably from any shown. The tables, or platens, are flat and are T-slotted so that various fixtures may be easily bolted in place. The maximum capacity for continuous service, is $2\frac{1}{4}$ in. round or other shape of equal section. Flats up to

¾×10 in. may be welded. The platens are of gunmetal and the T-slots will take ¾-in. bolts. These platens are recessed and water-cooled. Pressure is applied by means of an hydraulic jack, shown at the right. The switch is remote control magnetically operated. The main switch is controlled by a small shunt switch which is worked either by hand or foot, as desired. The transformer is 100 kva. It has an eight-step regulating coil. Floor space occupied is 38×88 in., height 50 in., weight 5,600 lb. This machine is intended to weld auto-rims, heavy forgings, steel frames, shafting, high-speed steel and work

Fig. 214.—Federal Heavy-Duty Butt-Welding Machine.

requiring accurate alignment and rapid production in quantities.

A set consisting of a tube welder and roller is shown in Fig. 215. This will weld tubes from 1¼ to 3 in. It will also weld flat, round or square stock of equivalent cross section. The dies are water-cooled, and the work is clamped in position by air cylinders operating on a line pressure of 80 to 100 lb. The switch is on the main operating lever, so that the heat is at all times under the control of the operator. The transformer is 65 kw. air cooled. Eight current steps are obtained. The machine occupies a floor space of 30×51 in., is 42 in. high, and weighs 2,100 lb. By using the set, a tube may be welded and immediately transferred to the rolling machine and the

TABLE XXII.—COST OF ¼ TO 2 IN. WELDS PER THOUSAND

Diameter of Stock		Area in Square Inches	K. W. Required	Horse Power	Time in Sec. Per Weld	Cost Per 1000 Welds at 1 c. Per K.W. Hour	Average No. of Welds Per Hour	Labor Cost Per 1000 at 30c. Per Hour
¼	Inch	.05	2	3	3	.02	400	.75
⁵/₁₆	"	.08	3	4	4.5	.05	375	.80
³/₈	"	.11	4	5	6	.07	350	.85
⁷/₁₆	"	.15	5	7	6.5	.10	300	1.00
½	"	.20	6	8	7	.12	250	1.20
⁹/₁₆	"	.25	7	9	7.5	.15	200	1.50
⁵/₈	"	.31	8	11	8	.18	150	2.00
¹¹/₁₆	"	.37	9	12	9	.23	130	2.30
³/₄	"	.44	10	13	10	.28	100	3.00
¹³/₁₆	"	.52	10.5	14	12	.35	95	3.20
⅞	"	.60	11	15	15	.46	90	3.30
¹⁵/₁₆	"	.69	11.5	15.5	17	.55	85	3.50
1	"	.79	12	16	18	.60	80	3.70
1⅛	"	.99	16	21	20	.89	75	4.00
1¼	"	1.23	19	25	25	1.32	70	4.30
1⅜	"	1.48	25	33	30	2.08	65	4.60
1½	"	1.77	31	41	35	3.00	60	5.00
1⅝	"	2.07	38	51	37	3.90	55	5.50
1¾	"	2.41	45	60	40	5.00	48	6.20
1⅞	"	2.76	53	71	43	6.34	40	7.50
2	"	3.14	60	80	45	7.50	30	10.00

flash rolled out. The time consumed in rolling down the flash on a 2¼-in. tube is given as approximately 20 seconds.

FIG. 215.—A Tube-Welding Set.

Welding Rotor Bars to End Rings.—In the *General Electric Review* for December, 1918, E. F. Collins and W. Jacob describe the welding of rotor bars to the end rings used in squirrel-cage induction motors, employing the machine shown in Fig. 216. This machine has a double set of welding jaws, the front set being used to butt-weld end rings to make them seamless, while the rear set is used to weld the rotor bars to the end rings. As shown, the machine is welding rotor-bars to the end-rings. The description of the work as carried out in the General Electric shops is as follows:

"The projecting rotor bars surround a toothed end ring,

Fig. 216—General Electric Machine for Rotor Work.

which is of slightly smaller diameter than the rotor. A small block of copper is placed so that it covers the copper end surfaces of a rotor bar and the corresponding tooth on the end ring, after which it is butt-welded into place.

The projecting rotor bars are shown at A in Fig. 217 and the toothed end ring just inside the circle of rotor bars is shown at B. Finished welds as at C show blocks in place. The actual operation is as follows: A rotor bar is tightly clamped to the corresponding tooth of the end-ring between the jaws D and E. The copper-block end-connection is placed so that it covers the combined area of tooth and bar ends. The movable jaw F holds the end connection in place, and heavy pressure is then applied through compression springs. The welding current, furnished by a special transformer having a one-turn secondary, passes from jaw F through the surfaces and out through jaw E. This heavy current at low voltage causes intense heating due to the comparatively high resistance

FIG. 217.—Details of the Welding Mechanism and Work.

at the surface junction, and raises the temperature of the copper to welding heat, at which point the metal is plastic.

At this stage spring pressure forces the jaw F toward the rotor and squeezes out any oxide which may have formed between the welding surfaces. A small stream of water, playing upon the hot area, forms an atmosphere of super-heated steam which prevents the formation of oxide and also guards against excessive heating of the copper. No flux is used in the operation as the mechanical squeezing-out of the oxide is sufficient to form a homogeneous connection between the two surfaces.

As the welding jaws approach one another when the metal becomes plastic, an electrical connection is automatically made which operates a solenoid-controlled switch that opens the primary transformer circuit. Thus the current is interrupted as soon as the surfaces have knitted together. The contacts of this automatic switch are placed one on each movable jaw, and are so adjusted that they are separated by the distance necessary for the jaws to approach one another in forming

Fig. 218.—Butt-Welding the End Rings.

the weld and in forcing out the oxide. In this way, the end connection is butt-welded to the rotor bar and the end ring, forming a junction of great mechanical strength and low resistance.

Another example of non-ferrous butt welding is the making of seamless end rings, which operation is performed in the same machine. The operation is shown in detail in Fig. 218, which shows a finished end ring in place. One end of the ring is placed in the vise-jaws G and H, and the other is held in the opposite jaws I and J. As the jaws approach pressure is applied by means of the springs. In all other respects the operation is similar to that of welding the end connections.

Rotors up to 14 ft. in diameter are welded and Fig. 219 shows the rotor for a 1,400-hp. motor being welded.

The work is done rapidly; for example, end connections with a welding surface of about 0.6 by 0.4 in. are welded at the rate of about 90 an hour.

Welding Brass.—Brass rotor bars and end rings are also butt-welded in a similar manner, but the operation is slower. Brass, being an alloy, has a lower melting point than copper,

FIG. 219.—Welding End Ring and Rotor Bars for 1400-H.P. Motor.

and less pressure is necessary to effect a weld. The pressure is determined by the thickness of the piece to be welded, and should be just enough to form a small "flash" at the point of union. Excessive pressure will cause the molten metal to spurt out from the point of weld. In one fundamental particular the butt-welding of brass differs from that of copper, the pressure on brass must not be released after the stoppage of current until the metal has hardened sufficiently so that it will not crack on cooling. This delay retards the rate of welding to the extent that about 60 brass end connections, of the size previously mentioned, require the same time as 90 of copper.

Butt-welding has been the means of producing a rotor having low resistance, high mechanical strength, and ability to permanently withstand vibration and centrifugal force without excessive heating, all of which are essential factors in an efficiently operated squirrel-cage induction motor.

WELDING ELBOWS ON LIBERTY CYLINDERS

In making Liberty motors in the Ford shop, the valve elbows were butt-welded on as shown in Fig. 220. The holding

FIG. 220.—Welding Valve Elbows.

fixture is shown with the hinged top thrown back and a cylinder in the cradle. One elbow has already been welded on, and the other is held in the jaws of the sliding fixture, ready to be welded in place. This work was done before the cylinders were finish bored and by so doing all cylinder distortion, due to welding was cut out in the finish boring.

An automatic straight-link chain making machine, built by the Automatic Machine Co., Bridgeport, Conn., is shown in

Fig. 221. This machine took the material from a reel, shown at the right, formed it, butt-welded the ends of the links and turned out the chain as indicated. The machine was so made that the welded part of each link was pressed between special dies while still hot, the operation practically eliminating the

Fig. 221.—Automatic Chain Making Machine.

flash formed in welding. Aside from the welding features, the machine was a marvel of mechanical ingenuity and simplicity.

ELECTRO-PERCUSSIVE WELDING

The joining of small aluminum wires has always presented much difficulty on account of the oxide film which prevents the metal parts from flowing together, unless brought to a point of fluidity at which the oxide film can be broken up and washed away. If this be attempted with small sections, the whole mass is likely to be oxidized, and the resulting joint will be brittle or "crumbly."

In 1905 L. W. Chubb, of the Westinghouse Electric and Manufacturing Co., Pittsburgh, Penn., discovered that if two pieces of wire were connected to the terminals of a charged condenser, and then brought together with some force, that enough electrical energy would be concentrated at the point

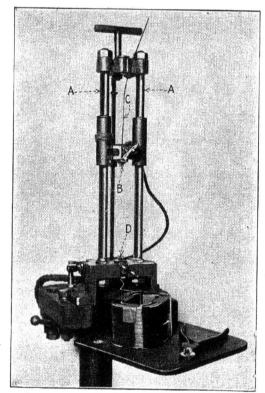

FIG. 222.—Electro-Percussive Welding Machine.

of contact to melt the wires, while the force of the blow would weld them together. Accordingly, a welding process was developed and used by the Westinghouse company, and machines made which are capable of welding all kinds of wire up to No. 13 gage. The process was called electro-percussive

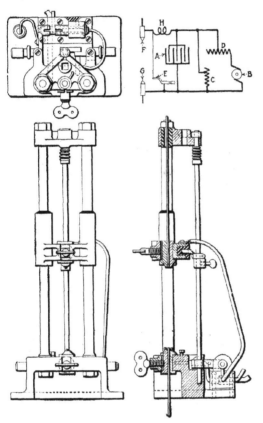

FIG. 223.—Details of Percussive Welding Machine and Wiring Diagram.

welding and a machine for doing the work is shown in Fig. 222. This machine has vertical guides A between which travels a chuck *B* holding one wire *C*. The other wire is held below in chuck *D* in such a position that the end of the moving wire strikes it squarely. Each chuck is connected by flexible cable to a circuit as shown in Fig. 223. An electrolyte condenser *A*, shown in the wiring diagram, is connected across a source of direct current from *B*, which charges it to a potential determined by the resistances *C* and *D*. A switch *E* keeps the chucks *F* and *G* at the same potential during placement and removal of work.

After the wires to be welded have been chucked, they are clipped short by a cutter which gives each a chisel, or wedge-shaped end. These ends are set at right angles to each other. The switch is opened and the sliding chuck is released and allowed to fall. At the instant when the two narrow edges come into contact, the current discharged generates intense heat at the center of the section. The metal melts and is forced out by the impact and eventually the entire surface of each wire is melted. Due to the very large body of cold metal adjacent, the thin film of molten metal solidifies quickly and since it is under momentarily heavy pressure it forms a homogenous mass absolutely continuous with the wires on each side. In practical operation, the inductance *H* is required to lower the rate at which the condenser discharges, that is, to maintain the current at a lower rate until the entire surface of the weld has been forced into contact. The correct action can be told by the sound made by the contact. It should be a splash or thud, rather than a sharp crack. The mass and drop of the falling part must be great enough to slightly forge the material. Once set for the proper drop, the machine will make a perfect weld every time.

Actual tests on two No. 18 B. & S. aluminum wires, using an oscillograph, show that the power being expended at the weld reaches a value of 23 kw. for an instant. However, the entire weld is made in 0.0012 sec., and the total energy used at the weld is 0.00000123 kw.-hr. The cost of this weld, figured at 10 cents per kw.-hr., would be twelve millionths of a cent.

A chart of the oscillograph aluminum-wire test just referred to, is shown in Fig. 224. At *A* the right-angled chisel-ends are shown almost in contact as the upper chuck falls. As the ends contact at *B* the voltage drops as indicated by the curve

G, but the current and power consumption suddenly increases as shown by the curves H and I respectively.

At C the wire ends have separated, caused by the melting and vaporizing of the chisel edges. At D the chucks are closer together but the arc is still burning away the wire ends. At E the second contact has been made, the arc eliminated and upsetting begun. At F the weld is shown completed.

One of the principal uses for this process is in welding copper to aluminum, as for example copper lead-wires to

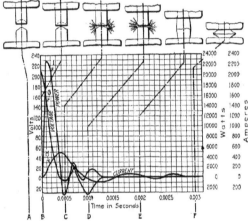

Fig. 224.—Chart of Oscillograph Test on 18 B. & S. Gage Aluminum Wire, Showing Power Consumed and Time to Complete a Percussive Weld.

aluminum coils. The advantage of copper for connecting is self-evident, as it is easily soldered. It was thought at first that a weld of the two metals would result in a brittle joint, but tests show that after several years the joint is apparently as strong and ductile as when first made. Similar ductility has been noted in almost every combination of metals when first welded, but disintegration and loss of ductility eventually result in such welds as silver to tin or aluminum to tin, the welds being affected by what is known as "tin disease" or "tin pest"—a disintegration of the molecules.

Alloy of practically any composition can be welded to each other, and there is little diffusion of one metal into the other across the welded surface. Thus this method is quite suitable

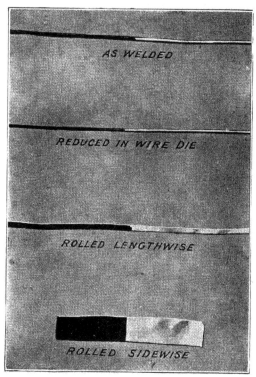

Fig. 225.—Copper Welded to Aluminum.

for *attaching contact points to flat plates* and making small welds required by jewelers.

Another important quality of the process is that metals which soften with heating, such as hard-drawn copper and silver, can be welded without change of condition since the length of metal heated to an annealing temperature will not be more than 0.004 in. long and this amount of metal is negligibly small. As will be seen from the specimens in Fig. 225, which show copper welded to aluminum, then drawn and rolled, there is no loss of ductility at the weld and no tendency for the two metals to separate.

CHAPTER XIII

SPOT-WELDING MACHINES AND WORK

Spot welding, as the name indicates, is simply welding in spots. Two or more overlapping metal plates or sheets may be welded together at intervals, by confining electric current to a small area of passage by means of suitable electrodes, or "dies" which are pressed against the metal from opposite sides. Spot welding is a form of resistance welding. Due to the way the metal is heated and forced together no oxidizing takes place, and in consequence no flux of any kind is needed.

While the process of spot welding is more commonly used at present for welding thin sheet iron, steel or brass articles, practical machines have been made for welding two pieces of $\frac{3}{4}$-in. ship plate together. Experimental machines have also been made capable of spot-welding three 1-in. plates together, and which can exert a pressure of 36 tons and have a current capacity of 100,000 amperes.

To weld soft cold-rolled steel in a satisfactory commercial manner, three conditions should be observed, if possible:

First, the surfaces to be welded should be free from rust, scale or dirt. If the work is not clean a higher secondary voltage will be required to penetrate through the scale or dirt of any given thickness of sheet. This means that a larger machine and more current must be used than would be required for clean stock of the same thickness.

Second, the sheets should be flat and in good contact at the spots to be welded, so that no great pressure is required to flatten down bulges or dents.

Third, the stock should not surround the lower horn, as in the case of welding the side seam of a can or pipe.

It must not be understood that spot welding cannot be done except under the conditions outlined, for it can, but if the conditions named are not followed the cost of welding will be greater. However, it is often necessary to violate these conditions in actual manufacturing work. This is especially true of the third one. Where the lower horn must be surrounded by the work, as in welding can seams, the capacity of the machine is cut down because of the "induction effect" which tends to choke back the main current and in this way cuts down the heating effect at the die points. This so-called induction effect is only present when welding steel or iron, no such action being noticeable in welding brass.

Light gages of sheet metal can be welded to heavy gages or to solid bars of steel if the light-gage metal is not greater than the rated single sheet capacity of the machine. Soft steel and iron form the best welding material in sheet metals, although it is possible to weld sheet iron or steel to malleable-iron castings of a good quality.

Galvanized iron can also be welded successfully, although it takes a slightly longer time than clear iron or steel stock, in order to burn off the zinc coating before the weld can be made. Contrary to common opinion, the metal at the point of weld is not made susceptible to rust by this burning off of zinc, since by some electrochemical action it has been found that the spots directly under each die-point and also around the point of weld between the sheets, are covered with a thin coating of zinc oxide after the weld has taken place. This coating acts as a rust preventive to a very noticeable degree. On spot-welded articles used in practice for some time, such as galvanized road-culverts, refrigerator-racks and pans, raingutters, etc., it has been found that no trace of rust has appeared on the spot-welds from their exposure to ordinary atmospheric conditions. Extra light gages of galvanized iron below 28 B. & S. gage cannot be very successfully welded, due to the fact that so little of the iron is left after the zinc has been burnt off that the metal is very apt to burn through and leave a hole in the sheets.

Tinned sheet iron is ideal for welding, giving great strength at the weld, but the stock will be discolored over the area covered by the die-points. Sheet brass can be welded to brass or steel if it contains not more than 60 per cent copper. It is not practical to attempt to spot-weld any bronze or alloy containing a higher percentage of copper than this as the weld will be weak.

Another class of work that can be successfully handled on a spot-welding machine, although it is not strictly spot welding, is the construction of wire-goods articles. This consists principally in "mash-welding" crossed wires. It may be done with the same copper die-points as are used for ordinary spot welding, except that the points are usually grooved to hold the wire in the required position. Among the common wire goods put together in this way are lamp-shade frames, oven

Fig. 226.—Typical Construction of Light Spot-Welding Machine.

racks, dish drainers, waste baskets, frames for floral make-ups and so on. Certain classes of butt-welding may also be done on a spot-welding machine by using special attachments.

Details of Standard Spot-Welding Machines.—Spot-welding machines are made in various sizes and designs to meet different requirements, but the general principle of action is the same in all. The illustration, Fig. 226, shows a Thomson No. 124-A10 machine with the cover removed. This gives an idea of the principal mechanism of all this line of light spot-welding

machines. Fig. 227 shows a typical head of one of their line
of heavier machines. This type of machine is designed for
heavy work on flat sheets or pieces, where considerable pressure is required to bring the parts together to be welded. To
withstand heavy pressures, the lower horn is made of T-section
cast iron and the current is conducted to the lower copper
die-holder by flexible copper laminations, protected on all sizes

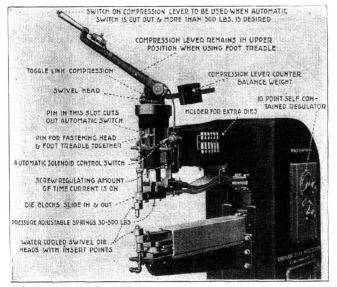

FIG. 227.—Spot-Welding Machine for Heavy Work, with Parts Named.

having over 15-in. throat, by a brass cover, insulated on the
inside from the copper by a coating of asbestos sheet.

The sliding head of the machine which carries the upper
die-holder is a hollow steel plunger, sliding in a cast-iron head,
which bolts to the body of the machine and on which are
mounted the control-switches. The pressure is applied by a
toggle-motion above the plunger, actuated both by a swiveled
hand-lever on top of the head, which may be swung into any

position through an arc of 260 deg., and a foot-treadle at the base, which also may be swung in an arc of 30 deg. This enables the operator to control the machine by hand or foot from any position around the front of the machine.

The current-control can be set to work automatically with the downward stroke of the upper die. In this case the pressure at the die-point is through an adjustable spring-cushion in the hollow cylinder-head. The current is automatically turned on after the die-points have come together on the work by further downward pressure of either lever. With the application of final pressure, to squeeze out any burnt metal as the weld is forced together, the current is automatically turned off. When working on pieces where more pressure is required to bring the parts together before welding than can be effected by the spring-cushion without turning on the current, it is possible to set a plug in the head of the machine so that direct connection is obtained from the hand-lever to the upper die-point while the foot-treadle still operates through the spring-cushion and with the automatic current-control. When it is desired to secure maximum pressure, the plug in the head can be set again so that both the hand-lever and the foot-treadle give direct connection to the die-point, the current being controlled by a push-button on the outer end of the hand-lever.

The regular line of spot-welding machines of different makes, operate on 110-, 220-, 440- and 550-volt, alternating current. A welding machine of this kind can only be connected to one phase of an a.c. circuit. The transformer must be made to furnish a large volume of current, at a low voltage, to the electrodes. For further transformer details, the reader is referred to the article on butt-welding.

The Thomson Foot-, Automatic-, and Hand-Operated Machines.—The machine shown in Fig. 228 is representative of the Thomson line of small, foot-operated spot-welding machines. These are intended for use on light stock where but little pressure is required. The die-holders are water-cooled, and the lower horn bracket allows the horn to be adjusted up or down for the use of various kinds of holders. The automatic switch and adjustable throw-in stop are plainly shown at the back of the machine.

The model is made in several sizes. The first size will weld from 30 to 16 B. & S. gage galvanized iron or soft steel, or to 24 gage brass. It will mash-weld wire from 14 gage to ¼ in. in diameter. Its throat depth is 12 in.; the lower horn drop clearance is 9 in.; size is 22×45×51 in. high; net weight

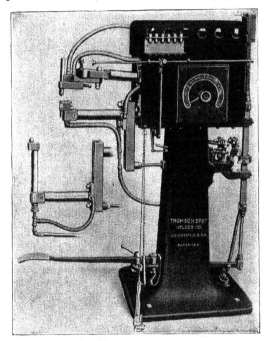

Fig. 228.—The Thomson Light Manufacturing Type Spot-Welding Machine.

is 825 lb.; full load rating is 5 kw., or 8 kva. The largest machine of this particular series, will weld 26 to 7 gage, B. & S., galvanized iron or soft steel, or 18 gage brass; it will mash-weld 10-gage to ⅜-in. diameter wire; has an 18-in. depth of throat; is 28×60×56 in. high; weighs 1,550 lb. and full load rating is 15 kw. or 25 kva.

On repetition work, where the operator has to work the foot-treadle in rapid succession for long periods, it is very tiresome. For such work, power-driven machines similar to the one shown in Fig. 229 are made. These machines are supplied either with individual motor drive or pulley drive, as desired. The control is effected through the small treadle shown. The regular foot-treadle is used while setting up dies,

FIG. 229.—The Thomson Semi-Automatic Type Spot-Welding Machine.

etc. If the operator desires to make but one stroke, he depresses the shorter treadle and immediately releases it, whereupon the machine performs one cycle of operation, automatically turning on the current, applying the pressure, turning off the current, and stopping. A ¼- to ½-hp. operating motor is used according to the size of the machine. Otherwise the capacity of the various sizes is the same as in the regular foot-operated

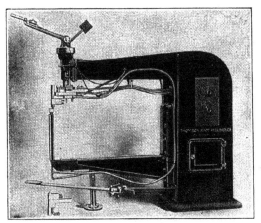

Fig. 230.—A Thomson Heavy-Duty Spot-Welding Machine.

Fig. 231.—Spot-Welding a Sheet Steel Box.

machines. The lower horn and upper arm may be of either style illustrated.

The machine shown in Fig. 230 is a hand-lever operated machine, although supplied with a foot-treadle which can be

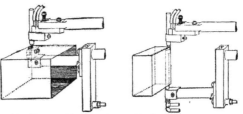

FIG. 232.—Showing How the Horn and Welding Points May Be Set.

swung back out of the way when not needed. This machine is typical of the Thomson designs used for the heavier run of commercial work. On the various sizes, the capacity for spot-welding is from 22 B. & S. gage galvanized iron or steel

FIG. 233.—Welding Small Hoe Blades to the Shanks.

up to No. 0 gage, or to 14 gage brass. Mash-welds may be made on from ⅛- to ⅝-in. diameter wire. The throat capacities run from 15 to 51 in. and the lower horn adjustment is from 12 to 24 in. The smallest size is 28×62×75 in. high and the

FIG. 234.—Welding Stove Pipe Dampers.

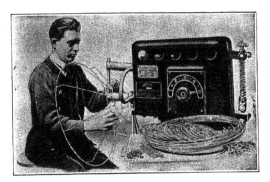

FIG. 235.—Mash-Welding Lamp Shade Frames.

FIG. 236.—Butt-Welding Attachment for a Spot-Welding Machine.

FIG. 237.—Welding Galvanized Iron Pipe.

largest size 28×98×75 in. high. The weights run from 2,335 to 3,225 and the full load ratings from 20 to 40 kw. or 35 to 67 kva. Various shaped horns, dies and other equipment are furnished to meet special demands.

Examples of Spot-Welding Work.—In connection with the Thomson machines, the welding of the corners of a sheet-steel box is shown in Fig. 231. The illustrations in Fig. 232 show how the lower horn is raised for welding side seams and dropped for welding on the bottom of a box.

The welding of small hoe blades to the shanks is shown

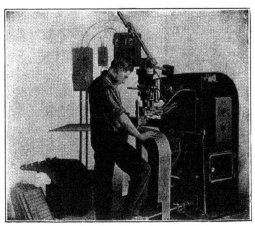

Fig. 238.—Welding 12-Gage Iron for Guards.

in Fig. 233. These are welded at the rate of 840 per hour, the shanks being bent afterward. Stove-pipe dampers are welded as shown in Fig. 234, and wire lamp-shade frames are mash-welded as shown in Fig. 235. Ordinary wire and sheet-metal oven gratings or racks, with seven cross-wires welded to the end pieces, have been made at the rate of 100 racks per hour, or 1,400 mash-welds. On certain kinds of wire work, it is desirable to butt-weld, and for this purpose the attachment shown in Fig. 236 is used. In general, however, where any amount of this kind of work is to be done, it is better to employ a regular butt-welding machine of the small pedestal or bench type.

The spot-welding of galvanized ventilating pipe is shown in Fig. 237, and in Fig. 238 is shown the welding of 12 gage sheet steel machine guards. In this illustration the operator is using the foot-treadle which leaves his hands free to manipulate the work. In Fig. 239 the operator is welding gas-stove parts and the foot-treadle is thrown back out of the

Fig. 239.—Welding Stove Parts, Using a Swinging Bracket Support.

way. A special bracket is employed to hold the work. The joints of this bracket are ball-bearing, making it very easy to swing the work exactly where it is wanted to obtain the spot-welds.

POINTS FOR SPOT WELDING

The form of spot-welding points shown in Fig. 240, says A. A. Karcher, has been developed by the Challenge Machinery Co., Grand Rapids, Mich., with gratifying results. Fig. 241 shows a typical weld and indicates the neatness, slight dis-

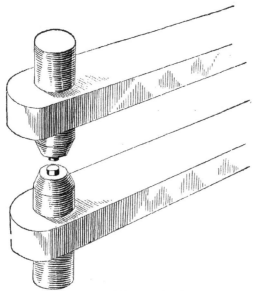

FIG. 240.—Form of Points for Spot Welding.

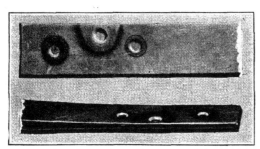

FIG. 241.—Spot Weld Showing Slight Discoloration and Freedom from Flash.

coloration of the metal and entire freedom from flash either on the outside or between the parts. In one view the discolorations give an erroneous impression of the existence of bosses on the face of the metal, which is actually flat except for the depressions at the points of the welds.

The shape of the points would lead one to expect that the small projections would require a lot of attention to keep them in shape. Experience shows, however, that this is not the case, as the points actually lengthen slightly and occasionally have to be filed down.

Even when a weld is made close to the edge the operation is quicker and consumes less current. A little practice in determining the correct amount of current to use is all there is to learn in handling these points.

SIZES OF DIE-POINTS FOR LIGHT WORK

The data on the size of die-points in Fig. 242 are given on the authority of Lucien Haas, and may be considered good

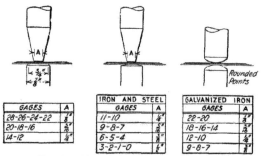

Fig. 242.—Sizes of Die Points for Light Work.

GAGES	A
28-26-24-22	3/16"
20-18-16	3/16"
14-12	1/4"

IRON AND STEEL	
GAGES	A
11-10	1/4"
9-8-7	5/16"
6-5-4	3/8"
3-2-1-0	1/2"

GALVANIZED IRON	
GAGES	A
22-20	1/4"
18-16-14	3/16"
12-10	1/4"
9-8-7	3/8"

general practice. These points are intended for welding two pieces of the same gage and material.

On certain kinds of heavy spot-welding work circular metal disks are placed between the plates in order to localize the current and to provide good contact. In other cases, projections are made in one or both of the plates. These latter, of course, necessitate a mechanical or press operation, previous

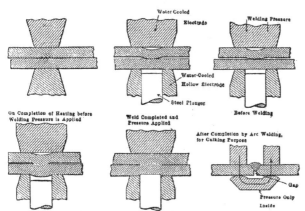

FIG. 243.—The Tit or Projection Method of Welding.

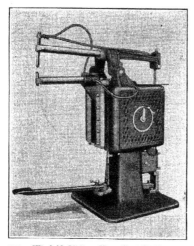

FIG. 244.—Winfield Sliding Horn Spot-Welding Machine.

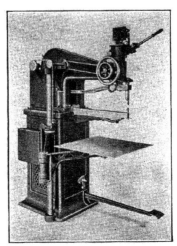

FIG. 245.—Winfield Heavy-Duty Machine with Adjustable Table.

FIG. 246.—Winfield Portable Spot-Welding Machine.

to welding. Heavy plate work is shown in Fig. 243. At the upper left are shown plates as commonly arranged for welding. Next to this is a plate with a projection under the upper die-

FIG. 247.—Winfield Portable Machine with Swivel Head.

point. A steel plunger is used in the lower die to give the needed pressure after the metal is heated. This saves crushing or distorting the soft copper. In the lower right-hand corner

FIG. 248.—Small Winfield Bench Machine.

FIG. 249.—Winfield Machine with Suspended Head for Welding
Automobile Bodies.

is shown a ridge or tit weld, after the seam has been arc-welded.

The Winfield Machines.—The machines made by the Winfield Electric Welding Machine Co., Warren, Ohio, comprise a varied line for every conceivable spot-welding purpose. In general, Figs. 244 and 245 may be taken as typical of their

Fig. 250.—Convenient Setting of Machine for Sheet Metal Work.

light and heavy spot-welding machines. Fig. 246 shows a very convenient form of portable machine. In Fig. 247 is shown a much heavier portable machine with swiveling head, and in Fig. 248 is a small bench machine that is exceedingly useful for light work.

A very interesting machine is shown in Fig. 249. This has the entire head suspended from the ceiling, so that work, like the automobile body shown, may be worked under it.

FIG. 251.—Federal Welding Machine with Universal Points.

This machine is in use in the plant of the Herbert Manufacturing Co., Detroit.

A good way to place a machine for some work is shown in Fig. 250. This is employed in the shop of the Terrell

Equipment Co., Grand Rapids, Mich., in the manufacture of steel lockers, steel furniture and the like.

Federal Welding Machines.—A feature of the spot-welding machines made by the Federal Machine and Welder Co., Warren, Ohio, are the "universal" welding points used on most of their output. The principle will be instantly grasped by

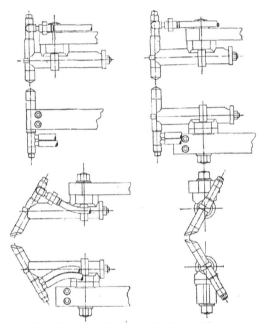

Fig. 252.—A Few Positions of the Universal Points.

referring to Fig. 251. Some of the different positions possible are shown in Fig. 252.

Another feature of these machines, is the use of the type of water-cooled points shown in Fig. 253. The welding point is copper and it is attached to the holder in such a way that the water flows within half an inch of the actual welding contact.

In general form, size and capacities, the Federal line does not differ materially from the machines already shown.

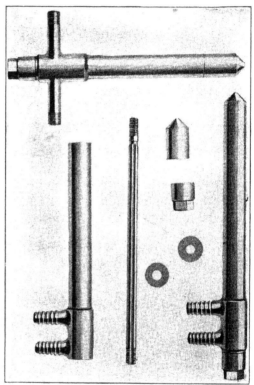

FIG. 253.—Federal Water-Cooled Points.

FEDERAL ROTATABLE HEAD TWO-SPOT WELDING MACHINE

The rotatable head two-spot, air operated welding machine, shown in Fig. 254, a 60-in. throat depth and is guaranteed to weld from two thicknesses of 24-gage up to two thicknesses of 8-gage steel stock. Twelve welds per minute may be made in the latter size.

The machine is built with a 4 kva. welding transformer in the upper and lower rotating heads. Primaries are in parallel while the secondaries are in series, so that two spot welds must be made at the same time.

The welding electrodes or points are $1\frac{1}{2}$ in. in diameter, are carried in water-cooled holders, and are so arranged that

Fig. 254.—Federal Rotatable Head Two-spot Welding Machine.

welds from 3 to 8 in. apart may be made. The ends of each set of welding points can be separated a maximum of 5 in. The heads can be rotated through an angle of 90 deg. to permit welding at different angles on the stock being handled.

Four air cylinders are used, each operating an independent point. The air control is hand operated and so arranged that an initial air line supply pressure of 80 lb. will give from 300 to 700 lb. pressure between the points during the heating period. A second step on the air control makes it possible to apply 1,200 lb. pressure between the points for the final squeeze. The air is exhausted into the reverse side of the cylinders to withdraw the points. The regulating transformer supplies power to the welding transformer in eight voltage steps.

FEDERAL AUTOMATIC SPOT-WELDER FOR CHANNELS

The machine shown in Fig. 255 was made for spot-welding two rolled steel channels together to form an I-beam. It is

FIG. 255.—Federal Channel Welding Machine.

capable of welding two spots at a time on two pieces of material ¼ in. thick, at the rate of 60 welds per min. The two welding transformers are for 220 volts primary, and are air cooled. Four copper disks are used for welding contacts. These are securely bolted to bronze shafts to insure good electrical connections. The secondaries of the welding transformers are connected to the brass bearings of these shafts, completing the welding circuit.

The welding current is controlled by auto transformers

in the primary circuit in eight equal steps from 65 per cent to full line voltage.

The welding disks can be adjusted to handle from 4 to 16 in. channels. Simultaneous spot welds from 4 to 12 in. apart may be made. A variable speed motor is used to control the feeding of the work through the machine at from 25 to 60 ft. per min.

AUTOMATIC PULLEY WELDING MACHINE

The machine shown in Fig. 256 was made to weld the ring section of pressed-metal pulleys, known as the filler, to the

Fig. 256.—Automatic Electric Pulley Welder.

rim itself. This ring, or filler, not only acts as a stiffener for the rim, but is the part to which the outer ends of the spokes are attached.

In welding, one-half of a pulley rim is locked by means of a chain-clamping device to a rotating carrier, with the filler and spokes in place as shown. An adjustable mandrel on the carrier insures the proper distance between the center of the pulley and the rim face. Duplicate welding sets operate on each side of the filler, and spot weld intermittently as the work is automatically indexed around.

The mechanical part of the machine is motor driven, and with the work in place, the machine will properly space and weld around the filler until it reaches the end, when it automatically trips. The points are water cooled and will make

FIG. 257.—Taylor Cross-Current Spot-Welding Machine.

about 60 welds per minute. These welding points can be set to weld within $2\frac{1}{2}$ in. of the center of the mandrel or supporting shaft, and have a maximum distance adjustment of 12 in. between them. The automatic indexing or feeding device is so arranged that welds from $\frac{1}{2}$ to 3 in. or more apart may be made. Pulleys from 12 in. up to 5 ft. in diameter may be handled, all the necessary adjustments being easily and quickly made to accommodate the various sizes.

This machine occupies a floor space of about 30×66 in., weighs about 3,500 lb.

The Taylor Welding Machines.—While the machines made by the Taylor Welder Co., Warren, Ohio, differ radically from others on the market, in that they employ double electrodes and cross current, the forms of the machines are about the same as those previously shown. An automatic belt-driven machine of the lighter type, is shown in Fig. 257. It may

FIG. 258.—Taylor Heavy-Duty Machine.

be operated by the foot-treadle also when desired. This machine has a capacity up to two ⅛-in. plates. The horns are water-cooled and the adjustable points are locked in with a wrench as shown. Fig. 258 shows a heavier type of machine. This has a capacity of two ¼-in. plates; overhang is 36 in.; distance between copper bands and lower horn, 6 in.; base, 26×42 in.; extreme height, 72 in.; greatest opening between welding points, 3 in.; weight about 2,400 lb. The transformer is 35 kw. and there is a ten-step self-contained regulator for controlling the current. This firm makes other sizes and styles of machines, to meet all the demands of the trade.

The general principle of the cross-current welding method employed in these machines is illustrated in Fig. 259. Two separate currents are caused to flow in a bias direction through the material to be welded. A high heat concentration is claimed for this method. In operation, the positives of two separate

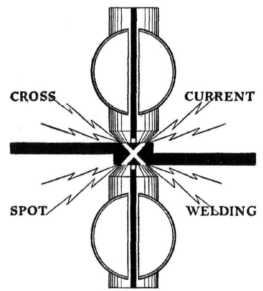

Fig. 259.—Diagram of the Current Action in a Taylor Machine.

welding currents are on one side of the material and the negatives on the other, with the co-working electrodes of each set so that the current travels diagonally across. An advantage claimed is that the electrodes on each side of the material may be set far enough apart to allow of the insertion of some hard material which will take the pressure instead of the softer copper welding points. These hard dies may be operated independently of the copper ones and make it possible to weld heavier material without crushing the copper die points, as these need to be pressed together only enough to give good

FIG. 260.—Automatic Hog-Ring Machine.

FIG. 261.—Partial Rear View of Hog-Ring Machine.

electrical contact with the work. The process is also unique in that it can be operated with a multiphase circuit without unbalancing the lines, which is not the case with any spot-welding machine employing a single current.

Some Special Welding Machines.—An automatic machine for forming and mash-welding 11 gage wire hog rings, at the

FIG. 262.—Close-Up of Front of Hog-Ring Machine.

rate of 60,000 per day, is shown in Fig. 260. This machine takes wire from two reels and turns out the complete hog rings. A partial rear view is shown in Fig. 261. A close-up of the front of the machine, with two hog rings lying on the platen, is given in Fig. 262.

A machine in use in the punch press department of the General Electric Co., Schenectady, N. Y., is shown in Fig. 263. This machine welds small spacers to the iron laminations for motors and generators for ventilating purposes, and hence is

Fig. 263.—General Electric Space-Block Welding Machine.

called a "space-block welder." A number of these machines are in use in this plant, and they are capable of welding 60 spots per minute when working continuously, not allowing for time to shift the stock.

A combination spot- and line-welding machine, used in the

General Electric Co.'s shops, is shown in Fig. 264. This is employed for welding oil switch boxes up to $\frac{1}{8}$ in. thick. As shown, the machine is fitted with a fixture for holding the boxes while line-welding the seams. A separate fixture is put

Fig. 264.—Combination Spot- and Line-Welding Machine, Set Up for Line-Welding Can Seams.

on for spot-welding work. A seam 6 in. long can be line-welded on this machine.

Another combination machine, used in the same shops, is shown in Fig. 265. This machine carries both the spot- and the line-welding fixtures at the same time. Fig. 266 shows the machine from the line-welding side. As shown, the machines are ready for welding straight plates. Machines of this kind should find a considerable field where it is desired to tack seams before line welding them. These machines have

Fig. 265.—A Combination Machine from the Spot-Welding Side.

a capacity of 20 kva., and will weld up to $^3/_{16}$ in. thick, and seams 18 in. long.

Line welding machines, as developed in the Schenectady plant, comprise a transformer with a one turn secondary, through which a heavy current is delivered at low voltage to the material through the medium of a stationary jaw and rolling wheel. Both the jaw and wheel are water-cooled and pressure is applied to the wheel the same as to a spot-welding tip. A small revolving switch mechanically geared to the driving motor and welding wheel operates a set of contactors

FIG. 266.—Machine from the Line-Welding Side.

or solenoid switches to throw the power on once a second, the power being on $\frac{2}{3}$ of a second, and off $\frac{1}{3}$ of a second. The mechanism is synchronized so that during the $\frac{2}{3}$ of a second the power is on, the welding wheel is rolling, and during the remaining $\frac{2}{3}$ of a second the wheel is stationary under pressure while the soft metal is solidifying, thus completing the weld.

Spot-Welding Machines for Ship Work.—During the World War, welding of all kinds took huge steps forward. Spot-welding developed at least as much as any other kind. Writing in the *General Electrical Review*, J. M. Weed says:

The machines to be described are two portable welders, one with 12-in. reach and the other with 27-in. reach, for use in the fabrication of structural ship parts, and one stationary machine with 6-ft. reach designed for welding two spots at the same time on large ship plates.

A preliminary survey of the structural work in shipbuilding indicated that about 80 per cent of this work could be done by a machine of 12-in. reach, and that a 27-in. reach would include the other 20 per cent. Since both the weight of the machine and the kva. required for its operation are about 33 per cent greater for the 27-in. reach than for the 12-in., it seemed advisable to develop two machines rather than one with the longer reach.

These machines were to a certain obvious extent patterned after the riveting machines, which they were intended to replace as will be seen from Fig. 267. They are necessarily considerably heavier than the riveting machines, but like these they are provided with bales for crane suspension, for the purpose of carrying the machines around the assembled work or parts to be welded.

The maximum welding current available in these machines, with a steel plate enclosed to the full depth of the gap, is about 37,500 amperes, with the maximum applied voltage of 534 volts at 60 cycles. Reduced voltages, giving smaller currents, are obtained in six equal steps, ranging from 534 down to 267 volts, from the taps of the regulating transformers furnished with the machines.

This wide range of voltage and current was provided in order to meet the possible requirements for a considerable range in thickness of work, and for experimental purposes. Tests have shown, however, that the machines will operate satisfactorily on work of thicknesses over the range on which they are likely to be used when connected directly on a 440-volt, 60-cycle circuit, with no regulating transformers. Two plates $\frac{1}{4}$-in. thick are welded together in spots from 1 in. to $1\frac{1}{4}$ in. in diameter, in from 12 to 15 seconds. Thicker plates require more time and thinner plates less time.

The welding current under these conditions is about 31,000 amp.; the primary current is about 600 amp. for the 12-in. machine and about 800 amp. for the 27-in. machine, the corresponding kva. at 440 volts, being 265 and 350 respectively.

Since the reactance of the welding circuit is large as compared with the resistance, the voltage necessary for a given current, and consequently the kva. necessary for the operation of the machine, is almost proportional to the frequency. Thus, these machines operate satisfactorily from a 25-cycle circuit at 220 volts, with the advantage that where the power-factor is from 30 to 40 per cent at 60 cycles, it is from 60 to 75 per cent at 25 cycles, and the kva. required at 25 cycles is about one-half that required at 60 cycles.

The maximum mechanical pressure on the work for which those machines are designed is 25,000 lb. This is obtained from an 8-in. air cylinder, with an air pressure of 100 lb. per square inch, acting through a lever arm of 5 to 1 ratio. Lower pressures on the work are obtained with

FIG. 267.—Portable Spot-Welding Machine with 27-in. Throat Depth. Capable of Welding Two Plates ⅜ In. Thick in Spots 1 In. in Diameter. Made by the General Electric Co.

correspondingly reduced air pressures. A pressure-reducing valve is provided for this purpose, and also a pressure gage for indicating the pressure on the machine side of the valve.

The pressure required to do satisfactory welding depends upon the thickness of the plates. It is necessary that the areas to be welded should at the start be brought into more intimate contact than the surrounding areas, in order that the current may be properly localized, and the heat generated in the region where it is needed. It is therefore necessary, on account of irregularities in the plate surface, that the pressure should be great enough to spring the cold plate sufficiently to overcome the irregularities. The pressure which will do this with heavy plates is ample for effecting the weld after the welding temperature is reached.

It should be explained in this connection that the rate of heating at the surfaces to be welded depends largely upon the contact resistance, and consequently upon the condition of the plates and the pressure used. If the plates are clean and bright, and the pressure high, the rate of heating with a given amount of current is slow and the welding efficiency is poor. This makes it difficult to weld heavy plates if they are clean, since, as stated above, it is necessary to use large pressure with heavy plates to insure a better contact of the areas to be welded than that of surrounding areas. It is much easier to weld plates which carry the original coat of mill scale, or a fairly heavy coating of rust or dirt, affording a considerable resistance which is not sensitive to pressure. If this necessary resistance is too great, the necessary current will not flow, of course, but if the scale is not too heavy it has little effect upon the current, the high reactance of the welding circuit giving it practically a constant current characteristic and making the rate of heating proportional to the resistance within certain limits. The scale melts at about the welding temperature of the steel, and is squeezed out by the high pressures used, permitting the clean surfaces of the steel to come together and effect a good weld.

A gage pressure of about 70 lb., giving 17,500 lb. pressure upon the work, has been found to give good results under these conditions in $\frac{1}{2}$-in. plates.

Both the mechanical pressure and the current are transmitted to the work in these machines through heavy copper blocks or welding electrodes. The shape of the tips of these electrodes is that of a very flat truncated cone.

The severity of the conditions to which the tips of the electrodes are subjected will be understood when it is considered that the current density in the electrode material at this point is approximately 60,000 amp. per square inch, and that this material is in contact with the steel plates which are brought to the welding temperature, under pressures of 15,000 to 20,000 lb. per square inch. It must be remembered, also, that copper, which is the best material available for this purpose, softens at a temperature considerably lower than the welding temperature of steel. The difficulty of making the electrode tips stand up under the conditions to which they are subjected has, in fact, constituted the most serious problem which has been met in the development of these machines.

The shape of these electrodes gives them every possible advantage in freely conducting the current to and the heat away from the electrode tips, and in giving them the mechanical reinforcement of the cooler surrounding material. However, it has been found necessary to reduce, as far as possible, the heat generated at the tips of the electrodes by cleaning the rust and mill scale from the surfaces of the plates beneath the electrodes. The most convenient way which has been found for doing this is by means of a sand blast. The bodies of the electrodes are also internally water-cooled by a stream of water flowing continually through them. Still, after all of these things have been done, a gradual deformation of the tip of the electrode will occur, increasing its area of contact with the work, and thus reducing the current density in the work and the pressure density below the values needed for welding. This would make it necessary to change electrodes and to reshape the tips very frequently, and the total life of the electrodes would be short on account of the frequent dressings.

An effort has been made to overcome this difficulty by protecting the tip of the electrode by a thin copper cap, which may be quickly and cheaply replaced. As many as 160 welds have been made with a single copper cap, $1/16$ in. thick, before it became necessary to replace it. Unfortunately this does not entirely prevent the deformation of the electrode tip, but it stands up much better than it does without the cap.

Another method which has been tried for overcoming this trouble is by making the tip portion of the electrode removable, in the form of a disk or button, held in place by a clamp engaging in a neck or groove on the electrode body. While this protects the electrode body from deformation and wear, the tip itself does not stand up so well as does the combination of electrode and cap, where the tip of the electrode is not separated from the body.

Some electrodes have been prepared which combine the features of the removable tip and cap. These give the advantage of a permanent electrode body, and the removable tip with the protecting cap stand up better than the unprotected tip.

Some interesting features were introduced in the design of the transformers which are integral parts of these machines, owing to the necessity for small size and weight. Internal water cooling was adopted for the windings, which makes it possible to use current densities very much higher than those found in ordinary power transformers. The conductor for the primary windings is $\frac{3}{8}$-in. $\times \frac{1}{2}$-in. copper tubing, which was obtained in standard lengths and annealed before winding by passing it through an oven which is used for annealing sheathed wire during the process of drawing. No difficulty was found in winding this tubing directly on the insulated core, the joints between lengths being made by brazing with silver solder. The entire winding consists of four layers of thirteen turns each in the 12-in. machine and three layers of thirteen turns each in the 27-in. machine.

The U-shaped single-turn secondaries were slipped over the outside of the primary windings in the assembly of the transformers. These were constructed of two copper plates each $\frac{3}{8}$ in. thick and $6\frac{3}{8}$ in. wide, which were bent to the proper shape in the blacksmith shop, and assembled one inside the other with a $\frac{1}{4}$-in. space between them. Narrow strips of copper were inserted between the plates along the edges, and the plates were brazed to these strips, thus making a water-tight chamber or passage for the circulation of the cooling water.

At 31,000 amp. the current density in these secondaries is about 6,200 amp. per square inch, the corresponding densities in the primary windings being about 7,000 for the 12-in. and 9,000 for the 27-in. machine.

In case these machines are started up without the cooling water having been turned on, the temperature rise in these windings will be rapid, and in order to avoid the danger of burning the insulation, asbestos and mica have been used. The copper tubing was taped with asbestos tape, and alternate layers of sheet asbestos and mica pads were used between layers of the primary winding, and between primary and secondary and between primary and core. Space blocks of asbestos lumber, which is a compound of asbestos and Portland cement, were used at the ends of the core and at the ends of the winding layers. The complete transformer, after assembly, was impregnated with bakelite. The result is a solid mechanical unit which will not be injured by temperatures not exceeding 150 deg. C. Several welds could be made without turning on the cooling water before this temperature would be reached.

The transformers are mounted on a chamber in the body of the frame. The long end of the U-shaped secondary runs out along the arm of the frame and bolts directly to the copper base upon which the bottom electrode is mounted. The short end connects to the base of the top electrode through flexible leads of laminated copper, to permit of necessary motion for engaging the work.

The copper bases upon which the electrodes are mounted are insulated from the frame by a layer of mica, the bolts which hold them in place being also insulated by mica.

The cooling water for these machines is divided into two parallel paths, one being through the primary winding, and the other through the secondary and the electrodes in series. Separate valves are supplied for independent adjustment of the flow in the two paths. The resistance of ordinary hydrant water is sufficiently great as to cause no concern regarding the grounding or short-circuiting of the windings through the cooling water, although it is necessary to use rubber tubing or hose for leading it in and out.

Some pieces of $\frac{1}{4} \times 2$-in. machine steel were welded in seven seconds with a current of 33,000 amp. They were afterward clamped in a vise and hammered into U-shapes. Small pieces were sheared from the seam where two $\frac{1}{4}$-in. plates had been welded together in a row of spots. The pieces of the plates were then split apart with a cold chisel in one case, and an effort was made to do so in the other, with the result that one piece of plate broke at the welds before the welds would themselves break. Such tests as these show that the welds are at least as strong as the material on which the welds were made. Some samples of the $\frac{1}{4} \times 2$-in. stock welded together in the same manner were tested by bending in an edgewise direction, thus subjecting the welds to a shearing torque. The ultimate strength calculated from these tests was in the neighborhood of 65,000 lb. per square inch. These tests showed also a very tough weld, the deflection being almost 45 deg. in some cases before the final rupture occurred. The maximum load occurred with a deflection of from 3 to 5 deg. with a very gradual reduction in the load from this time till the final rupture.

The Duplex Welding Machine.—The machine shown in Fig. 268 was developed for the application of electric welding as a substitute for riveting on parts of the ship composed of large-sized plates, which may be fabricated before they are assembled in the ship. The specification to which it was built stated that it should have a 6-ft. reach and should be capable of welding together two plates ¾ in. thick in two spots at the same time. A machine capable of doing this work, with a 6-ft. gap, is necessarily

FIG. 268.—Duplex Spot-Welding Machine. Made by the General Electric Co. 6-ft. Throat Depth, and Capable of Welding Together Two Steel Plates ¾ In. Thick, in Two Spots 1¼ In. in Diameter.

so heavy as to preclude even semi-portability, and no effort was made in this direction.

With the welding circuit enclosing a 6-ft. gap, and carrying the very heavy current necessary to weld ¾-in. plates, the kva. required would be very large. A great reduction in the kva. and at the same time a doubling of the work done, is obtained in this machine by the use of two transformers as integral parts of the machine, and two pairs of electrodes, thus providing for the welding of two spots at the same time. The transformers are mounted in the frame of the machine, on opposite sides of the work, and as near to the welding electrodes as possible, so as to obtain the minimum reactance in the welding circuit. The polarity of the electrodes on one side of the work is the reverse of that of the opposed electrodes, thus giving a series arrangement of the transformer secondaries, the current from each transformer flowing through both of the spots to be welded.

The bottom electrodes are stationary, and the copper bases which bear them are connected rigidly to the terminals of their transformer, while the bases which carry the top electrodes are connected through flexible leads of laminated copper, to permit of the motion necessary for engaging the work.

Previous tests with an experimental machine had shown that, to successfully weld two spots at the same time in the manner adopted here, it is necessary that the pressures shall be independently applied. Otherwise, due to inequalities in the thickness of the work, or in the wear and tear of the electrodes, the pressure may be much greater on one of the spots than on the other. This results in unequal heating in the two spots. The resistance and its heating effect are less in the spot with the greater pressure. The two top electrodes in this machine were therefore mounted on separate plungers, operated by separate pistons through independent levers.

The pressures obtained in this machine with an air pressure of 100 lb. per square inch, are 30,000 lb. on each spot, giving a total pressure of 60,000 lb. which must be exerted by the frame around the 6-ft. gap. The necessary strength is obtained by constructing the frame of two steel plates, each 2 in. thick, properly spaced and rigidly bolted together.

The use of steel in this case is easily permissible on account of the restricted area of the welding circuit and its relative position, resulting in small tendency for magnetic flux to enter the frame. However, the heads carrying the electrodes, being in close proximity to the welding circuit, were made of gun metal.

The two air cylinders are mounted on a cast-iron bed-plate in the back part of the machine. The levers connecting the pistons to the electrode plungers, which are 7 ft. in length, were made of cast steel, in order to obtain the necessary strength.

The maximum welding current for which this machine was designed is 50,000 amp. This current is obtained with 500 volts at 60 cycles applied.

The distance between the electrode bodies for this machine is fixed at 8 in., center to center, but the distances between the centers of the tips may be easily varied from 6 in. to 10 in. by shifting the tip from the center of the body toward one side or the other.

Provision has been made for shifting the electrodes on their bases to positions 90 deg. from those shown in the picture, thus spacing the welds in a direction along the axis of the machine instead of traverse to it.

The transformers are insulated and cooled in the same manner as those in the semi-portable machines. The windings are interlaced in order to obtain minimum reactance, the primary being wound in two layers of 14 turns each, one inside and the other outside of the single turn secondary.

With 50,000 amp. in the secondaries of these transformers, the current in the primary is 1,800. The respective current densities are 7,000 and 9,000 amp. per square inch. The kva. entering the transformers on this basis, the two primaries being in series on 500 volts, is 450 for each transformer.

This machine also has been provided with a regulating transformer for applying different voltages to give different values of welding current,

Fig. 269.—General Electric Co.'s Experimental Spot-Welding Machine. Current Capacity 100,000 Amp. Pressure Capacity 36 Tons. Has Welded Three Plates, Each 1 In. Thick.

and with a panel carrying the necessary selector switches and contactor. The maximum voltage provided by this regulating transformer as at present constructed is 440. If it is found that the current obtained with this voltage is not sufficient for the heaviest work which it is desired to do with this machine, the maximum voltage may be changed to 500.

The kva. entering the transformers of 440 volts will be approximately 350 each, instead of 450.

In order that this machine may be operated from any ordinary power circuit, it will be necessary to use a motor-generator set provided with a suitable flywheel. This will eliminate the bad power-factor, distribute the load equally on the three phases, and over a much larger interval of time for each weld, thus substituting small gradual changes in power for large and sudden changes. On account of the high reactance the welding current will remain practically constant as the speed of the motor-generator set falls away, thus favoring the utilization of the flywheel. The total maximum power drawn from the circuit with this arrangement would be about 100 kilowatts.

FIG. 270.—Portable Machine for Mash-Welding Square or Round Rods.

A Heavy Experimental Spot-Welding Machine. — The machine shown in Fig. 269 was built in 1918 by the General Electric Co., in order to investigate the possibilities of welding plates from $\frac{1}{4}$ in. up. Three plates each 1 in. thick have been welded with it. The machine is provided with a 2,000-kva. transformer, having a capacity of 100,000 amp. at 20 volts. Hydraulic pressures up to 36 tons are obtained at the electrodes. Motor-generator sets of 500- and 6,000-kva. capacity

were used. From the nature of the service, it was apparent
that some form of cooling was needed at the contact points.
It was found, however, that it was impossible to water-cool
the points sufficiently to give a reasonable life to the electrodes
if they were kept the same diameter for any distance from
the work. In consequence heavy masses of copper were placed

FIG. 271.—Lorain Machine for Spot-Welding Electric Rail Bonds.

as close to the points of contact as practicable. By doing this
it was possible to have a very large cooling surface at the
top of the electrode and by passing water through this part
at the time of welding and between welds, the joints were kept
cool enough for all practical purposes.

A portable machine for making mash-welds for splicing or
attaching round or square rods cross-wise, is shown in Fig.

270. This was made by the General Electric Co., for ship-yard use.

A big machine for spot-welding electric railway bonds, is shown in Fig. 271. This is made by the Lorain Steel Co., Johnstown, Pa. It will weld two plates 18 in. long and 3 in. wide by 1 in. thick, each plate having three raised "welding bosses." Pressure as high as 35 tons is obtainable and current up to 25,000 amp. may be used.

Spot-Welding Data.—It is difficult to give definite costs for spot welding, as much depends on the operator. A careless or inexperienced operator will waste more current than a good one, and various conditions of the metal being worked on will make a considerable difference at times. However, the information given in Table XXIII, which is furnished by the Winfield Electric Welding Machine Co., will prove of value as a basis for calculations. Tables XXIV and XXV will also be useful to use in connection with the measurement of the thickness of sheets, and in comparing different gages.

TABLE XXIII.—SPOT-WELDING POWER AND COST DATA

Gauge Number	Thickness of Sheets in Fractions of an Inch	Thickness of Sheets in Decimals of an Inch	K. W. Required	H. P. Required	Time in Seconds to Make a Weld	Cost 1000 Welds at one Cent per K. W. Hour
30	$1/80$	.0125	3.0	4.2	.25	.002
28	$1/64$	.0156	4.0	5.6	.3	.003
24	$1/40$	.0250	5.0	7.0	.45	.006
20	$3/80$	.0375	6.5	9.2	.6	.011
18	$1/20$	.0500	8.0	11.3	.8	.017
16	$1/16$	.0626	9.5	13.5	1.0	.026
14	$5/64$	.0781	10.0	14.2	1.3	.036
12	$7/64$	.1093	12.0	17.0	1.6	.052
11	$1/8$	.1250	13.0	18.5	1.7	.061
10	$9/64$	.1406	14.0	19.9	1.8	.070
9	$5/32$	.1562	15.0	21.3	1.9	.079
8	$11/64$	.1715	16.0	22.7	2.0	.088
7	$3/16$	.1875	17.0	24.1	2.1	.099
6	$13/64$	.2031	18.0	25.6	2.2	.110
5	$7/32$	.2187	19.0	27.0	2.4	.124
4	$15/64$	.2343	20.0	28.4	2.7	.148
3	$1/4$	.2500	21.0	29.8	3.0	.174

As the cost of current varies in different places, we have figured the current at one cent per K. W. hour to give a basis for calculating the cost. Multiply the cost of current given above by the rate per K. W. hour you pay and you will have your cost per 1000 welds for current.

TABLE XXIV.—THICKNESS AND WEIGHT OF SHEET IRON AND STEEL, U. S. STANDARD.

Number of Gauge	Approximate Thickness in Fractions of an Inch	Approximate Thickness in Decimal Parts of an Inch	Weight per Sq. Foot Iron	Number of Gauge	Approximate Thickness in Fractions of an Inch	Approximate Thickness in Decimal Parts of an Inch	Weight per Sq. Foot Iron
30	1-80	.0125	.5	13	3-32	.09375	3.75
29	9-640	.0140625	.5625	12	7-64	.109375	4.375
28	1-64	.015625	.625	11	1-8	.125	5.
27	11-640	.0171875	.6875	10	9-64	.140625	5.625
26	3-160	.01875	.75	9	5-32	.15625	6.25
25	7-320	.021875	.875	8	11-64	.171875	6.875
24	1-40	.025	1.	7	3-16	.1875	7.5
23	9-320	.028125	1.125	6	13-64	.203125	8.125
22	1-32	.03125	1.25	5	7-32	.21875	8.75
21	11-320	.034375	1.375	4	15-64	.234375	9.375
20	3-80	.0375	1.50	3	1-4	.25	10.
19	7-160	.04375	1.75	2	17-64	.265625	10.625
18	1-20	.05	2.	1	9-32	.28125	11.25
17	9-160	.05625	2.25	0	5-16	.3125	12.50
16	1-16	.0625	2.5	00	11-32	.34375	13.75
15	9-128	.0703125	2.8125	000	3-8	.375	15.
14	5-64	.078125	3.125				

TABLE XXV.—DECIMAL EQUIVALENTS OF AN INCH FOR MILLIMETERS, B. & S. AND BIRMINGHAM WIRE GAGES

Decimal Inch	Mill.	Fra. In.	B&S	Birm Gge.
.00394	.1			
.00787	.2			
.010025			30	
.011257			29	
.01181	.3			
.012				30
.012641			28	
.013				29
.014				28
.014195			27	
.015625		1/64		
.01575	.4			
.01594			26	
.016				27
.0179			25	
.018				26
.01968	.5			
.02				25
.0201			24	
.022				24
.022571			23	
.02362	.6			
.025				23
.025347			22	
.02756	.7			
.028				22
.02846			21	
.03125		1/32		
.03149	.8			
.03196			20	
.032				21
.035				20
.03543	.9			
.03589			19	
.03937	1.0			
.04030			18	
.042				19
.0433	1.1			
.04525			17	
.46875		3/64		
.04724	1.2			
.049				18
.05082			16	
.05118	1.3			
.05512	1.4			
.05766			15	
.058				17
.05905	1.5			
.0625		1/16		
.06299	1.6			
.06408			14	
.065				16
.06692	1.7			
.07086	1.8			
.07196			13	
.072				15
.0748	1.9			
.078125		5/64		
.07874	2.0			
.080801			12	
.08267	2.1			
.083				14
.08661	2.2			
.09055	2.3			
.09074			11	
.09375		3/32		
.09448	2.4			
.095				13
.09842	2.5			
.10189			10	
.10236	2.6			
.10629	2.7			
.109				12
.109375		7/64		
.11023	2.8			
.11417	2.9			
.11443			9	
.11811	3.0			
.12				11
.12204	3.1			
.125		1/8		
.12598	3.2			
.12849			8	
.12992	3.3			
.13385	3.4			
.134				10
.13779	3.5			
.140625		9/64		
.14173	3.6			
.14428			7	
.14566	3.7			
.148				9
.14960	3.8			
.15354	3.9			
.15625		5/32		
.15748	4.0			
.16141	4.1			
.16202			6	
.165				8
.16535	4.2			
.16929	4.3			
.171875		11/64		
.17322	4.4			
.17716	4.5			
.180				7
.1811	4.6			
.18194			5	
.18503	4.7			
.1875		3/16		
.18897	4.8			
.19291	4.9			
.19685	5.0			
.20078	5.1			
.203				6
.203125		13/64		
.20431			4	
.20472	5.2			
.20866	5.3			
.21259	5.4			
.21653	5.5			
.21875		7/32		
.22				5
.22047	5.6			
.2241	5.7			
.22834	5.8			
.22942			3	
.23228	5.9			
.234375		15/64		
.23622	6.0			
.238				4
.24015	6.1			
.24409	6.2			
.24803	6.3			
.25		1/4		
.25196	6.4			
.2559	6.5			
.25763			2	
.259				3
.25984	6.6			
.26377	6.7			
.265625		17/64		
.26771	6.8			
.27165	6.9			
.27559	7.0			
.27952	7.1			
.28125		9/32		
.28346	7.2			
.284				2
.2874	7.3			
.2893			1	
.29133	7.4			
.29527	7.5			
.296875		19/64		
.29921	7.6			
.3				1
.30314	7.7			
.30708	7.8			
.31102	7.9			
.3125		5/16		
.31496	8.0			
.31889	8.1			
.32283	8.2			
.32495			0	
.32677	8.3			
.328125		21/64		
.3307	8.4			
.33464	8.5			
.33858	8.6			
.34				0
.34251	8.7			
.34375		11/32		
.34645	8.8			
.35039	8.9			
.35433	9.0			
.35826	9.1			
.350375		23/64		
.36220	9.2			
.3648			00	
.36614	9.3			
.37007	9.4			
.37401	9.5			
.375		3/8		
.37795	9.6			
.38				00
.38188	9.7			
.38582	9.8			
.38976	9.9			
.390625		25/64		
.3937	10.0			
.39763	10.1			
.40157	10.2			
.40551	10.3			
.40625		13/32		
.40499	10.4			
.4096			000	
.41338	10.5			
.41732	10.6			
.42125	10.7			
.421875		27/64		
.425				000
.42519	10.8			
.42913	10.9			
.43307	11.0			
.437	11.1			
.4375		7/16		
.44094	11.2			
.44488	11.3			
.44581	11.4			
.45275	11.5			
.453125		29/64		
.454				0000
.45669	11.6			
.46			0000	
.46062	11.7			
.46456	11.8			
.4685	11.9			
.46875		15/32		
.47244	12.0			
.47637	12.1			
.48031	12.2			
.48425	12.3			
.484375		31/64		
.48818	12.4			
.49212	12.5			
.49606	12.6			
.49999	12.7			
.5		1/2		
.50393	12.8			

CHAPTER XIV

WELDING BOILER TUBES BY THE ELECTRIC RESISTANCE PROCESS

About 1912 the resistance, or Thomson, process of electric welding was first tried out in a locomotive shop for the purpose of replacing the oil-furnace welding equipment in safe-ending boiler tubes up to 2½ in. in diameter, says P. T. Van Bibber, in the *American Machinist*. At the present time, in shops in different parts of the country where electric welding machines have been installed, one will find many enthusiastic "boosters" for this process. It is to these users that we are indebted for the information contained in this article and for the benefit of those who are unfamiliar with this adaptation of resistance welding, an endeavor has been made to cover all the details possible.

In using the resistance type of machine for welding safe-ends onto locomotive-boiler flues, the old tube and the new safe-end are gripped securely in heavy copper jaws with the ends to be joined held in alignment. As these ends are pressed together a large volume of current from the secondary winding of the transformer is passed through them. Since the junction of the abutting ends is the point of greatest resistance to the electric current, the greatest heating effect is there and, usually, on a 2½-in. tube it requires only about 15 sec. to secure a perfect running or welding heat. A slight push-up by the pressure device on the welding machine sticks the two parts together solidly enough so that the tube can be removed to the mandrel of a rolling machine, exactly as is done when welding by the oil-furnace method, and the weld is then completed in a few seconds by rolling down the joint.

Since it is always necessary to scarf the ends of a tube and new safe-end before welding by the oil-furnace method, the first question that the practical boiler-shop man

324

will ask is, How much preparation is needed for electric resistance welding? The first step in any method is to clear the
tube from heavy scale, if in use under bad water conditions,
by rolling in a large tumbling barrel. After this, the tubes
are cut to the desired length to remove the old end that is
to be replaced by the new section.

In some shops it is the practice to never allow more than
one or two welds in a tube, which means that after removing
the second time, the tube must be used in a shorter boiler than
before. This procedure is carried out until the tube can only

Fig. 272.—Machine for Cutting Off Flues.

be used for small switching locomotives—if it lasts that long
—after which it is scrapped. By this method, only one length
of tube is bought new, which is that required for the longest
boilers.

In other shops the writer found tubes with many welds,
showing that the safe-ending was continued in order to maintain the same length each time until the tube was worn out,
when it was replaced by a new one of the required length.
This latter method necessitates buying several lengths new
but in localities where the water is not very hard on tubes,
it prevents a tube from going to the scrap pile as long as there

is any good in it. After cutting off the old tubes, as shown in Fig. 272, which represents a common type of machine for this purpose, the tubes are next scarfed, or cut off square, according to which method of welding is to be employed.

If a scarf weld is to be used, the old tube is generally

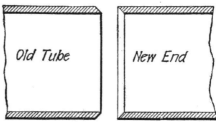

FIG. 273.—Ends Prepared for Scarf-Weld.

FIG. 274.—Bolt Threading Machine Made Into a Scarfing Machine.

beveled on the outside at an angle of from 45 to 60 deg., according to the length of scarf desired, about as shown in Fig. 273. The bevel is wholly a matter of personal opinion for just as good welds can be made with a 30-deg. scarf as when one of 60 deg. is used.

One type of machine used for scarfing is shown in Fig. 274. This has been rigged up from an old bolt-threading machine. The jaws shown at the left are for gripping the old tube which is then fed into a revolving chuck by means of the handwheel. This chuck contains the necessary cutters for forming the desired bevel on the outside of the tube end. The jaws on the right-hand side of the same machine grip the new short ends as they are fed onto a revolving tapered reamer, which cuts a scarf from the inside. In some shops, the scarfing is done on an old lathe with special fixtures, but the remodeled bolt-threading machine seems to offer the most efficient proposition for, with this type of machine, it is possible for one man to scarf over 60 tubes and ends per hour.

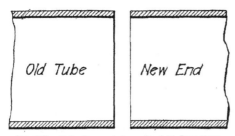

FIG. 275.—Ends Prepared for a Straight Butt-Weld.

If a straight butt-weld is to be made instead of scarfing the ends to be joined, they are cut off squarely, as shown in Fig. 275. This is done in an old pipe-threading machine, or a lathe, so that when placed in the welding machine, the abutting ends will be in contact practically all the way around their circumference. Although this last method of preparing work may sound shorter than scarfing, nevertheless, from actual observation of both methods in different shops, the former is faster by nearly two to one.

After preparing the ends for welding, if the tubes have not already been tumbled to remove all scale, which usually leaves the outside surface quite bright and clean, it is necessary to grind the surface of both old tube and new ends back to a distance of about 8 in. in order to secure a good electrical contact between the tube metal and the copper jaws of the welding machine.

There are three distinct methods of welding boiler tubes, which are called butt-, scarf- and flash-welding, the latter producing the same effect as a scarfed joint when completed. In the straight butt-weld, the ends to be joined are first brought firmly together by means of the pressure device on the welding machine, and the current is then turned on There is always some point around the circumference of the tube which starts to heat first, due to the impossibility of making the two ends to abut with the same pressure at all points of their contacting surfaces. However, the heat will gradually become uniform all around the circumference before the welding temperature is reached. The current is maintained through the tubes until the joint reaches a good running heat, as evidenced by a "greasy" appearance of the surface, when the pressure is applied sufficiently to push up the hot metal about $\frac{1}{4}$ in. which partly completes the weld. The jaws are then released and the tube is immediately thrust onto the mandrel of the rolling apparatus, which is described further on, and the bulge at the joint, caused by the pushing up of the hot metal, is rolled down until the joint is of the same diameter as the original tube.

This rolling-down operation, in addition to reducing this bulge of the tube, also forces a complete union of the plastic metal of the two pieces, thereby completing the weld. From this it may be seen that in welding boiler tubes, the welding machine is only used for a heating device to supplant the oil furnace, requiring only sufficient pressure to stick the ends together to hold it while removing work to the rolling machine where the welding is finished.

In the scarf weld, the beveled end of the old tube is pushed into the chamfered end of the new piece and the current then turned on the same as in making the butt-weld just described. Due to the "feather" edge of the short new piece, it is often necessary to apply the current intermittently until the joint is well heated all around the circumference; otherwise points of the sharp edge, which come in contact first with the opposite member, will be burned off before the heat is evenly distributed around the tube. Owing to the expanding effect of the scarfed ends, it is not necessary to apply so much pressure as with the butt-weld when the metal is plastic in order to stick the pieces together before rolling down.

With either of the above welds, it is necessary to give the old tube more projection beyond the copper clamping jaws than is given the new short piece. This is because the wall thickness of the old tube has been slightly reduced by wearing away in service and if the two parts were given the same projection, the end of old tube would heat much more rapidly than that of the new piece since its resistance to the electric current would be greater, owing to the reduced sectional area. It is always necessary for the heat to form uniformly in each

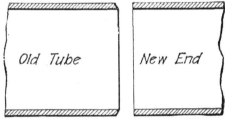

Fig. 276.—Ends Prepared for a Flash-Weld.

of the abutting ends or one will burn away before the other reaches the plastic stage.

In making a flash-weld, not so much preparation is required as for the two other methods just described; hence it is a much cheaper job and yet, from all tests made so far, it is the only type of joint which is always 100 per cent perfect when considering the number of defective welds in any lot of tubes. The old tube is cut off the right length in a machine, which has a cutting wheel so beveled as to give an angle of 30 deg. from the vertical on the end of the tube, as shown in Fig. 276. The new ends are bought direct from the tube manufacturers with both ends cut square and the surface cleaned well so that there is no preparation needed on the new pieces. After cutting off the old tube it is only necessary to grind it on the outside about 8 in. back from the end to insure good electrical contact. The old tube is placed in the clamps with about 4 in. of projection and the new end with about 3 in. The current is turned on first and the pressure is then applied very slowly and steadily to bring the abutting ends into contact. As soon as they meet, a small arc or "flash" is formed which commences to burn away the points of metal coming into contact first. This flashing is continued until the abutting ends are arcing all the way around the circumference and by this time the sharp edge of the old tube, although somewhat burned away itself, has burned its way into the square-cut end of the new piece. A sudden application of more pressure stops the flashing and the joint then quickly attains the running or welding heat as in the butt- or scarf-welding method. The ends are now shoved together and as the current is turned off, the end of the old tube will have forced itself into the end of the new piece sufficiently to form a scarf-weld when rolled down in the rolling machine.

Using a Flux.—From statements made by every operator interviewed, the use of flux does not help the welding in any way; yet it is used in each shop because it clears up the surface of the metal when the plastic stage is reached and enables the operator to judge the appearance of the heat more easily. The writer is confident that if a new operator were to be broken in on a welding machine, he would soon be able to correctly judge the right welding heat of the metal by its appearance without any flux, as there are many pipe shops using electric-welding machines for making joints in long coils, where flux was never heard of. Each railroad shop uses a slightly different kind of flux, but generally this material is nothing more than a common yellow clay, streaked with quartz formation, which has been pulverized and thoroughly dried out before using.

There are several methods and machines employed in the various shops for rolling down and completing the weld after heating the joint properly. One of the simplest machines in use is shown in Fig. 277. It consists of a power-driven mandrel slightly smaller than the internal tube diameter, above which is a power-driven roller. This roller is held a short distance above the mandrel by a spring. When the hot tube is thrust onto the mandrel, the upper roller is brought firmly down onto the outside surface of the joint by pressure on a foot treadle located under the table on which the device is mounted. The pressure is maintained until the joint has been rolled down to outer tube size. The main disadvantage of this style of apparatus is that the speeds of the roller and the mandrel must be in the correct ratio so as to not allow any slip on either inner or outer surface of the tube, otherwise the tube will roll unevenly and when finished will have a thicker wall on one side than on the other. However, this is the earliest form of rolling machine used with the electric-welding method and

Fig. 277.—Simplest Form of Rolling Machine.

is still giving fairly satisfactory service in two well-known shops today.

Another type, which is more elaborate but more positive, is a three-roller machine, shown in Fig. 278. The mandrel here is stationary and the three idling rollers, being mounted on a power-driven head, continually revolve around it. After inserting the tube, which is also held stationary, pressure is applied by means of a hand lever which closes the three rollers in toward the center of the mandrel and the joint is rolled down by the surface pressure of the three rollers revolving around it. In order to still further insure uniform rolling, the tube is turned slightly on the mandrel three or four times during the rolling operation since the mandrel is slightly smaller than the tube and if the latter were to be held in only one position, a difference in wall thickness on one side might result.

Rolling machines of the types just described are sometimes located in **direct** alignment with the jaws of the welding machine, **so that** after obtaining the proper heat, it is only necessary **to release the jaws and** shove the hot tube directly

Fig. 278.—The Three-Roller, or Hartz Type, Machine.

onto the mandrel. If the three-roller type is being used, the tube is held stationary by locking one jaw of the welding machine. When a new position on the mandrel is desired the jaws are released and the tube allowed to turn slightly with the friction of the revolving rollers.

Another method is to have the rolling machine in back of the welding machine so that when the correct heat is obtained, the tube is lifted out of the jaws by the operator's assistant who shoves it onto the rolling mandrel, leaving the operator free to get the next tube lined up in the machine for heating. In this last method, the assistant must act quickly so as not to allow the joint to cool down before the rolling, as he cannot transfer the tube from the welding to the rolling machine as quickly as the operator could shove it forward onto the mandrel as first mentioned.

As to speed in welding, the writer observed that the same production could be obtained in different shops by either method of locating the rolling machine; hence it is purely a matter of space available around the welding machine, and local opinion.

A third way of handling the rolling down is to have the rolling machine built onto the welding machine, as shown in Fig. 279. In this particular apparatus, the mandrel is made long enough to permit welding in to a distance of 10 ft. from the joint, so as to reclaim old short tubes by making a new long one with a joint in the middle. This reclaiming of tubes has proved to be perfectly practical, having been forced in one locomotive shop during the war due to the inability to obtain new tube stock. The mandrel is power driven as well as the upper roller, while the two lower rollers are idlers. After obtaining the welding heat, it is only necessary to move the tube about one foot to bring the joint onto the rollers. A clutch at the rear end is then thrown in to revolve the mandrel and upper roller, and pressure is applied through the latter by means of an air cylinder mounted above it. While being rolled the tube is allowed to revolve freely in the open jaws of the welding machine. The rear end of the tube is supported on idling rollers.

After the rolling-down process, which is the same as has always been used with the oil-furnace method of welding, the tubes are subjected to the annealing and end-swaging processes. They are then usually tested hydrostatically for possible leaks and stacked away ready for assembling in the boiler. The percentage of leaks is less than 5 per cent in any shop, and in one shop they are so sure of their welding that the tubes are not tested until completely assembled in the boiler when the latter is subjected to a hydrostatic test as a complete unit. This particular shop uses the flash-weld method and has never

FIG. 279.—Electric Welding Machine with Built-On Rolling Device.

had a defective joint since the welding machine was installed over four years ago.

Merits of Electric and Oil Heating.—When asked to compare the electric welding with the oil-furnace method on boiler tubes of any size, one of the oldest users of the former replied that there was "no comparison." Using oil it was never possible to average over 30 or 40 welds per hour on tubes up to 3 in. with one furnace and one gang. This meant that the tube shop was always behind the rest of the repair departments and working overtime a great deal in order to catch up. Fuel oil will vary greatly in different lots as well as under different atmospheric conditions, so the oil furnace itself is a constant source of aggravation and calls for continual adjusting, which means an interruption in production while the fire is regulated.

As to production with an electric-welding machine, the average output on tubes up to 3 in. in diameter, taken from all shops using this process, will run 60 completed welds per hour, requiring one operator and a helper at the machine and a third man to prepare the work for welding. In the days of piecework, in some of the shops, records show that the maximum number of small tubes turned out in any shop, with the same number of men, was 125 per hour or a little better than one tube every 30 sec. and this could be kept up for two hours at a time without greatly tiring the men. This speed was obtained by three different shops, each using a different style and arrangement of rolling-down apparatus, which shows that all of the methods outlined previously in this article are equally fast.

On welding superheater tubes at the reduced section, where the diameter at the point of weld is about $4\frac{3}{8}$ in., the production will run about 10 to 20 welds per hour, although better time has been made on piecework. By comparing these figures with the oil-furnace welding production, even under the best of working conditions, nothing further need be said as to the speed of the electric process.

As to cost, there are no figures available later than 1916, which of course would be much lower than at the present day, but by comparing costs of both methods at that time, taking into consideration upkeep, labor, cost of heat either way and cost of time lost by making adjustments or repairs to either apparatus, the electric costs per 1,000 tubes welded, is about one-third that of the oil-furnace method.

The only wear on the welding machine is the surface of the copper dies or jaws which grip the pieces and this is so slight as to only require smoothing off a few times a week. The machine does not cost anything for heating energy except when the weld is being made and it is always ready for action as soon as the operator has placed the work in the jaws. Hence there is no delay in starting up the fire in the morning or after lunch hour nor from the fire balking at any time during the welding. The replacements on welding machines in all the shops visited by the writer could be easily covered by $100 during the last six years.

In recapitulating the three methods of electric welding flues, it is safe to say that the flash-weld, which produces a scarfed joint when finished, takes the lead for simplicity of preparation, speed of actual welding and reliability as to percentage of failures in any lot of tubes.

Next to this comes the straight scarf-weld, which requires machining of the ends before welding but insures a good joint after welding although occasionally a small leak will show up on the first hydrostatic test. As stated before, the percentage of leaks is very low with this type of weld and practically negligible with the flash-weld.

The butt-weld, which was originally employed in all the shops, is now only used in one shop in the whole country, probably due to the difficulty in making a perfect weld each time as compared to the ease of making a scarf weld. However, this one shop claims very high efficiency with a butt-weld, both as to tensile strength, which will average over 85 per cent of original tube section, and as to tightness of the joint under pressure.

The principal objection offered by most shops against butt-welding is that should the weld prove tight under pressure, but still be a weak joint mechanically, it might break apart in service. This has happened in a few cases, allowing the tube to drop down in the boiler and subjecting the engine crew to the danger of scalding. With a scarf-weld, which generally shows a tensile strength equal to that of the original tube, due to the area of the weld, should the tube not be welded strongly as just cited and a break should occur inside the boiler, the scarf would prevent the tube from pulling away from its end and only a slow leak could result. This sometimes actually happens with oil-furnace welded tubes.

The Kind of Machine to Use.—As there are different styles and sizes of welding machines being used at the present time on flue-welding, the writer will endeavor to specify special characteristics that should be sought when selecting a machine for this class of work, which is different from any other pipe-welding job. The machine should be constructed to be as efficient electrically as possible; that is, the clamping jaw should be as close to the transformer as is practical in order not to

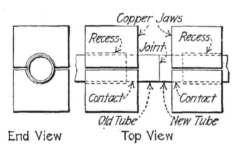

Fig. 280.—Recessed Copper Clamping Jaws.

have large inductive losses caused by the large gap due to the long secondary leads widely spaced. The fewer the joints between the secondary loop of the transformer and the copper jaws which grip the tube, the less chance will there be for resistance losses that cut down the heating effect gradually as oxides form in the joints or by dirt collecting from allowing them to become loose. Although the jaws should be long to permit thorough water cooling, it is only necessary to grip the pipe over a length of about 2 in. This length is bored out to exactly fit around the tube as shown in Fig. 280.

The pressure device does not need to be as heavy as would be used on the same welding machine for joining ordinary pipe or solid stock, since the squeezing together of the plastic metal is really done in the rolling machine. For fastest operation the clamping jaws should be operated by air cylinders so that only a slight movement of two valves is necessary to lock or unlock the tube in the jaws.

For welding up to 3-in. size tubes, a machine of 30-kw. rating ought to be large enough to stand constant use. Any form of toggle lever or screw-wheel pressure device, which permits the operator to stand close to the work will be suitable, as not over 1,000 lb. effective pressure is required on this size of work to stick the ends together sufficiently hard for placing in the rolling machine.

To handle up to 5⅜-in. superheater tubes, a machine of about 75-kw. rating should be employed. For its pressure device, an air cylinder or hydraulic apparatus may be used to best advantage so as to secure up to three or four tons' maximum effective pressure.

For ordinary butt- or scarf-welding, a hand-operated oil jack may be used, although trouble has been experienced in the past with this type of pressure device due to sticking of the valves at critical times, often spoiling a weld.

Flash-Welding.—For flash-welding, a toggle lever or hand-screw wheel on small machines and an air cylinder or hydraulic pressure device on large machines must be used, to effect a slow steady forward movement of the movable jaw in order to maintain the arc of the flashing, yet to have available a quick reverse to break the parts away should they stick too soon from too rapid movement of the pressure device. In small shops, it is advisable to install a 75-kw. machine to handle all sizes of tubes up to the largest superheater. If the shop is large enough to keep a small machine busy all the time on tubes up to 3 in., it will no doubt pay to install in addition, a large machine just to handle the superheater tubes as well as any overflow lot of small tubes. While the large machine will handle any size, it is not so rapid in operation on small tubes as the smaller one, and the bulk of flue-welding is on small tubes, less than 10 per cent of the total being represented by the larger sizes for superheaters.

WELDING IN THE TOPEKA SHOPS OF THE SANTA FE RAILROAD

Supplementing the foregoing, we give the following extract from an article published in the *American Machinist*, June 8, 1916:

In order to give the gripping jaws of the welder good, clean contact the ends of the pieces are ground on the outside for about 6 or 7 in. back from the ends, the operator simply

Fig. 281.—Close-Up Showing Inside Mandrel.

revolving the tube end against the grinding wheel. The ground pieces are sorted out into suitable lengths to form full-length flues when two pieces are butted together, keeping in mind that only two welds are allowed to a flue.

The butt-welding machine itself is practically as received, but the inside mandrel and outside rolls, together with the driving mechanism, were added in the shop after considerable experimenting. Without these the method would be a failure.

A close-up view of the machine, from the back, is given in Fig. 281. This shows the mandrel *A* that works inside the

FIG. 282.—Flue Parts Ready for Welding.

FIG. 283.—Flue Ends Just Beginning to Heat.

FIG. 284.—Almost Hot Enough for Welding.

FIG. 285.—Rolling Out the Upset Metal.

flue as the outside is rolled between the three rolls after the parts have been heated and butted together. The action of the mandrel and rolls is to take out the upset and give a weld that is smooth on the outside and with very little extra metal inside. The gripping jaws are water-cooled, and the operating air cylinders are plainly shown.

Fig. 282 shows two parts of a flue in place in the jaws and illustrates how it is slipped over the mandrel. It will be observed that the mandrel does not extend far enough beyond the rolls to interfere with the welding or become heated from the current passing between the jaws. As it is impossible always to have the two parts to be welded of the same thickness, the setting of the pieces in the jaws must be done with judgment. If one piece is thinner than the other and they were both set in the jaws the same distance out, the thin one would burn before the thick one was hot enough to weld properly. To avoid this, a thick and a thin piece are placed about as shown at *A* and *B*. In this case the thick one is at *A* and the thin one at *B*. As the thick one is in closer to the jaw, it will heat faster. The thin one, being set out farther, gives practically the same amount of metal for the current to heat. The result is an even heating and a perfect weld.

Fig. 283 shows two pieces the reverse of the ones just shown. As the work gradually heats, it looks as in Fig. 284. At the proper heat, the operator butts the work together to form the weld, which leaves a considerable amount of upset. He then shoves the tube along over the mandrel until the weld is between the rolls, when he throws in the clutch and brings down the upper roll. The work spins between the rolls, as shown in Fig. 285 and the result looks almost like a new tube.

CHAPTER XV

ELECTRIC WELDING OF HIGH-SPEED STEEL AND STELLITE IN TOOL MANUFACTURE

The cost of solid high-speed cutting tools is high. At the same time their remarkable cutting qualities make them a necessity in up-to-date shop practice. The electric process of butt-welding has made it possible to obtain all the advantages of a solid high-speed cutting tool and yet at a cost that is not a great deal higher than the ordinary tool-steel product. Stellite, which has recently become more widely known, has been rather limited in its use owing to the fact that it cannot be machined, and it has been thought by many that it could not be successfully joined to any other metal for holding it. This has limited its use to special forms of toolholders, which are often very clumsy in getting into difficult corners on special shapes. The electric process of butt-welding has made it possible to join Stellite bits of any common size and shape to a shank of ordinary steel, giving all the advantages of a solid cutting tool and yet employing only a small amount of the Stellite metal just where it is needed for cutting.

The Thomson welding process consists of passing a large volume of electric current at a low pressure through the joint made by butting two pieces of metal together. The electrical resistance of the metals at the contacting surface is so great that they soon become heated to a welding temperature. Pressure is then applied mechanically and the current turned off, thereby producing a weld. The metal is in full view of the operator at all times instead of being hidden by the coal of a forge or by flame in an oil furnace. No smoked glasses or goggles are required any more than would be if welding by the forge method. Due to the way the metal is forced together there is no oxidation such as there would be in an open fire and therefore no welding compound is ordinarily required.

It is this feature alone which makes it possible to weld high-speed steel and Stellite, the former being very difficult to weld by the forge method and the latter practically impossible. With this process of electric welding the heat is first developed in the interior of the metal. Consequently, it is welded there as perfectly as at the surface. When welding with other methods, however, the outer surface is heated first and very often the interior part does not reach welding heat, the result being an imperfect weld. There is no blistering or burning of the stock when welding electrically, whereas it certainly requires a very expert welder indeed to secure the proper heat on high-speed steel in a forge fire without burning at some point. The process is the most economical known, due to the fact that no energy in the form of heat is being wasted in heating more of the material than is required to make a weld and as soon as it has been completed the current is turned off so that the machine then is not using up any energy whatever. The operator has complete control of the current at all times so that he can obtain any color desired on the metals, where are always visible, and waste by accidental burning of metal is reduced to a minimum.

The only preparation of stock necessary for welding by this process is that when very rusty or greasy it should be thoroughly cleaned, as the presence of either rust or heavy grease affords poor contact with the copper clamping jaws, retarding the flow of electricity and seriously reducing the heating effect.

It is often asked if the electric current has any effect on the welded metal. This question arises from the fear that there may be some mysterious condition connected with electricity that will change the characteristics of the metal, particularly of high-speed steel or Stellite. The answer is, of course, in the negative, as the only effect of the electric current is to heat the metals being welded.

The rapidity of work will depend largely on the operator, the size and shape of the pieces to be welded and the size of machine being used, as there is a wide range in welding time between heavy pieces requiring careful alignment in the clamping jaws and light pieces which can be rapidly and easily handled.

Welding High-Speed to Low-Carbon Steel.—In tool welding

there are various kinds of welds to be made, which require different designs of holding jaws and often two distinct types of welding machine.

Three butt-welding machines shown in Figs. 286, 287, and 288 are especially suitable for welding drills, reamers or other

Fig. 286.—Thomson 10-A6 Butt-Welding Machine.

tools that can be made up of a combination of high-speed and low-carbon steel. The machine shown in Fig. 286, known as the 10-A6 machine, will weld iron or steel rods from $\frac{1}{4}$ to $\frac{3}{4}$ in. in diameter, or an equivalent cross-section in squares, rectangles or flats. An operator can make from 50 to 200 welds per hour, according to the size and nature of the work being handled.

The clamps are of the horizontal operating type, adjustable for different sizes of stock as well as for horizontal alignment of the work. A close-up view of the left-hand clamping mechanism is shown in Fig. 287. The jaw blocks are water cooled and have a maximum movement of $1\frac{1}{2}$ in. by means of the hand-operated clamping levers. There is also a possible $\frac{3}{4}$-in. adjustment of both front and rear jaw blocks. Stops are provided for backing up the work. There are four copper jaws to a set, two being used on each clamp. These jaws are

Fig. 287.—Closeup View of Left-Hand Clamp.

$2\frac{1}{2}$ in. square by $1\frac{7}{16}$ in. thick. The pressure device for forcing the heated ends of the work together is a hand-lever-operated toggle movement, which enables the operator to "feel" his work. This toggle device gives a movement of 1 in. to the right-hand jaw. The maximum space possible between the jaws is $3\frac{1}{4}$ in. There is an automatic current cutoff mounted on the machine. The standard windings are for 220, 440 and 550 volt, 60-cycle alternating current. The current variation for different sized stock is effected through a five-point switch mounted on the machine. Standard ratings are 15 kw., or 25. k.v.a., with 60 per cent. power factor. This size of machine covers a floor space 43×57 in., is 65 in. high and weighs about 1100 pounds.

The machine shown in Fig. 288, or the No. 6 machine, is for heavier work, its capacity being from ¼ to 1 in. in diameter on iron or steel rods, or the equivalent in other shapes. Its production is from 50 to 125 welds per hour. The maximum jaw opening is 3 in.; the four jaws are of hard-drawn copper, 2⅛×2⅜ in. and 1¼ in. thick; toggle-lever movement 1½ in.;

FIG. 288.—No. 6 Butt-Welding Machine.

maximum space between jaws, 4 in.; current standards are the same as for the previous machine. There are 10 points of current variation for different sized stock, effected through double-control switches mounted on the machine. Standard ratings are 30 kw. or 45 kva., with 60 per cent. power factor. The jaws are air cooled, but the copper slides to which the jaws are bolted, as well as the secondary copper casting of the transformer, are water cooled. It occupies a floor space 22×44 in. and the height to center line of the jaws is 37½ in. The weight is 3100 lb. Its operation is practically the same as the first machine described.

Another machine of very similar characteristics is shown

in Fig. 289. This is known as the Special 5-D machine and is intended for the use of makers of small taps and twist drills up to ⅝ in. in diameter. It has very accurate adjustments on

FIG. 289.—Special 5-D Machine.

the clamps and special jaws with steel inserts to prevent wear. To use these, however, requires that the pieces to be welded must be finished to uniform size so as to accurately fit the jaws in order to conduct the current properly.

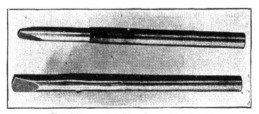

FIG. 290.—Stellite-Tipped Roughing Drills.

The machines shown in Figs. 286 and 288 are not only good for welding the steels mentioned, but also for Stellite work, samples of which are shown in Fig. 290, since the com-

monly used bits of this metal are within their range. The
hand-lever toggle action is quicker and is better suited to this
work than the hydraulic-pressure device used on some of the
larger machines.

In welding twist drill or reamer blanks, such as shown in
Fig. 291, not over ¾ in. in diameter, it has been found practical

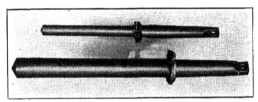

Fig. 291.—Twist-Drill Blanks Just Welded.

to use a pair of jaws on each side that will handle all work
from the smallest up to the ¾-in. size. These jaws are made
as shown in Fig. 292. The two rear, or movable, jaws on each
side of the machine are flat faced, while the front, or stationary,
jaws, have a V-groove cut in them just deep enough to give
clearance for the smallest size of stock to be handled in contact

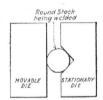

Fig. 292.—Copper Jaws for Various Sizes.

with the face of the opposite jaw. The work is held in the
jaws with a three-point contact, which has been found to be
sufficient for stock of this size, although it is not to be recommended for larger work, since not enough current could be
carried into the pieces without applying pressure sufficient to
squeeze the work into the surface of the copper jaws. This
would soon spoil all accuracy of alignment of the V-grooves.

In this connection it may be well to mention that a welding machine is not a micrometer and the welding of finished pieces is not recommended in commercial production, although such welding is done right along for special jobs. By "special jobs" is meant the putting on of an extension to a drill, tap or small reamer and the like.

In welding high-speed to low-carbon steel the low-carbon steel should project approximately twice as far out from the jaws as the high-speed steel does in order to equalize as much as possible the heating of the two pieces.

Where a tool is to be made with a head larger than the shank, as shown at A, Fig. 293, holding copper jaws should

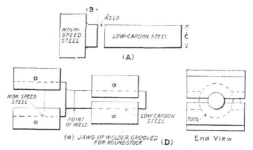

Fig. 293.—Copper Jaws for Holding Large Heads and Small Shanks.

be made as shown at D. In work of this kind the dimension B should always be about one-half of the diameter of C. The same rule holds good with this type of tool blank when placing it in the jaws as with steel of the same relative size; that is, the low-carbon steel should project about twice as far from the jaws as the high-speed steel since the high-speed steel has the higher resistance and has a tendency to become plastic sooner. To still further reduce its tendency to heat up quickly, the resistance should be reduced as much as possible by having the jaws as good a fit for the high-speed piece as it is possible to make them. Where different sizes are to be welded it is advisable to have special holding jaws for each separate size of high-speed steel head, although the low-carbon steel pieces may be held in V-grooved jaws made up to hold several sizes.

Fig. 294.—No. 9 Butt-Welding Machine.

This is the practice of some of the largest makers of reamers and large drills.

The actual use of the machines shown for the work outlined is simplicity itself. The work is placed in the respective jaws and securely locked in place by pulling forward the two levers shown projecting upward on each machine. In addition to the grip of the jaws the work is kept from any possible slip by means of stops against which the outer ends of the work are butted. With the work solidly in place the operator pulls

FIG. 295.—Close-up of Machine with Work in Jaws.

on the pressure lever at the right of the machine until the ends of the work are in firm contact. He then turns on the current by means of a push button conveniently located in the pressure lever, and when the proper heat is reached, which is judged by the color, the push button is released. This shuts off the current and the operator then applies full pressure and the weld is made.

The maximum capacity of the largest of the three machines described is 1 in. round or its equivalent in other shapes. For larger work a machine similar to the one shown in Fig. 294

is used. This is known as a No. 9 butt-welding machine, and its capacity is from $\frac{1}{2}$ to $1\frac{1}{4}$ in.; the output is from 50 to 100 welds per hour; the maximum jaw opening is $1\frac{7}{8}$ in.; the four hard-drawn copper jaws are 3 in. high, $3\frac{1}{4}$ in. wide and $1\frac{1}{2}$ in. thick; the pressure device is a 5-ton hand-operated hydraulic oil jack; maximum movement with jack, 2 in.; maximum movement with one stroke of jack, $\frac{1}{4}$ in.; maximum opening between jaws, 4 in.; standard windings the same as for the previous machines; standard ratings, 40 kw. or 55 kva., with 60 per

Fig. 296.—Steps in the Making of a Large Reamer.

cent. power factor; width of machine, 27 in.; length, 60 in.; height, 46 in.; weight, 3900 pounds.

A closeup of this machine, with a large reamer blank in the jaws, is shown in Fig. 295, and progressive steps in the making of the reamer are shown in Fig. 296. The high-speed steel piece is 3 in. long by $1\frac{3}{8}$ in. diameter, and the machine-steel piece is 6 in. long.

Two other machines (10-B and 40-A2 models) of this type suitable for heavy tool welding may be mentioned. They are made with a capacity of from $\frac{1}{2}$ to $1\frac{1}{2}$ and from 1 to 2 in.

The first of these has a hand-operated pressure device capable of exerting a pressure of 12 tons and it weighs 7800 lb. The second has a pressure device which receives its initial pressure

FIG. 297.—A Welded and a Finished Lathe Tool.

from an external accumulator, which gives an effective pressure of 23 tons; it weighs 8000 lb. and is 64×105×48 in. high.

The Welding of Other Than Round Tools.—The welding

FIG. 298.—How the Parts Are Arranged for Welding.

of tools similar to the ones shown in Fig. 297, intended for lathe or planing-machine tools, may be done in any of the foregoing machines. The cutting parts may be of either Stellite

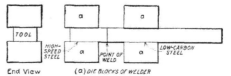

FIG. 299.—How the Parts Are Clamped in the Jaws.

or high-speed steel. This kind of welding is usually employed by manufacturing concerns in their own toolrooms in order to use up odd bits of high-priced steel or Stellite. The pieces are

prepared about as shown in Fig. 298. Jaws for holding work
of this kind are outlined in Fig. 299.

Another way to make tools for lathe or planing-machine
work is outlined in Fig. 300. This method may often be
employed when the one just given could not. As can be seen,

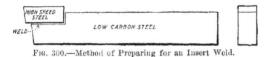

FIG. 300.—Method of Preparing for an Insert Weld.

in order to properly support the high-speed steel piece, the
low-carbon steel shank is milled away to form a recess for
the reception of the high-speed steel bit. The welding can
be done on any of the machines shown provided the parts are
not of too great cross-section. The method of recessing the
copper clamping jaws is clearly shown in Fig. 301.

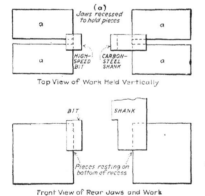

FIG. 301.—Jaws Used for Holding Work in Insert Welding.

The perfect success of a welded high-speed tool depends
not only on the correct welding but also upon the correct
treatment after the welding itself has been accomplished. It
is easily seen that if a piece of high-speed steel is welded to
a piece of ordinary carbon steel and the joint allowed to cool

fairly quickly in the air strains will be set up at the joint for the reason that the high-speed steel in cooling so quickly, both metals become hardened more or less but to a different degree. Hence if the weld is subjected to any great strain under these conditions it will break either at the joint or close by, due to the strain. *It is therefore very evident that immediately after welding a piece of high-speed steel to carbon steel the work should be immediately put into some sort of furnace to be annealed.* The amount of time that the tools should be left in the furnace for thoroughly heating through and the amount of time required to allow the pieces to cool down to room temperature depend entirely upon the size and

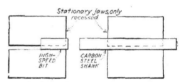

Top View of Work Held Horizontally

End View of Work in Right-Hand Jaws

Fig. 302.—Jaws Used for Stellite Butt Welding.

character of tool being made. However, the annealing of any piece of any size requires that the work be left in the furnace heated to at least a dull cherry red for a few hours and allowed to cool very slowly in the furnace.

If a welded tool is not properly annealed before machining much difficulty is often experienced from hard spots being encountered in the machining of the pieces, which of course is more or less disastrous to the cutting edges of the tools being used in the machining process.

The best method of hardening high-speed steel tools after the welding and machining depends also greatly upon the shape and size.

Welding Stellite.—Although the welding of the various

grades of Stellite is not difficult there is a certain knack in the welding and also in the clamping of the stock which must be fully acquired to produce satisfactory results.

The welding should be done in a horizontal butt-welding machine with a quick-acting hand-lever pressure device. In butt-welding round drill stock or rectangular tool stock the pieces should be held as shown in Fig. 302. It will be noticed that the projection of the Stellite beyond the copper jaws is very short indeed while the projection of the carbon-steel

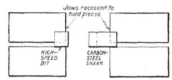

Top View of Work Held Vertically

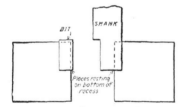

Front View of Rear Jaws and Work
FIG. 303.—Jaws Used for Stellite Insert Welding.

piece is comparatively long. This is because Stellite has a very high resistance compared with the carbon steel. Since in this work the heating effect varies directly with the resistance of two metals the heating in the Stellite should be retarded as much as possible by surrounding it almost completely with the copper jaws. The correct amount of projection of the carbon steel will have to be determined by experiment in each case after observing with each setting of two pieces which has the tendency to heat the fastest.

In welding in cutting bits of Stellite by the insert-weld method the pieces should be held as shown in Fig. 303.

It will be seen from this cut that the copper jaws holding the small bit nearly surround it and at the same time back up the piece to take the pressure of the squeezing up of the

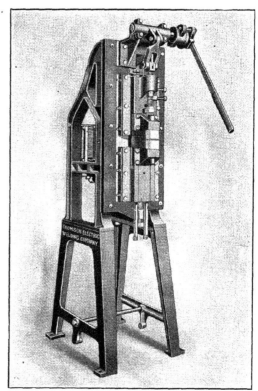

FIG. 304.—Vertical Type of Welding Machine.

stock. The opposite jaws holding the carbon-steel shank do not have to grip very much of the metal but they serve to back it up to receive the force of the pressure.

In the welding itself the current is applied intermittently, as the Stellite usually has a tendency to heat very rapidly, until the carbon steel is fast approaching the plastic state. The current is then held on steadily and the instant the Stellite metal "runs," the pressure lever is given a quick jerk as the current is turned off. It will be found that with a good weld there is scarcely any push up of the stock and very little of the

Fig. 305.—Making a "Mash" Insert Weld in a 20-AV Machine.

metal flows out at the joint, requiring little grinding, if any, to finish the tool.

Unlike high-speed steel Stellite requires no further heat treatment or attention of any kind if it is welded correctly. When it is taken out of the welding machine the tool is ready for use at once after grinding off the resulting burr.

Where large numbers of tools of the lathe and planing-machine types are to be made, such as shown in Fig. 300, the highest production can be obtained by using a vertical

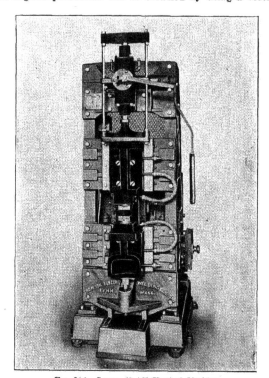

Fig. 306.—Large 40-AV Vertical Machine.

type of welding machine built on the lines of the one shown in Fig. 304.

This machine (10-AV model) has a capacity of two pieces with contact areas between 0.40 and 0.30 sq. in. for pieces with a total thickness of $\frac{3}{4}$ to $1\frac{1}{4}$ in. The production is 35 to 85 tools per hour, depending on the size; the upper and lower jaws are of hard-drawn copper $1\frac{3}{4}\times2\frac{1}{4}$ in. and $1\frac{1}{2}$ in. thick; the jaw blocks are water cooled; the machine has a current variation through a five-point switch for different sizes of stock; standard windings are for alternating current 220 440 and 550 volt, 60 cycles; standard ratings, 15 kw. or 25 kva. with power factor of 60 per cent.; the pressure device is hand operated, giving a movement of $2\frac{3}{4}$ in.; maximum space between jaws, $3\frac{1}{4}$ in.; floor space occupied, 21×53 in.; height, 75 in.: weight, 1200 pounds.

A larger machine (20-AV model) of the same type in operation is shown in Fig. 305. This machine gives a maximum area of contact ranging from $1\frac{1}{4}$ to 1 sq. in. on pieces with a total thickness from 1 up to 2 in.; production is from 50 to 75 welds per hour; there is a throat clearance of 10 in.; the copper jaws are 2×3 in. and $1\frac{1}{2}$ in. thick; pressure is by hand-toggle

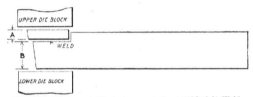

Fig. 307.—Jaws and Work Arranged for a ''Mash'' Weld.

lever and spring cushion; current control, as in the other machines, is by push button in the lever operating through a magnetic wall switch; the jaw blocks are water cooled; standard ratings are 30 kw. or 50 kva. with 60 per cent. power factor; weight, 2200 pounds.

Another still larger machine (40-AV model) is shown in Fig. 306. Except for its size it is but little different from the two just described, the main difference being the hydraulic-pressure device, which gives an effective pressure of 5 tons. This machine has a maximum contact area of 3 sq. in. and will weld pieces from $1\frac{1}{2}$ to 3 in. total thickness; production, 15 to 50 welds; throat depth, $6\frac{1}{4}$ in.; jaws, $2\times4\times1\frac{1}{2}$ in. thick; maximum movement of upper jaw block, 2 in.; movement with one stroke of lever, $\frac{3}{4}$ in.; space possible between jaws, 3 in.; standard ratings, 60 kw. or 86 kva. with 70 per cent.

TABLE XXVI—CURRENT CONSUMPTION FOR WELDING VARIOUS SIZES

Diameter of rod, inches — Decimal	Fraction	Dia. of rod, millimeters	Area of section, sq. in.	Current consumption per 1000 welds	Cost per 1000 welds at 1 cent per K.W.H.*
.25	1/4		.04909	10	$0.10
.2755		7	.0596	11	.11
.3125	5/16		.0767	12	.12
.3149		8	.0779	12	.12
.3543		9	.0987	14	.14
.375	3/8		.11043	15	.15
.3937		10	.1217	16	.16
.4724		12	.1753	19	.19
.5	1/2		.19635	20	.20
.5612		14	.2472	26	.26
.625	5/8		.3068	30	.30
.6299		16	.3115	34	.34
.7087		18	.3946	45	.45
.75	3/4		.44179	52	.52
.7874		20	.487	60	.60
.8661		22	.585	80	.80
.875	7/8		.60132	85	.85
.94488		24	.701	105	1.05
1.	1		.7854	130	1.30
1.0236		26	.822	135	1.35
1.1023		28	.944	180	1.80
1.125	1 1/8		.994	190	1.90
1.1811		30	1.094	230	2.30
1.25	1 1/4		1.2272	265	2.65
1.2598		32	1.245	270	$2.70
1.3385		34	1.407	320	3.20
1.375	1 3/8		1.4849	340	3.40
1.4173		36	1.576	360	3.60
1.496		38	1.757	425	4.25
1.5	1 1/2		1.7671	430	4.30
1.5748		40	1.946	470	4.70
1.625	1 5/8		2.0739	530	5.30
1.6535		42	2.146	540	5.40
1.7322		44	2.356	600	6.00
1.75	1 3/4		2.4053	640	6.40
1.811		46	2.576	700	7.00
1.875	1 7/8		2.7612	780	7.80
1.8897		48	2.802	810	8.10
1.9685		50	3.089	870	8.70
2.	2		3.1416	930	9.30
2.0472		52	3.286	1000	10.00
2.125	2 1/8		3.5466	1100	11.00
2.1259		54	3.55	1130	11.30
2.2047		56	3.82	1200	12.00
2.25	2 1/4		3.9761	1280	12.80
2.2834		58	4.095	1350	13.50
2.3622		60	4.387	1460	14.60

* Multiply these values by the rate you are paying per K.W Hour for current, to determine what the cost per 1000 welds for any size would be at your plant.

TABLE XXVII—SIZES OF COPPER WIRE FOR CONNECTING UP DIFFERENT SIZES OF WELDING MACHINES

Type Machine	K.V.A. Demand	220-Volt Circuit		440-Volt Circuit		550-Volt Circuit	
		Size of Wire	Size of Switch and Fuses	Size of Wire	Size of Switch and Fuses	Size of Wire	Size of Switch and Fuses
10-A6 10-AV }	25	No. 4 B. & S.	100 Amp	No 10 B & S	50 Amp	No. 10 B & S	50 Amp
No. 6	45	No. 1 B. & S.	200 Amp	No. 6 B. & S.	100 Amp	No. 6 B. & S.	100 Amp.
20-A10 20-AV }	50	No. 1 B. & S.	200 Amp	No. 6 B. & S.	100 Amp	No. 6 B. & S.	100 Amp.
No. 9	55	No. 00 B. & S.	350 Amp.	No. 3 B. & S.	175 Amp.	No. 3 B. & S.	150 Amp
10-B	75	No. 000 B. & S.	400 Amp.	No. 2 B. & S.	175 Amp.	No. 3 B. & S.	150 Amp
40-A2	86	No. 000 B. & S.	400 Amp.	No. 2 B. & S.	175 Amp.	No. 3 B. & S.	150 Amp
*40-A2	107	No. 0000 B. & S.	600 Amp.	No. 0 B. & S.	250 Amp.	No. 0 B. & S.	200 Amp.

*With oil transformer

power factor; size, 34×60 in. by 79 in. high; weight, 3600 pounds.

For welding tools on these machines the relative thickness of the two parts should be about that shown in Fig. 307. Under ordinary conditions the dimension *A* should be about one-third of *B* in order to have the point of the weld nearest the jaw in contact with the high-speed steel, so that the heating effect

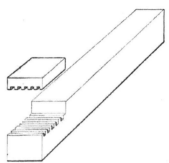

FIG. 308.—Pieces Grooved to Make Better Welds with Less Current.

will be lessened and its fusion point retarded until the low-carbon steel has a chance to heat up properly.

In order to obtain the best results tools wider than 1 in. and with a recess longer than 1½ in. should be grooved as shown in Fig. 308. This reduces the section in actual contact, thereby requiring less current, is easier and quicker to heat and assures a better weld over the entire area of contact.

In order to assist those who have tool or other butt-welding to do some useful data are given in Table XXVI.

In Table XXVII is given the proper size of copper wire to use to connect up the various machines mentioned for tool welding.

CHAPTER XVI

ELECTRIC SEAM WELDING

Seam or line welding is the process of joining two overlapping edges of sheet metal for their entire length without the application of any solder or spelter along the joint. In the Thomson process of lap-seam welding, the heat is produced by passing a large volume of electric current through the edges to be welded by means of a copper roller on one side of the joint and a copper track or horn underneath. In any electrical path, wherever high resistance is interposed, heating will result, and the higher the resistance to the current, the greater will be the heating effect. In the electric lap seam welding machines, the copper roller and horn are good conductors and the joint between the edges of the metal to be welded is the point of highest resistance. On this account it is evident that the greatest heating effect will be at that point. As the roller passes over the joint, heating the stock to a plastic state beneath it, pressure is applied by springs on the roller which forces the two edges together as fast as they are heated. Since 20 B. & S. gage or lighter metal heats very rapidly, the pressure and heating can be effected at the same instant of contact by the roller, and it is possible to weld as fast as 6 in. per second.

The only preparation necessary for seam welding is that the stock must be absolutely clean, that is, free from any traces of rust, scale, grease, or dirt, if a tight, well-appearing joint is desired. If it is not necessary for the joint to be tight, it will not be necessary to have the stock so clean, although heavy scale or rust will obstruct the passage of current, so that little or no heating effect can be secured under these conditions.

In welding sheet brass of 22 to 30 B. & S. gage, to secure a perfect joint the metal should be carefully pickled and washed to remove all traces of grease and tarnish which tend to prevent

365

the passage of current across the joint of the edges. The metal should be welded soon after pickling, as, no matter how carefully it may be washed, oxidation is always sure to start very shortly after the brass has been removed from the pickling acid.

Steel, to be successfully seam welded, should not have a carbon content of over 0.15 per cent., for a higher carbon steel than this has a tendency to crystallize at the point of weld, due to the rapid cooling of the welded portion from the surrounding cold metal. After welding, the joint will be found to be about one-third thicker than the single thickness of the metal. It is possible, by applying more pressure, to reduce this finished thickness still more, but it wears more on the copper roller to do so.

In welding brass, a soft, annealed metal should be used, for although hard-rolled brass can be welded, it does not force the two edges together very much and the finished joint under these conditions is almost twice the original metal thickness. However, with a soft, annealed brass the finished joint will be not over a third greater than the single metal thickness, and by applying sufficient pressure can be reduced down to be not over 10 per cent. thicker.

The principal advantage of electric seam welding is that no spelter and no flux are required, the metal itself forming its own cohesive properties, which allows great speed in production. The greatest efficiency of a seam welding machine lies not only in its welding qualities but in the use of a suitable jig to properly hold the work. The jig used should be made so as to enable the operator to place or remove the work in the shortest possible time, since the welding itself is very fast compared with any other known method of making a continuous joint.

In order that their seam welding machines may operate in every installation with the highest efficiency possible, the Thomson Electric Welding Co., Lynn, Mass., build them standard only up to a certain point and then design a special holding jig to best fit the work to be done in each individual case. The amount of lap allowed in making lap seam welds is usually about twice the single sheet thickness of the metal.

The operation of a lap seam welding machine is very simple, once the machine is set for any given piece of work for which a special jig has been built. After placing the piece in the jig and securely locking it there, the operator depresses a foot-treadle which throws in a clutch and starts the copper roller across the work. By the proper setting of adjustable control-stops on the control-rod at the top of the machine, the current is automatically turned on as the roller contacts

Fig. 309.—Model 306 Lap Seam Welding Machine.

with the overlapping edges of the piece to be welded and is automatically turned off when the roller reaches the end of its stroke; another stop reverses the travel of the roller and brings it back to the starting position. The control-stops may be adjusted to turn the current on or off at any point along the stroke of the roller for doing work with a seam shorter than the maximum capacity of the machine. The roller stroke may be also shortened so that the complete cycle of operation will be accomplished in the shortest space of time on seams shorter than maximum seam capacity of any machine. In order to keep the copper roller from overheating in action, water is introduced through its bronze bearings on each side. This same water circulation, also passes through the under copper horn or mandrel and then through the cast-copper secondary of the transformer, so that the machine can be operated continually, 24 hours per day if desired, without overheating.

Lap Seam Welding Machines.—The lap seam welding

FIG. 310.—Details of Welding Roller Head.

machine, known as Model 306, shown in Fig. 309 will weld a seam 6 in. long in soft iron or steel stock up to 20 gage in thickness, or brass and zinc up to 24 gage thick. This machine will make from 60 to 600 welds per hour, depending on the nature of the work and the quickness with which the pieces can be placed in and removed from the jig. The copper horn is water-cooled and has an inserted copper track on which the work rests. The upper contact consists of a copper roller 6¼ in. in diameter, mounted on a knockout shaft supported in water-cooled bearings. Pressure is exerted on the copper roller by means of a series of springs on each side which are adjustable to give the proper tension for various thicknesses of stock. Current control is automatic through a magnetic wall switch carrying the main current. The latter is controlled from a mechanical switch which is thrown in or out by the action of the roller-carrying mechanism as it starts

FIG. 311.—Thomson No. 318 Lap Seam Welding Machine.

and completes the stroke for which it is set. Standard **windings** are for 220-, 440-, and 550-volt, 60-cycle, alternating current. Current variation for different thicknesses and kinds of stock, is effected through a regulator which gives 50 points of voltage regulation. A variable-speed $\frac{1}{2}$-hp. motor gives a wide variation in the speed with which the roller may be fed over the work. The standard ratings for the machine are 15 kw. or 25 kva., with 60 per cent. power factor. This machine covers 32×96 in. floor space, is 68 in. high and weighs 2750 lb.

A close-up view of the type of roller-carrying head used on all the lap seam welding machines, is shown in Fig. 310. In this view the roller is shown operating between the clamping bars of a special holding jig on the horn. As the roller itself occasionally requires smoothing off around its contacting surface, its bearing has been designed to knock out quickly so

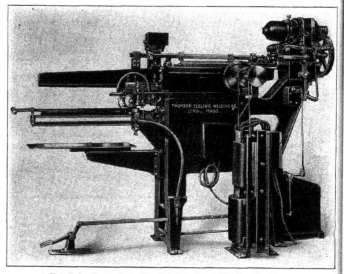

FIG. 312.—Large Size, No. 324, Lap Seam Welding Machine.

that removal and replacement of the roller is very simple and easy to accomplish. The cleaner the stock being welded is kept, the longer a roller will operate without requiring smoothing off, as dirt and scale on the stock cause a slight sparking as the roller passes along, which tends to pit up its contact surface.

The machine shown in Fig. 311, known as Model 318, is a larger and heavier machine than the one previously described and will weld a lap seam 18 in. long on the same gages of metal quoted. Another very similar but smaller machine (Model 312) is also made for welding seams up to 12 in.

In Fig. 312 is seen a considerably larger machine, Model 324, capable of welding a lap seam up to 24 in. in length. The production is from 30 to 120 welds per hour. The machine covers a floor space of 36×90 in., is 72 in. high, and weighs 3500 lb. All other specifications are the same as given for Fig. 309.

Examples of Holding Jigs.—The machines shown may be fitted with numerous forms of holding jigs from the simple

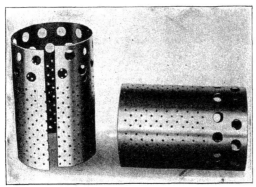

Fig. 313.—Oil Stove Burner Tubes Before and After Welding.

bar clamps shown on the horns in Figs. 311 and 312, to various more complicated forms, some of which may be mounted on the knee below the horn or bolted direct to the face of the machine column.

The small oil stove burner tubes shown in Fig. 313 lend themselves nicely to the seam welding process. Cylindrical pieces such as the shell tubes for automobile mufflers shown in Fig. 314, need a rather elaborate holding jig. A machine fitted up for this work is shown in Fig. 315. To insert a muffler shell into this jig the hinged end is swung outward and downward; the two halves of the holder are spread apart by pressing down on the left-handle treadle; the shell is then thrust into the holder; the treadle is released, which allows the holder sides to be pressed in by the springs and hug the muffler shell around the horn of the machine, with the edges overlapping enough for the weld; the end gate is then closed and the welding roller started over the seam. The principal function of the gate is to hold the muffler shell square in the jig and prevent it being pushed out by the welding roller.

FIG. 314.—Seam Welded Automobile Muffler Tubes.

A jig for holding large cans is shown in Fig. 316. The side clamps of this jig are operated by means of the lever shown at the left. An end gate, shown open, is used in the same way as in the muffler shell jig. Work of this kind is of course much slower than with a smaller jig, yet it is faster than by any other process of closing the seams.

Bucket bodies are held as shown in Fig. 317. The holding jig is made to slide in a channel bolted to the machine knee. The jig is slid back clear of the horn and, with the gate in the flaring end open, the bucket blank is inserted. The gate

FIG. 315.—Holding Jig for Automobile Muffler Tubes.

is then closed by means of the handle, the jig and work is pushed over the horn to a stop, and the weld is made as usual.

Another application of seam welding, is to use it for welding the ends of strip stock together, end to end, so as to facilitate continuous passage of the strip through the dies of a punch press. A machine fitted up for this work is shown in Fig. 318.

The ends of the two strips to be welded are inserted in the jig from opposite sides and the edges brought together. The pieces are then clamped by means of the two levers shown in front of the jig, which operate eccentrics over the clamping

Fig. 316.—Holding Jig for Large Sheet Metal Cans.

plates. The welding roller is then run over the ends as in other work of this kind.

Flange seam welding differs from lap seam welding in that instead of the metal being lapped a slight fin or flange is formed along the edges of the metal parts, the flanges being welded together and practically eliminated in the process. This class of welding is especially adapted to the manufacture of light gage coffee and teapots spouts or similar work.

A machine built especially for flange seam welding, known

FIG. 317.—Jig for Holding Bucket Bodies.

as Model 26, is shown in Fig. 319. The work being done is the welding of the two halves of teapot spouts. In the operation the two halves of the spout are clamped securely in a special copper jig, Fig. 320, which has been carefully hand-cut to fit the halves of the spout perfectly on the entire contacting area. The jig is pushed around on the flat copper table, which constitutes the top of the welding machine, so that the seam of the edge to be welded is allowed to ride along the small

FIG. 318.—Jig for Welding Ends of Metal Strips Together.

power-driven copper roller which is mounted on a vertical shaft, as illustrated in Fig. 321. The halves which are welded by this process must be blanked out by special steel dies to give the correct amount of fin or flange on each edge. This fin is heated to the plastic stage by contact with the roller and the slight pressure applied not only forces the metal of the two fins to cohere but also forces the projection into a level with the outer surface of the spout, thus giving a finished job direct from the welder which is smooth enough without

Fig. 319.—Machine for Flange Seam Welding.

any grinding to be ready for the enamelling or agate-coating process.

The secret of success of this work lies wholly in the proper preparation of not only the copper holding-dies, but also the steel flanging and forming dies. A finished spout, just as it

TABLE XXVIII.—COMPARATIVE THICKNESS AND APPROXIMATE CURRENT CONSUMPTION FOR 6-IN. SEAM.

| THICKNESS OF SINGLE SHEET | | | | K.W.H. CONSUMED PER 1000 WELDS | COST PER 1000 WELDS @ 1c PER K.W.H.* |
Decimals of inch	Millimeter	B. & S. Std. Gauge	Birmingham Gauge		
.00394	.1			.075	.0007
.00787	.2	30		.175	.0017
.01002		29		.25	.0025
.01126			30	.3	.003
.01181	.3			.35	.0035
.012		28		.35	.0035
.01264			29	.375	.0037
.013			28	.4	.004
.014				.45	.0045
.01419		27		.46	.0046
.01575	.4			.525	.0052
.01594		26		.55	.0055
.016			27	.56	.0056
.0179		25		.675	.0067
.018			26	.68	.0068
.01968	.5			.75	.0075
.02			25	.78	.0078
.0201		24		.78	.0078
.022			24	.95	.0097
.02257				.975	.0097
.02362	.6			1.05	.0105
.025		23		1.175	.0117
.02535			23	1.257	.0126
.02756	.7	22		1.35	.0135
.028			22	1.4	.014
.02846		21		1.425	.0142
.03149	.8			1.65	.0165
.03196			21	1.7	.017
.032		20		1.7	.017
.035			20	1.925	.0192
.03543	.9			1.95	.0195
.03589		19		2.	.02

* Multiply these values by the rate you are paying per K. W. Hour for current, to determine what the cost per 1000 welds would be at your plant.

TABLE XXIX—SIZE OF COPPER WIRE TO USE TO CONNECT UP THE WELDING MACHINE.

(Where the machine is not over 150 ft. from source of supply.)

Type Machine	K.V.A. Demand	220-Volt Circuit		440-Volt Circuit		550-Volt Circuit	
		Size of Wire	Size of Switch and Fuses	Size of Wire	Size of Switch and Fuses	Size of Wire	Size of Switch and Fuses
No. 26	8	No. 12 B. & S.	35 Amp.	No. 14 B. & S.	20 Amp.	No. 14 B. & S.	15 Amp.
No. 306 No. 312 No. 318 No. 324	25	No. 4 B. & S.	100 Amp.	No. 10 B. & S.	50 Amp.	No. 10 B. & S.	50 Amp.

Fig. 320.—Jig for Holding Teapot Spouts for Welding.

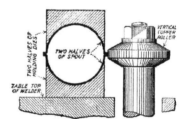

Fig. 321.—Diagram of Flange Seam Welding Operation.

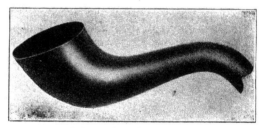

Fig. 322.—A Finish Welded Teapot Spout.

comes from the welding machine, is shown in Fig. 322. The welded seam is barely visible.

In order to assist those who have welding jobs to do, to calculate the current cost on various jobs, Table XXVIII is given. This table shows the approximate current consumption, and multiplying the rate given by the local rate charged, the cost of 1000 welds can be easily ascertained.

Table XXIX is very convenient for ascertaining the size of copper wire needed to connect the different machines mentioned to the main source of current supply.

CHAPTER XVII

MAKING PROPER RATES FOR ELECTRIC WELDING AND THE STRENGTH OF WELDS

The uncertainty which seems to exist regarding electric welding rates among central-station interests, says S. I. Oesterreicher in *Electrical World*, is no doubt due to the indifference of the welding industry, which during a long period in the past did not assist those affected by the rates as much as its unquestionable duty would have suggested.

While welding installations of only comparatively small sizes had to be considered—say from 25 to 100 kva.—no great harm was done by such tactics to either interest. However, with the installation of large equipments and the operation of large unit welding machines, central stations suddenly experienced disturbances upon their lines and in their stations, which were anticipated but partly and were blamed entirely upon the welding equipment. Thus, to protect themselves, central-station interests launched into a partially retroactive policy, greatly to the detriment of the welding industry as a whole.

Since welding installations of several thousand kva. capacity are not unusual, it is proper that all points of doubt should be considered as broadly and fairly as possible, and a far-reaching co-operative policy inaugurated. The revenue from such large installations may easily reach several thousand dollars a month. It is therefore obvious that, from a purely commercial standpoint, a welding load is a very desirable constant source of income to the central station.

Looking at the reverse side, it should be recalled that central-station engineers, on account of past sad experiences, had jumped to the following conclusions:

1. That a welding installation is a very unreliable metering proposition.

382

2. That it has a poor load factor.

3. It has a constantly fluctuating load varying between extreme limits, and

4. It has a bad power factor.

The first important point is, no doubt, the metering. The time-honored opinion on one side that, due to the short period involved, an integrating wattmeter does not respond quickly enough, is contradicted by the claim on the other side that the deceleration of the meter disk compensates for the lagging acceleration. As far as the writer is aware, not the slightest positive proof has been offered to support either contention. Considering for instance a 200-volt, 300-amp., single-phase, two-wire wattmeter, whose disk at full load makes 25 r.p.m., and assuming the total energy consumption to be integrated within 0.2 second, it will be found that to register correctly the meter disk has to travel about 0.08 of a revolution. It is scarcely possible that by merely looking upon a meter disk any one could guess within 100 per cent the actual travel during such a short time interval. A stop watch will scarcely be of any assistance; neither will a cycle recorder with an ammeter and voltmeter check be of any value, since no instrument is of such absolute dead beat as to come to rest from no load to full load within 0.2 second. Such methods therefore are of no value in ascertaining the behavior of a wattmeter under sudden intermittent heavy loads.

The next step of the metering proposition was to take the rated energy consumption of the welding machine as given by the manufacturer, assume a certain load factor, calculate from these data the energy consumption, correct for the power factor and check the answer periodically on the meter dial. The result obtained on the meter was usually a constantly varying, lower energy consumption than calculated, and no doubt this was the cause of the great distrust of the meter. This method is worse than no check at all, and it is so for the following reasons:

1. The energy consumption at a welder depends upon the welding area of the metal, but is not a proportionate variable. That is, all other factors being the same, two square inches of a certain weld do not consume twice as much energy as one square inch does. Fig. 323 shows this fact plainly. It

is also of common knowledge that on a spot welder the area of the weld varies from weld to weld just as much as the electrode contact area does. Assuming an electrode at the start as $^3/_{16}$ in. diameter at the tip, after about 200 welds it might be anything from $\frac{1}{4}$ in. to $^5/_{16}$ in. diameter, thus gradually increasing its contact area anywhere from 75 per cent to 175 per cent.

2. On butt welders the energy consumption does not depend

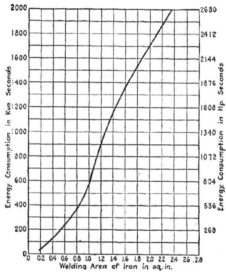

FIG. 323.—Energy Consumption of Resistance Welding for Commercial Grades of Sheet Iron.

upon the size of the weld alone, but also upon the clamping distances. Fig. 324 gives some information about the influence of variable clamping distances upon the energy consumption of welding machines. On a butt welder, the clamping distances increase with the gradual wear of the electrode; thus the above spot welder conditions are duplicated on butt welders also.

3. If no compensation is made to vary the impressed emf.

of the welder—and this is never done—then the time must vary from weld to weld according to the condition of the electrode. If the time is changing constantly, the assumed load factor changes correspondingly; thus there are three constantly changing factors in the estimated energy consumptions, beyond any reasonable approximation of the actual facts.

A more reliable method would be a periodic oscillograph test, but this method is rather complicated and expensive and could be done only by large central stations which have both the equipment and the trained personnel for such work.

Such tests, once they are made for certain types of welders

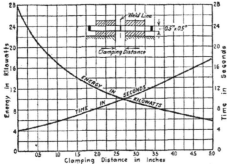

Fig. 324.—Effect of Clamping Distance Between Electrodes Upon Time and Energy Demand.   Area, 0.25 Sq. In.

and work, will give excellent data from which to check the actual behavior of the standard type of wattmeter. If such comparisons are made, it will be found that the integrated energy consumption of the wattmeter will be larger than the oscillograph test indicates. It is not intended to claim that the wattmeter registers "fast." Laboratory tests are usually made by skilled men, who before the test carefully ascertained all important factors entering into the test, as area of weld, condition of electrodes, welder, emf., cleanliness of material, etc., whereas under normal operating conditions almost no attention is paid by the operator to these considerations. In fact, if the operator works on a piecework or bonus basis, he will conceal as much as possible all discrepancies which have a tendency even temporarily to curtail his earnings. The result of his policy has a very important effect upon the wattmeter.

Summing up the metering proposition and speaking from experience on large welding installations with capacities over 250,000 sq. in. of welding per month, where ten to fifteen butt welding machines are constantly thrown on or off the supply circuit, it is safe to claim that in such installations the standard alternating-current integrating wattmeter is on the job.

The Load Factor.—The present-day tendency in resistance welding practice is to perform the weld as quickly as possible without injury to the metal, but fast enough to prevent imperfection at the weld. Having in mind large welders with 5 to 15 sq. in. weld capacities, this tendency will give a unit load factor not much over 10 per cent per welder. From the central-station viewpoint, this factor is certainly very low and undesirable.

However, two important circumstances alter the condition considerably. The first point is that in large installations one large welder will not suffice to do all the required work, therefore several will have to be installed. Owing to the big energy demands these large welders never operate simultaneously. While one welds the next is cleaned, the third is prepared, the fourth is waiting for the signal to weld, etc.; thus the load factor of the installation as a whole is considerably over 10 per cent and nearer to 20 per cent. Another natural circumstance of large installations is the fact that not all work requires large welders. There are usually ten to fifteen smaller welders installed, of which 30 per cent might work intermittently with the larger welders. Thus it will be seen that the load factor is bad only in small installations connected to small central stations, while large installations, which necessarily must receive their supply of energy from comparatively larger central plants, have rather a good aggregate load factor, reaching well up to 25 to 30 per cent.

Another point for consideration is the fact that, owing to its temperature, large work cannot be handled immediately after welding. The work must cool off before additional operations can be performed upon it. The cooling takes some time. In several instances it was found desirable to shift the working hours of the welding crew several hours ahead or behind the working hours of the rest of a factory, for the sole reason that there should be on hand sufficient cool welded work for the successive manufacturing steps. If this time-shifting is selected to coincide with the low-point period of the load factor of a central station, then there results an actual all-around improvement. For this the welding installation should be entitled to a certain proportionate consideration.

Maximum Demand.—Owing to the instantaneous severity of a welding load, demand upon a supply station seems to be of considerable importance. However, the shifting of a load factor toward an off-load period, as described, will certainly take the severest effects off the system. Under such conditions regulation of the supply system suffers only in small plants, and only in places where lighting and power loads are fed from the same mains

But large welding installations are usually direct-connected through transformer banks to the station buses, where the fluctuating character of the welding load will be almost negligible and certainly will not affect the regulation of a system in a degree commensurate with the size of the connected welding installation. Of course in all these discussions it is assumed that the station apparatus, transformers and supply feeders are properly selected, with equipment properly calculated to fit the particular welding load. In the past this has not always been the case, and this is one of the causes of so many different maximum demand charges.

The ratio which the maximum demand should bear to the connected load will always remain a local issue between producer and consumer. The ratio should, however, be made to depend on the average kilovolt-ampere energy demand of all the welders (and not on their rated capacities as given by the manufacturer) and of the rated capacity of the primary supply installation. If the welding customer bears a part of the installation charges caused by larger transformers and larger supply mains, he should benefit by the resultant mutual advantages. However, no demand charge should be based upon a mixed welding and motor load supplied from a common primary installation. The importance of this claim will be more evident if it is stated that by separating a certain mixed welding and motor circuit, and by installing an additional

100-kw. equipment, the maximum-demand charge in a single supply circuit in one month was reduced over $200.

To be sure that no more disturbing overloads are thrown upon the line than have been contracted for, overload relays, time clocks and maximum-demand indicators will be found sufficiently reliable for all honest purposes on both sides of the controversy.

Proper grouping of the single-phase welding loads upon a three-phase supply system will give perfect satisfaction in almost all installations but those of small size.

Power Factor.—So much has been said and so much worry caused about the poor power factor of a welding installation that it is now universally accepted that the power factor is bad, and nothing further is done about it. The outstanding feature about this condition is that the central stations, in a most unfortunate moment, decided to "penalize" the power factor. It is not the charge for the condition, but the adoption of the word for the charge, which makes the customer balk and is the cause of no end of distrust toward the welding machine. The word "penalty" conveys to the lay mind the impression that a poor power factor exists only with welding installations, and naturally the conclusions are not flattering for the welding equipment.

No attempt is made here to describe the well-known methods of improving the power factor of a welding installation with synchronous apparatus. The adoption of such methods is more of a commercial than an engineering problem. Upon investigation it will be found that, with few exceptions, it is cheaper to pay for the poor power factor than to invest in additional apparatus. However, the average power plant usually has, besides a welding installation, a number of other consumers, the effects of whose poor power factor are felt in considerable measure at the generators. If all such sources are investigated and segregated upon one common bus, together with a welding load, it might be found that either a synchronous or static apparatus would more than pay for itself, if installed at the proper place.

If this fact is explained to a welding customer, there can be no doubt that he will be only too eager to bear a certain proportion of the investment for a special apparatus and thus

secure for himself a better rate for the consumed energy. With
proper co-operation between the central station and the welding
customer on all these points of mutual interest, much misunder-
standing and distrust could be eliminated, benefiting all parties
concerned in the welding industry.

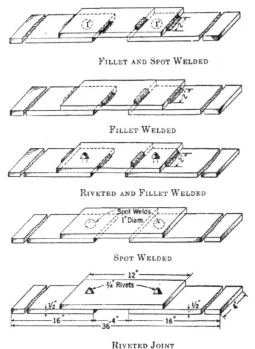

FILLET AND SPOT WELDED

FILLET WELDED

RIVETED AND FILLET WELDED

SPOT WELDED

RIVETED JOINT

FIG. 325.—Welded and Riveted Joints.

Strength of Resistance Welds.—In some of its applications, spot welding affords a method of preliminary joining
ship hull plates, after which the required additional strength
is obtained by arc welding. The Welding Research Sub-Committee made some progress in comparing combined spot and

arc welds, and combined rivet and arc welds with riveted, spot-welded and arc-welded joints. It is not a question in such an investigation, of spot versus arc welding, but of spot and arc welding.

According to Hobart, test specimens are made up of the following combinations:

(a) Spot and fillet welds (two samples made)

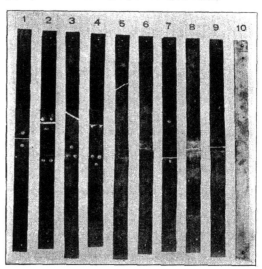

FIG. 326.—Spot-Welding Tests on Hoop Iron.

(b) Fillet welds, made by welding fillets about two inches in length at the ends of overlapping plates (two samples made)

(c) Rivet and fillet welds (one sample made)

(d) Spot welds, made by welding two spots approximately one inch in diameter, on the plates (two samples made)

(e) Riveted joint, made by riveting a $\frac{1}{2} \times 4 \times 12$ in. plate with two plates $\frac{1}{2} \times 4 \times 16$ in., using two $\frac{3}{4}$ in. rivets and a four inch plate lap (one sample made)

The way these plates were fastened is illustrated in Fig. 325. The results of the tests were as follows:

(a) Spot and fillet weld..................ultimate load........50,350 lb.
(b) Fillet welds ....ultimate load........37,000 lb.
(c) Rivet and fillet welds...............ultimate load.........35,000 lb.
(d) Spot welds ....ultimate load........28,000 lb.
(e) Riveted joint ....ultimate load........13,000 lb.

Spot-Welding Tests on Hoop Iron.—The Thomson Co. made up ten samples of spot-welded, riveted, butt-welded and plain pieces of hoop iron, and had them tested in the Lunkenheimer laboratory. The pieces after testing are shown in Fig. 326. The results were as follows:

No. 1. Spot-welded in one place—broke at weld at 1,625 pounds.
No. 2. Spot-welded in two places, also two rivets—broke at rivets at 1,555 pounds.
No. 3. Spot-welded in three places—broke outside weld at 2,715 pounds. (Notice elongation of metal.)
No. 4. Spot-welded in three places, also three rivets—broke at rivets at 2,055 pounds.
No. 5. Solid lap-weld—broke outside weld at 2,720 pounds.
No. 6. Butt-welded—broke at weld at 2,555 pounds.
No. 7. Spot-welded in one place, and riveted once—broke at rivet at 990 pounds.
No. 8. Solid lap-weld—broke at weld at 2,425 pounds.
No. 9. Spot-welded in two places—broke at weld at 2,275 pounds.
No. 10. Plain piece of hoop iron, not welded—pulled apart at 2,690 pounds.

Taking the average of the breaking points of the three pieces, 3, 5 and 10, that broke in the pieces themselves, we get approximately 2700 lb. as the strength of the hoop iron. This furnishes a basis for percentage calculations if such are desired. By grouping six of the tests, we get the following results for comparative purposes:

Test No. 1. One Spot-weld: broke at 1,625 pounds.
Test No. 7. One Rivet: broke at 990 pounds.
            The weld stood over 60 per cent more than the rivets
Test No. 9. Two Spot-Welds: broke at 2,275 pounds.
Test No. 2. Two Rivets: broke at 1,555 pounds.
            The weld stood over 60 per cent more than the rivets.
Test No. 3. Three Spot-Welds: broke outside weld at 2,715 pounds.
Test No. 4. Three Rivets: tore apart at 2,055 pounds.

Strength of Spot-Welded Holes.—It sometimes happens that a hole will by mistake be punched in a plate where it is not needed. The spot welder can be used to plug such holes and make the plate as strong as, or stronger than, it was originally. It is first necessary to make a plug of the same material as the plate which will fit in the hole and which is slightly longer than the plate is thick. The length required will depend on the snugness of the fit of the plug in the hole; there should be enough metal in the plug to a little more than completely fill the hole. The plate is placed in the welder with the hole which is to be filled centered between the electrodes, the plug is placed in the hole, the electrodes brought together upon it,

Fig. 327.—Sample Plates with Holes Plugged by Spot-Welding. At the Right Is Shown a Plate with Plug in Place Previous to Welding.

and upon the application of pressure and current the plug will soften, fill the hole, and weld to the plate.

Fig. 327 shows, at the extreme right, a piece of $\frac{1}{2}$-in. plate with a punched hole which is to be plugged, and the plug in place previous to welding. The three pieces at the left of the photograph have the plugs welded in place. A fact which the illustration does not bring out very clearly is that the surface, after the plug is fused in, is practically as smooth as the remainder of the plate, the maximum difference in thickness between the plugged portion and the remainder of the plate being not more than $\frac{1}{32}$ in. on a $\frac{1}{2}$-in. plate.

That there is a real and complete weld between the plug and the plate is shown by Fig. 328. The four samples illus-

trated were placed in a testing machine and broken by longitudinal pull, with the interesting result that not one of the
three plugged plates broke through the weld. The sample at
the right was broken to give an indication of the strength
of the samples after punching and before welding. Two sam-

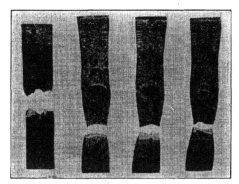

Fig. 328.—Plates Shown in Fig. 327 After Pulling in the Testing Machine.
Note That All Welded Plates Broke Outside the Weld.

TABLE XXX.

No. of Sample	Description of Sample	Sec-tion In.	Tensile Strength Lb.	Location of Fracture
1	Punched $\frac{9}{16}$-in. dia-meter hole and plugged by welding	2 by $\frac{1}{2}$	59,320	Outside weld
2	Punched $\frac{9}{16}$-in. dia-meter hole and plugged by welding	2 by $\frac{1}{2}$	59,320	Outside weld
3	Punched $\frac{9}{16}$-in. dia-meter hole and plugged by welding	2 by $\frac{1}{2}$	59,350	Outside weld
4	Punched $\frac{9}{16}$-in. dia-meter hole but not plugged	2 by $\frac{1}{2}$	31,590	Through hole
5	Original bar, not punched	2 by $\frac{1}{2}$	59,230	Through center
6	Original bar, not punched	2 by $\frac{1}{2}$	59,000	Through center

ples (not shown) from the same bar but without the punched holes were pulled to find the original strength of the material. The results are given in Table XXX.

It is interesting to note that the average of the breaking point of the three samples punched and plugged was 59,330 lb., whereas the average for the two samples not punched was 59,115 lb., or 115 lb. less. This proves that there was no weakening of the surrounding plate, due to the weld. That the ductility of the welded section was somewhat decreased is shown by the photographs of the samples after pulling.

The actual welding time required for plugging a hole in a plate is from five to ten seconds. Of course, it is necessary to have a plug of the proper size, but a variety of plugs, of all the standard rivet hole diameters and of lengths suitable for the various thicknesses of plates, could be made up and

Fig. 329.—Straight Rods Spot-welded to Angle Iron and then Bent by Hammer Blows, the Angle Being Supported only by the Unwelded Flange.

kept in stock in the yard. The method described should prove a valuable means of salvaging material which otherwise might have to be scrapped.

Strength of Rods Mash-Welded to Angle Iron.—While no figures are available, the illustration Fig. 329 will give an idea of the strength of welds where rods are mash-welded to angle iron or plate. Three straight iron rods were welded to an angle iron and then hammered over with a sledge, as shown. This is a very severe test of a weld.

Strength of Electric Resistance Butt-Welds.—According to Kent, tests of electric resistance butt-welded iron bars resulted as follows:

32 tests, solid iron bars, average.........52,444 lb.
17 tests, electric butt-welds, average......46,836 lb.

This is an efficiency of 89.1%.

Presumably the welds were turned to the size of the bars, although Kent does not say so.

In a number of tests on draw-bench mandrels the following results were obtained. The mandrels consisted of one piece of ⅝ in. dia., 30-40 point carbon steel, welded on to another piece of ⅝ dia., 110 point carbon Carnegie electric tool steel No. 4. The low carbon ends were drilled and threaded to receive the stud of the bench rod, and the high carbon ends were upset, machined, and used as working heads. Six samples of each kind of steel were prepared and sent to the Thomson Electric Welding Co. of Lynn, Mass., to be welded.

After welding the mandrels were subjected to the following heat treatments and operations:

1. Head-end annealed after upsetting.
2. Head-end machined, and hardened by quenching in water.
3. Mandrels worked on draw benches until worn out or broken.
4. Entire length of mandrels heated to 1450° F. and cooled in air.
5. Mandrels subjected to tensile test to destruction.

Mandrel No. 1.—Pulled 5125 ft. of 1×.112 in. to ⅞×.107 in., 17 point carbon. Rather heavy pull. Broke stud once, and used again after replacing same. Pulled to destruction in standard testing machine, and failed 2½ in. below weld on low carbon end, at a stress of 59,000 lb. per sq. in. Weld stronger than low carbon round.

Mandrel No. 2.—Pulled 3360 ft. of 1³/₁₆×.46 in. to ³/₄×.38 in., 17 point carbon. Not badly worn at end of load. Pulled to destruction in testing machine, and failed 1 in. below weld on low carbon end, at a stress of 58,800 lb. per sq. in. Weld stronger than round of 30-40 point carbon of same cross-section.

Mandrel No. 3.—Pulled 2400 ft. of 1×.112 in. to ⅞×.107 in., 17 point carbon. Broke at stud and replaced by another mandrel. Pulled to destruction in testing machine, and failed on weld at stress of 58,000 lb. per sq. in. Weld 98% efficient, referred to mandrel No. 1.

Mandrel No. 4.—Pulled 2250 feet of 1³/₄×.200 in. to 1¹/₁₆×.200 in., 17 point carbon. In good shape at end of load.

Pulled to destruction in testing machine and failed on weld, at a stress of 56,900 lb. per sq. in. Weld 96% efficient, referred to mandrel No. 1.

Mandrel No. 5.—Pulled 402 ft. of $1 \times .112$ in. to $\frac{3}{8} \times .108$ in., 17 point carbon. Broke off at stud of rod, tube being unduly oversize. Pulled to destruction in testing machine, and failed on weld at a stress of 53,700 lb. per sq. in. Weld 91% efficient, referred to mandrel No. 1.

Mandrel No. 6.—Mandrel broken at thread on first tube. Tube over-size. Mandrel lost.

Conclusion.—Out of five mandrels subjected to a tensile test to destruction after being worked on the benches, two show that the weld is stronger than the 30-40 point carbon round solid rod, and the other four showed efficiency of 91% to 98%, referred to 59,000 lb. per sq. in. The maximum required efficiency is not over 70%. Therefore the mandrels passed all requirements for strength and service.

Strength of High Carbon Steel Welds.—In order to throw some light upon the chemical and physical changes induced by the welding process, pieces of 0.97 per cent carbon drill steel, of $\frac{5}{8}$ in. diameter, were studied after butt welding, writes E. E. Thum in *Chemical and Metallurgical Engineering*, Sept. 15, 1918. Test pieces of the original stock and of both annealed and unannealed welds were made by mounting in a lathe, removing the excess metal of the fin, and then turning or grinding a short length of the bar accurately to a diameter of $\frac{1}{2}$ in., with the weld in the center of the turned portion. In the unannealed welds, the turned portion was but $\frac{1}{2}$ in. in length in order that the failure would be forced to occur within the portion of the bar altered in constitution by the welding heat. Tension tests of the unannealed welds showed, in all cases, a failure with little or no necking occurring at the end of the turned portion—that is to say, farthest from the weld and in the softest portion of the test piece. The strength this developed was much higher than even the strength of the original steel, and it is clearly evident that all parts of this weld have a higher ultimate strength than the original bar. The average results of the tension tests follow:

	Ultimate Strength Lb. per Sq. In.	Contraction in Area, Per Cent	Elongation in ¼ In. Per cent
Original tool steel....................	114,100	12	10
Unannealed weld	158,700	2	3
Weld annealed at 750° C. (1382° F.)..	100,800	24	16

In the annealed bars failure always occurred at the weld, accompanied by considerable necking, strictly limited to the close proximity of the point of failure.

The results of a series of tests on butt- and spot-welds made by G. A. Hughes, electrical engineer of the Truscon Steel Company, Youngstown, Ohio, were reported as follows:

TESTS MADE ON BARS OF SOFT STEEL, 1 IN. SQ., BUTT-WELDED AND MACHINED TO THE SIZE OF THE BAR.

Test No.	Volts	Amps.	Kw.	Power Factor
1	220	220	40.	91
2	220	220	40.	91
3	220	210	39.	84
4	218	210	39.5	86
5	220	210	39.	84

All tension tests were pulled at a speed of ½ in. per min. Nos. 1, 2 and 3 were pulled, while Nos. 4 and 5, were sheared. On the different tests, No. 1 failed in the weld at 48,800 lb.; No. 2 failed in the weld at 52,300 lb.; No. 3 failed back of the weld at 50,100 lb.; No. 4 failed at 51,500 lb. and No. 5 at 50,300 lb.

These tests indicate that the ultimate shearing strength of such a weld closely approaches the ultimate tensile strength.

Pieces of soft steel, $^3/_{16}$ in. thick and 5 in. wide, with an ultimate tensile strength of 56,150 lb., were butt-welded and pulled with the following results:

Test No.	Manner of Failure	Lb.	Per Cent
1	½ in plate and ½ in weld	51,000	91
2	In plate just back of weld	52,000	93
3	" " " " " "	53,400	95
4	" " " " " "	52,000	93
5	" " " " " "	46,100	82
6	" " " " " "	51,900	93

On six samples of spot-welded single lap-joint sheets of 14 gage steel, 3 in. wide, welded with a $^5/_{16}$ in. spot, the average at which the welds pulled out, was 4480 lb.

The ultimate tensile strength of a piece of plate of 14 gage, was 64,500 per sq. in. The ultimate shearing load per weld (two spots with an area of 0.0742 sq. in. each) averaged 8942 lb. Approximate total welded area, 0.1484 sq. in. This gives an ultimate shearing strength for 1 sq. in. of weld, of about 60,200 lb. On steel 3/8 in. thick and 2 in. wide, welded with a spot having an area, measured with a planimeter, of 0.476 sq. in., the failure under pull was at 34,650 lb. Examination of the welds showed them to be under both a tensile and a shearing action. A piece of the same steel tested for ultimate strength, failed at 66,800 lb. per sq. in. This shows that the weld was stronger than the original metal.

The final conclusions drawn by Mr. Hughes from his tests, are that, in general, the ultimate tensile strength of a properly made butt- or spot-weld, is about 93 per cent of that of the parent metal, and the ultimate shearing strength of a properly made butt- or spot-weld is also about 93 per cent.

ELEMENTARY ELECTRICAL INFORMATION

What is a Volt?—This is a term used to represent the pressure of electrical energy. In steam we would say a boiler maintains a pressure of 100 pounds. This term relates to pressure only regardless of quantity, just as the steam pressure of a boiler has nothing to do with its capacity.

What is an Ampere?—This term is used to represent the quantity of current. In the case of steam or water we speak of carrying capacity of a pipe in cubic feet, while in electricity the carrying capacity of a wire is given in amperes.

What is a Watt?—This is the electrical unit of power and equals volts×amperes. One mechanical horsepower is the equivalent of 746 watts.

What is a Kilowatt or kw.?—1000 watts, kilo merely indicating 1000. It is the most commonly used electrical unit of power and one kilowatt of electrical energy is equivalent to one and one-third mechanical horsepower.

What is a Kilowatt Hour or kw.-hr.?—This is the electrical equivalent of mechanical work, which would be stated in the latter in terms of horsepower hour. It means the consumption of 1000 watts of electrical energy steadily for one hour or any equivalent thereof (such as 5000 watts for 12 minutes) and is the unit employed by all power companies in selling electric power, their charges being based on a certain rate per kw.-hr. consumed.

What is kva.?—This means Kilovolt amperes or volts× amperes÷1000. This term is used only in alternating current practice and is used to represent the apparent load on a generator. In any inductive apparatus, such as a motor or welder, a counter current is set up within the apparatus itself, which is opposite in direction to and always opposes the main current entering the apparatus. This makes it necessary for the generator to produce not only amperes enough to operate the motor or welder but also enough in addition to overcome this opposing current in either of the latter, although the actual mechanical power required to run the generator is only that to supply watts or electrical energy (volts×amperes) *actually* consumed in the motor or welder. Hence, the kw. demand of a welder represents the actual useful power consumed, for which you pay, while the kva. emand represents the volts×total number of amperes impressed on the welder÷1000, to also overcome the induced current set up within, but it is the *kva. demand* that governs the size of wire to be used in connecting up the welder. Kw. divided by kva. of any machine, represents the power factor of that machine, which is usually expressed in per cent.

INDEX

401

Lightning Source UK Ltd.
Milton Keynes UK
UKHW020637010421
381372UK00005B/439